LLANBRADACH

1900–1950

Chapters in the later history

of a pit village

by

Dennis G. Sellwood

Published by

D.G. Sellwood 31 Maerdy Crescent Caerphilly

Printed by
Bruce Print Services Ltd. Llanbradach

To Daphne,
David, Judith, Jane,
with all my love

By the same author :
Llanbradach 1887-1914
Chapters in the early history
of a pit village
Published 1988
Re-printed 1989, 1991, 1992, 1995, 1998

Dennis G. Sellwood, 1998
ISBN 0 9512424 1 5

Author's Note

This book is based mainly on original records preserved in the Glamorgan Record Office as well as others held in Coedybrain Primary School, supplemented by newspaper reports. I wish to express my gratitude to the staff of the Record Office and the Bargoed Library for their assistance, and to Mr. Cliff Davies and Mrs. Aurelia Jones, past and present headteachers, for their co-operation and help.

My thanks are particularly due to those villagers, too numerous to mention individually, who have provided invaluable information, with my special thanks to those whose personal memories make up the final chaper, and to Mrs. Molly Tudor for permission to print her poem.

I also thank everyone who has allowed photographs to be used. I have acknowledged ownership wherever possible.

Finally, and most importantly, I thank Daphne, my wife, for giving me her unstinting support during the last ten years – without her the book would still be unfinished.

CONTENTS

INTRODUCTION

The response to "Llanbradach 1887 – 1914" surprised me greatly. I was unprepared for the warm welcome it had from many readers. Perhaps seeing Llanbradach's story in print enhanced people's sense of its worth. This former pit village, sometimes referred to by outsiders, only half jokingly, as "a hole", was seen to have an interesting history. I think the 1993 centenary celebrations were, in part, an expression of the villagers' heightened sense of identity, coupled with huge relief at the completion of the by-pass. The dedication in September 1994 of the memorial to those who were killed in the colliery was primarily a tribute to those men and boys but also a reaffirmation of Llanbradach as the pit village it once was, a reminder to ourselves and future generations of what the place was about until 1961, a coal mining community, one small part of a great industry and colourful way of life which extended over the whole of South Wales.

The southern aspect of Llanbradach, taken from the viaduct in the 1930s
by V.C. Hardacre

1

I was unaware of the large number of Llanbradach "exiles" living in the surrounding district, in England, and even overseas, for whom the book would provide an often nostalgic pleasure, reviving happy memories of childhood and youth, even though the book dealt with a period which had ended before most of the readers were born. The book, which I made as factual and accurate as possible, was not intended to set anyone off on a rose-tinted walk down Memory Lane. Nor is this one. It is for the most part severely factual. Dealing as it does, however, with a period at least partly within living memory, my own included, it may arouse personal memories which are predominately happy ones.

Two major wars and several lengthy miners' strikes or lockouts; loss of life in the colliery and on military service; deaths caused by now mostly extinct diseases; unemployment, short time working, and material deprivation; forced emigration to England and beyond. Surely, there must be many who lived through those times who had plentiful cause to be sad, and even bitter. Yet, it seems, most of us have pleasent and happy memories of growing up in Llanbradach, and even if we now live elsewhere we retain a strong sense of identity with our inward image of life as we knew it. We somehow belong to "The Brad" ("This dear, old dusty town", as it was fondly described in a 1912 local newspaper) in a way which we rarely know in any other place in later life. Of course, this is not an experience which is peculiar to Llanbradach and its inhabitants; any other small, close-knit community tends to inspire a feeling of attachment in its sons and daughters, perhaps expecially in the years before television and car-ownership radically altered the old way of life, before people's horizons, both physical and mental, were immeasurably widened.

As children, certainly, our horizons were extremely limited. Even within the narrow space of the village pupils in the Llanbradach schools and the Coedybrain schools, at opposite ends, were unlikely to know one another; children attended their separate Sunday Schools; and although the streets, back lanes, river and hills were our common playground we tended to stay within a small radius of our own homes, so that neighbours rather than classmates were our playfellows out of school. I remember at a certain age I would gaze across the valley in naive wonderment at the mysterious, ambiguous Monmouthshire hillside which I understood to be that foreign country called "England". If we ventured out of the village it might only be as far as Caerphilly (to the secondary schools if we "passed the scholarship"), to Cardiff (to visit the Christmas grotto in a department store), or to Barry Island (once or twice in the summer on a Sunday School outing by "charabang" or steam train).

In common with all other coal-mining communities in South Wales Llanbradach is remembered by those who lived there in the 1920s, 30s, and 40s as a predominately one-class society of families whose wage-earners toiled together in the colliery, whether underground or on the surface. We lived in similar houses, sparsely furnished by today's standards : no vacuum cleaner, washing machine, fridge-freezer, television, no gas or electric cooker, central heating, dishwasher or microwave oven; no wall-to-wall carpets, only linoleum and mats, no bathroom or shower, only a tin bath in front of the kitchen fire, no in-door toilet, only a lavatory at the bottom of the garden, no toilet paper, only

2

squares of newspaper nailed to the door, no hot water "on tap", only a kettle or pot on the black-leaded kitchen hob, some streets in the village had the cold-water tap outside the kitchen door. We had the minimum of clothing, a few items for daily wear and our "Sunday best" for chapel, church or dance hall. We had no cars, only shanks's pony, push bikes, or public transport. We had no hi-fi system or CDs, only a "wireless" set powered by a kind of car battery called an "accumulator" which had to be re-charged every week, a wind-up gramophone, and sometimes a piano.

To younger generations these living conditions of 50 and more years ago seem almost un-imaginably primitive. We were all, more or less, "in the same boat". There was very little money available after basic needs had been met and there was little pressure to consume any surplus cash in the purchase of material goods. We had little, and were content with little, we made do with what we had. This way of living is the backcloth to the "story" told in this book.

These new chapters about Llanbradach are an attempt to record the facts about the village schools, some outside living memory, based on a variety of official documents. I have tried to weave other facets of local and national life into the schools' history, events or developments which affected the children and their families directly or indirectly. Whereas the earlier book dealt with the birth of Llanbradach and its boom years, this one, although beginning during those years before 1914, carries on into the decades of foreign wars and industrial battles, gradual decline in coal production and population, a community which stabilised and to some extent stagnated. Yet in the same decades the provision of mains sewerage and a better water supply improved people's health, their homes were lit by gas and electricity instead of candles and oil lamps, they were entertained by "the pictures" and the wireless, the colliers had unpaid, and then paid, holidays. World War Two and the post-war years brought full employment, nationalisation of the coal mines, and the panoply of the Welfare State.

The education system of the first half of the 20th century aimed to give elementary schooling up to the age of 13 or 14 years to the vast majority of the nation's children, sufficient to prepare the children of the working class for their allotted positions in life, the boys to enter local industries, the girls to do domestic work (in their own or someone else's home) and bring up the next generation of children. The emphasis was on the basics of reading, writing and arithmetic. Spurred on locally by the Caerphilly Schools Manager, Mrs Catherine John (often known by her bardic name Megfam) and enthusiastically supported by some of the Welsh-speaking Llanbradach headteachers, Glamorgan County Council tried to encourage the use of the Welsh language and a knowledge of Welsh culture in all the schools, but in Llanbradach, as in so many other places, it was a losing battle. The original colliery managers were Lancashire men, a fact which introduced a bias into the recruitment of the workforce and gave a predominately Anglicised flavour to the population.

A minority of children, from the earliest years of the century, gained entry by examination to a secondary education. Before 1912 the scholarship children went to the Intermediate or County schools in Pontypridd (boys and girls), Pengam (boys) and Hengoed (girls). They were exposed to an academic

3

The northern aspect of Llanbradach in the 1930s, showing the fields of Tarranyonwrthwyl farm, on part of which Oakfield Street and Victoria Street were built.

Courtesy of Kevin Williams

curriculum intended to prepare them for the professions, teaching, and other white-collar careers. In December 1912 the Caerphilly Higher Elementary School, on the Crescent Road site which the building still occupies, opened its doors. This school, as its name implies, was intended to offer its pupils, also selected by examination, an extended elementary education to the age of 15 years. However, over the years it evolved into something very similar to the older County schools and was renamed Caerphilly Secondary School in 1921. The building became the Girls Secondary School when the newly built Boys Secondary School (now St Martin's Comprehensive) opened in September 1929. In 1931 the Caerphilly Junior Technical School opened (on the same site as the Boys Secondary School) and offered boys of 13 years of age a three year course somewhat less academic in nature. A few girls went to the Treforest Commercial College. Many children from Llanbradach attended these various "secondary" schools; an incomplete list of their names will be found in the appendix.

There are many aspects of Llanbradach's history which are not included in this book. I hope to produce a third volume, using material about the colliery, All Saints Church, the Workmen's Hall and Institute, and Pwllypant. The more I research, the more I realise that even with a place as small and as young as Llanbradach, there is too much work for one local historian to grapple with. Mr Ellis Stanbury is engaged in compiling a history of the Bowling Club, one of the oldest institutions in the village, and Mr Kevin Williams is performing an invaluable service by collecting and preserving memorabilia, postcards and photographs. There are many other facets which could be researched, written

4

up or recorded in other ways; chapels, farms, public houses and social clubs, football, rugby, tennis and cricket teams, political and trade union activities, water gas and electrical services, Boys and Girls Brigades, music making, plays and pantomimes, shops and home life, etc., etc. There may be documentary and photographic records in respect of some of these topics; oral evidence is a valuable but dimishing source of information. I would urge anyone who has an area of particular interest to pursue it – once the historical bug bites it doesn't let go!

110 YEARS : AN OVERVIEW

Until the late 1880s this part of the Rhymney Valley was an almost entirely agricultural area consisting of several valley-bottom farms and a few hill farms. Owned by wealthy families most of whom lived elsewhere they were worked by tenant-farmers, often by several generations of the same family. This centuries-old way of life was disturbed only by the quarrying and coal-mining near Pwll-yPant and by the railway tracks which passed through the valley on both sides of the river from the 1850s onwards.

All of this changed radically and swiftly after the Cardiff Steam Coal Collieries Company obtained a lease from Miss Clara Thomas to exploit the coal measures beneath her land. Two shafts were sunk between 1887 and 1893. Even before the first coal was brought to the surface in 1893 the demand for labour and the prospect of future employment brought men and their families to live near the new colliery. Houses were built, streets laid out and a public hall was provided. By the turn of the century there was an Anglican church, several

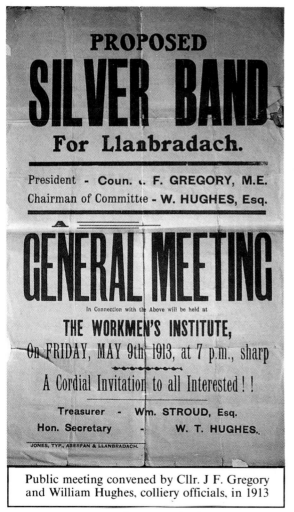

PROPOSED

SILVER BAND

For Llanbradach.

President - Coun. ... F. GREGORY, M.E.

Chairman of Committee - W. HUGHES, Esq.

GENERAL MEETING

In Connection with the Above will be held at

THE WORKMEN'S INSTITUTE,

On FRIDAY, MAY 9th 1913, at 7 p.m., sharp

A Cordial Invitation to all Interested!!

Treasurer - Wm. STROUD, Esq.

Hon. Secretary - W. T. HUGHES.

JONES, TYP., ABERFAN & LLANBRADACH.

Public meeting convened by Cllr. J F. Gregory and William Hughes, colliery officials, in 1913

Courtesy of Miss Kitty Hughes

6

Early success for the newly formed Llanbradach Silver Band

Courtesy of Ellis Stanbury

nonconformist chapels, schools for several hundreds of children, a half dozen pubs and clubs, the village had its own railway station and scores of trades people had set up shop in the High Street and elsewhere.

The colliery and the community flourished in these early decades despite fluctuations in the coal trade. There was a great movement of people into and out of the village as men and their families followed where the best work opportunities presented themselves. Yet there was a core of stability and many organisations and institutions grew and developed: churches and chapels, schools, workmen's clubs, political parties and trade unions, football, rugby and cricket teams, a bowling club, an annual flower show andcarnival, three public houses and two cinemas and then in the 1930s the village acquired a wonderful children's playground (with tennis courts and a putting green) and an open–air swimming pool.

The national coal miners' strikes of 1921 and 1926 caused much suffering and the economic depression of the late 1920s and the 1930s brought unemployment, short–time working and deprivation to the village. Some families emigrated to England and North America, but most chose to stay put in order to remain part of a close-knit community, bound together by family ties, adversity, and a shared way of life, with the social life centred in the village. There were a few excursions into the outside world: a Sunday School charabanc, or train, trip to Barry Island, a paddle–steamer crossing to Weston–super–mare or Ilfracombe. Few people had holidays before World War II unless they were able to stay with relatives in some other part of the country.

7

World War II brought changes to Llanbradach and Pwll–y–Pant; men and women left to serve in the Armed Forces and for the first time experienced new places and new faces; the colliery, even when wartime demand for coal was high, had difficulty in recruiting the men it needed; other employment opportunities had begun to open up outside the village; women replaced men who were doing military service e.g. in the colliery offices; hundreds of evacuee children with strange accents arrived from Kent, London, Birmingham, Cardiff.

The village, although changing, remained recognisably similar in the early post–war years and with full employment and the creation of the Welfare State, most people's lives experienced a material improvement. The colliery still provided most men and boys with a job and this shared experience, combined with reliance on public transport and the traditional forms of religious observance and entertainment, ensured the continuity of village life.

The 1950s saw the arrival of television, the 1960s the growth of car ownership. These developments brought about a decline in cinema attendance and greater opportunity to look for entertainment outside the village, resulting in the eventual closure of both cinemas. The importance of the church and chapels as religious institutions and as social meeting places diminished. The swimming pool closed down and the park was reduced to a shadow of its former self.

These changes would have occurred anyway, as they did all over the country, but the closure of the colliery at the end of 1961 removed the original "raison d'etre" of the community. From thousands of jobs in the early decades of the century the colliery workforce had gradually decreased to hundreds in the 1950s and then to none. The social cohesion produced by the colliery suddenly disappeared. The small amount of employment which has been created in the village in recent years is dispersed among tiny separate workplaces and the majority of the population works outside the village. Even the reorganisation of the school system at about the same time, sending all children of secondary school age out of the village, has reinforced this pattern.

As a commercial and retail centre Llanbradach, like other pit villages such as Abertridwr and Senghenydd, has almost ceased to exist. Whereas in 1914 there were at least 70 shops of all kinds spread throughout the village, the development of superstores and car ownership in the last 20 years has taken the commercial heart out of the village and, as with the decline of other aspects of community life, has reduced the opportunity for people to meet and gossip.

Throughout Llanbradach's history there has always been a flow of people coming and going, but whereas the colliery used to help to bind them together, since 1961 the newcomers had no such cohesive force to produce a sense of community and hence for many residents, Llanbradach is now simply where they happen to live, while their work, leisure activities, and family ties are elsewhere. However, the picture is not wholly negative : the village offers an attractive and pleasant place in which to live, and there are many activities to bring people together – although perhaps the revival of a Llanbradach Silver Band or a Choir would strengthen its image in the wider community?

Courtesy of Miss Kitty Hughes

Llanbradach Shakespearean Company. June 1918. This appears to be a production of "The Merchant of Venice". The cast and other members of the company are posing in front of the Workmen's Social Club, the building being the original Boulton and Paul public hall dating from 1891. Among those pictured here are John Bassett (extreme left, second row down). Edmund Evans, "Elfryn" (centre, third row down). Miss G S McCarthy, teacher (front row, extreme left). Kate Hughes, teacher (second left). Gertie Fuell, teacher (fifth left). The little girl on the left is Sibyl Warfield, the little girl on the right is Kitty Hughes (daughter of Kate and Ellis Hughes).

9

COEDYBRAIN MIXED SCHOOL 1900 - 1913

Rapid growth My earlier book recounted the setting-up of the Coedybrain Mixed and Infants Schools by the Eglwysilan School Board, opening the doors to their first pupils on 10 September 1900. The Mixed School, taking children between the ages of seven and fourteen years of both sexes, was immediately overcrowded, admitting 184 children into a building designed to accommodate only 150. The educational planners had not foreseen the rapid growth which Llanbradach was to experience over the next decade. In the years leading up to the outbreak of the Great War in 1914 the colliery, in common with the whole of the South Wales coalfield, greatly increased its production. In 1900 the colliery produced 429,635 tons of coal; by 1910 production had risen fifty percent to 638,118 tons. Over the same period the workforce had risen from 1600 to 2400. While most of the male population of Llanbradach from 14 years onwards worked in the local colliery the numbers were insufficient to make up the whole of the required work force. Many men and boys travelled daily from the surrounding district, especially from Caerphilly and even from Cardiff. The

A view of the village c. 1907: the boys with their iron "bowlies", the Rhymney Railway station and goods depot, the still-new Barry Railway viaduct spanning the valley. The police station does not yet appear to have been built in Station Road.

Courtesy of John Coppage

Rhymney Railway laid on special colliers' trains to bring them straight into the colliery sidings.

The population of the village rose correspondingly and in order to accommodate the families moving into the locality there was a frenzy of speculative building. During the first decade of the century Llanbradach largely took the shape which it kept until further expansion occurred after the 1939–45 War. The 1890s had seen the village begin to grow up along the old parish road from Caerphilly to Ystrad Mynach : Stanley Row and Stanley Terrace (both now demolished), more than half of Coedybrain Road, most of De Winton Terrace, all of Lewis Terrace and half of Oak Terrace, Station Road, most of High Street, Pencerrig Street, all of Ffrwd and Glenview Terraces, Wingfield Terrace (demolished), Wingfield Crescent and Oakfield Street (originally known as Abercarn Road the Charles Street). During the following ten years the village "filled out" : Horace Terrace, Richmond Terrace (also known as The Joinery, demolished), School Street, Thomas Street, James Street, most of Tynygraig Road, Tynygraig Terrace, Church Street, Park View (originally Central Terrace), Morgan Street, Rees Terrace, Garden Avenue, Garden Street, Plasturtwyn Terrace and Victoria Street. Also during this decade the Llanbradach Hotel was added to the older Wingfield and De Winton Hotels, the English Baptists (Ebenezer) and Congregationalists (Bethel) moved into their stone built chapels a few years later than their Welsh counterparts (Seion and Tabernacl) and the Glamorgan Constabulary acquired a permanent home in Station Road. The Church Rooms were built in 1904, and in 1909 All Saints, with the addition of a chancel, vestry and tower, was completed.

Between 1890 and 1910, in step with the increasing manpower and productivity of the colliery, the physical fabric of the village grew at an astonishing rate – it must have seemed to the pioneer settlers like living in a permanent builders yard – and the inflow and flux of humanity must have been, at times, a nightmare for the planners and providers of the services required by such a shifting population. The admission register of Coedybrain Infants shows that between September 1900 and September 1905 about 400 children came into and left the village; miners and their families were constantly coming and going. Some came directly from places such as Taunton, Plymouth, Manchester, Leeds, London, Sheffield, Bristol, Newcastle-on-Tyne, Dudley; many others had moved on from the adjacent Monmouthshire and Glamorgan mining districts as well as Cardiff, Newport and Swansea – but even some of these apparently "internal" migrants would have come originally from outside of Wales, e.g. my own grandfather, W H Selby, is recorded as having moved from Lower Ystrad Mynach in 1904, whereas he had lived there only temporarily after bringing his family from Somerset, awaiting accommodation in Llanbradach where he worked as an ostler in the colliery.

Serious overcrowding The headteacher, Tom Moses, and his little band of qualified and unqualified teachers, struggled to cope with a rapidly increasing, constantly changing, number of children. The first internal examinations held in April 1901, indicate the narrow, focused nature of the syllabus : Reading,

Oak Terrace c. 1910: the Post Office second from the right (still there today) and the original steepled public hall behind the wall on the left (before it was replaced by the present Workmen's Hall). Courtesy of Kevin Williams

High Street c. 1916: Llanbradach Hotel and Co-operative Stores on left, the Workmen's Hall on right. Courtesy of Kevin Williams

Recitation, Geography, Composition and Word–Building, Writing, Drawing, English Grammar. Mr Moses discussed with his staff the issues which concerned him : organisation, discipline, careful marking of books and registers, manners and morals. He was also concerned about the impending visit of the HMI, the result of whose examination of the school would determine not only the Board of Education grant towards the running of the school, but also, in part, his own salary. He brought to the HMI's attention the disadvantages under which the school had laboured during its first year: the overcrowding, having only two rooms to work in (the pupils were divided into seven classes), the constant change of teachers during the year – two of them being assistants who had never taught before. The HMI took these factors into account before concluding in December 1901 that "This new school has been already brought to a very efficient state, and is altogether well conducted. Some school excursions for educational purposes have been undertaken and the teaching is generally on sound lines; the staff was rather inadequate during some months of the year; but it is understood that it is to be strengthened. There is serious overcrowding". The difficulty caused by overcrowding is apparent in April 1902 when there were 246 on the register, with an average attendance of over 200; a teacher who left in February had not yet been replaced, resulting in Tom Moses, assisted by two young pupil teachers, having to take charge of the 79 children in Standard 1.

Tea and sermonising   There was the occasional welcome break from these conditions :

Friday 18 Oct 1901   Mrs Col. Lindsay, Ystrad Mynach, kindly gave the school a tea–treat as a memento of Col. Lindsay's safe return from the South African War.

In June 1902 the children received, as a Coronation gift, copies of a book entitled "The King's Realm". These were presented, on behalf of Eglwysilan School Board, by one of its members, Mr Tom Jones, who took the opportunity to lecture his audience on "obedience, truthfulness, honesty, cleanliness, thoroughness, temperance, loyalty, kindness, gentleness, bravery, modesty, punctuality, generosity – and exampled from the Royal Family and other great personages". The school was closed for a whole week at the time of Edward VII's coronation and on 26 June the children formed a procession along with the general public and various societies and marched to Taran y Morthwyl field where a free tea and medals were given.

7 July 1902   Sunday Schools excursion to Weston.
3 October 1902   Elementary Science walk. River dirty – why?
4 November 1902   Standard 1 taken for lesson in fields to see the direction of new viaduct and various features of the district.

In the midst of life   The children, most of whom were destined to work in the colliery or to be married to a miner, were almost as aware as their parents of the

Mr D J Davies, dairyman and undertaker, ran his business from 1 Tynygraig Terrace before transferring to 40 High Street. He is seen here with his funeral coach c. 1914.

constant danger hovering over their close-knit community. During 1901 the September explosion and individual accidents throughout the year had caused the deaths of thirteen underground workers, and in 1902 another three men died before the following logbook entry :-

23 October 1902   Advantage has been taken of many cases of carelessness of miners during the last few weeks and children have been told of the great responsibility that falls on each miner engaged in the pit. Careful children will make careful miners. They have also been questioned as to the dreadful nature of explosions.

Other fatalities in the immediate neighbourhood of the school would have reminded the children of the dangers inherent in the business of earning one's bread. The Pwllypant quarry, which could be seen from the Coedybrain playground, claimed the life of a workman who fell 100 feet from a crumbling edge in 1900, and in 1902, in separate incidents, two men engaged in blasting were killed when the gunpower ignited as they packed it into the holes. The viaduct, as it neared completion in August 1904, was the scene of another tragic accident when a young Bristolian, lodging at 33 Pontygwindy Road, fell more than 80 feet from the structure, hitting his head on a tree, dying almost at once from his injuries.

Have bike, will travel   The HMI's second report (September 1902) conveys more strongly than the first one his awareness of the difficult conditions :-

"All that can be said on this occasion is that the master has done his best for the children under most serious difficulties. It must be a great strain on him and his assistants to teach in rooms which are so overcrowded and it is very creditable to them that the work is as good as it is and that order is so well maintained.

Priscilla Lewis (mother of Miss Elsie Davies) was allowed to leave Coedybrain Mixed School before her fourteenth birthday after passing the "Labour Exam" and obtaining her Proficiency Certificate.

Courtesy of Miss Elsie Davies

In December 1902 the overcrowding was slightly eased when the School Board rented space in Bethel, the English Congregational chapel, and Standard 1 moved in with their teacher.

The HMI's 1903 report again highlighted the problem :-

"Considering the disadvantage under which the lessons are given, the condition of the school as regards instruction and discipline is very creditable. The singing and marching deserve high praise.
Addendum. Pending the completion of the enlargement of the school according to the plans approved on 24 August 1903 additional temporary accommodation should be secured to relieve the overcrowding".

But it was not until February 1904 that one of the classes was moved into the Public Hall, by which time the work of expanding the Coedybrain schools was already under way, although it was not completed until November. For the best part of two years the pupils of the Mixed School were split between three sites.

The HMIs worked for central government, at first for the London–based Board of Education, later for the devolved Welsh Education Office. After the Glamorgan Education Committee took over responsibility in 1903 for all the schools in its area formerly set up by the old School Boards and the religious bodies it appointed its own County Inspector of Elementary Schools. The qualifications for the post included: recent experience as a Head Teacher, aged 25–40 years; a knowledge of Welsh was important and "ability to ride a bicycle would be deemed a considerable advantage"!

Scholars   Despite the overcrowding and the disruption of the building work the school, almost from the beginning, had prepared some of its pupils to take the scholarship examination for entry to the County or Intermediate Schools:

20 June 1902	Six girls sent to Pontypridd to sit County School Scholarship: Mary Davies, Mary A James, Gert Llewellyn, Gwladys Williams, Evelyn Thomas, Daisy Bowen. Only Mary James and Gwladys Williams were successful.
7 September 1903	Edward Jarman, Standard V, has been successful at the County School entrance exam at Pontypridd, gaining a £3 scholarship ... only candidate from the school this year.
7 September 1905	Successful at Pontypridd County School Scholarship examination : David J Williams -- top boy of the division Edith Jones -- £5 scholarship
4 September 1908	County Scholarships : Edith Hughes, Florence Edwards, Susan Warren, James Beck (or Baker?).

In 1910 Elizabeth James and Maggie Evelyn White won scholarships to Pontypridd County School. All of these young students would have had a long day as they had to get to Caerphilly in time for the 8 o'clock train to Pontypridd and had a correspondingly late return home.

Gender differences   It is interesting to pause for a moment and speculate on the above information. Between 1902 and 1910 the available records (which may be incomplete) show that eleven children from Coedybrain Mixed and five from Llanbradach Mixed obtained scholarships to the local County Schools; of this number twelve were girls and only four were boys. Were the girls, in general, academically brighter than the boys? More motivated towards academic achievement and the greater career possibilities a secondary education would open up to them? Were the boys not looking beyond the assumption that they would follow their fathers down the mine? Did some parents feel they could more easily do without their daughter's domestic help than their son's pay packet? Whatever may have lain behind these early statistics, they seem to run counter to the then traditional view that "education is wasted on a girl".

The preponderance of girls over boys seeking a secondary education at this time was a reflection of the situation in the whole of thé County of Glamorgan, where the totals registered in the Intermediate or County schools in 1914 were 1894 girls and 1534 boys.

Another interesting set of figures for the same period can be considered alongside those for the County School Scholarships. At this time it was possible for children approaching the last year or two of their compulsory schooling to sit what was colloquially known as the Labour Exam. If the results showed that the pupil was "proficient" in reading, writing and arithmetic he or she was awarded a Proficiency Certificate and allowed to leave school. The figures available from Coedybrain Mixed School show that 23 boys and only 6 girls obtained such a certificate, which suggests that the boys, perhaps encouraged by parents, were much keener than the girls to enter the labour market as soon as possible. They might work as delivery boys for local tradesmen before going into the colliery on their fourteenth birthday, whereas the girls would only help their mothers to care for younger children or leave the village to go into domestic service.

Prosecutions   A matter of perennial concern to the headteacher was the non–attendance of pupils, but it seems not to have been a serious problem in Coedy-brain Mixed, the percentage of attendance rarely slipping below 85 per cent and settling between 90 and 94 per cent as the decade wore on. The authorities kept a steady pressure on the children and their parents through the activities of the Attendance Officer and the Magistrates :

4 July 1902	Jenny Maud Harris prosecuted for not attending school. Magistrates granted an attendance order and costs of 6/6d.
7 November 1902	Richard Jones, 53 De Winton Terrace, summoned at Caerphilly, was fined 10/– for irregular attendance.
2 July 1903	Mr Millward, Attendance Officer, reports three parties summonsed for irregular attendance last Tuesday. Richard Jones 10/– John Henry Thomas adjourned for 2 weeks Phoebe Williams 5/–
10 June 1904	4 or 5 very bad cases of non–attendance reported to Atten-dance Officer, but he is hampered by new resolution of managers to have all names on intended prosecutions at every managers' meeting which is monthly. In the mean-time many children will run about unimpeded.
30 June 1904	Attendance could be better. There are now flagrant cases of irregularity, particularly among children living in Stanley Row.
28 November 1904	Attendance not so good this morning. Mondays lately are idle days at the colliery and many families make it a habit

17

	of keeping their children home especially in mornings, cases of sleeping late very frequent.
4 October 1905	Prosecutions :
	George Haines — 54 De Winton Terrace
	George Llew Jones — 8 Stanley Row
	Florence Morris — 12 Stanley Row
	Arthur Morgan — 2 Coedybrain Road
	Edwin Barnes — 29 De Winton Terrace
	– parents fined 7/6d.
	Lily Smart — 41 Joinery Terrace
	Lottie Clarke — 13 Joinery Terrace
	– parents fined 5/-
	Margaret Welsh — – parent cautioned
11 May 1906	Prosecutions –
	Arthur Morgan — Truant School
	Ethel Jones — Adj. two weeks

Sometimes the counter-attractions to school were so strong that the head-teacher and local manager, J P Charles, wisely gave way :-

24 April 1903	Circus – closed early
4 May 1903	Band of Hope meetings, many children attend. School closed in afternoon.
13 June 1904	School closed today on account of general holiday of miners – Sunday School outings and Demonstration of miners. The place will be busy, advantage being taken of holiday to open Bowling Green.
27 February 1905	School closed this afternoon by order of manager – laying memorial stones of English Baptist Chapel.
11 September 1905	School closed – miners demonstration.
14 May 1906	Closed this afternoon owing to circus.
7 September 1906	School will close on Monday in accordance with Managers orders owing to demonstration of miners and sports in proximity of school buildings.

Travelling fairs also visited the village from time to time, setting up on the patch of land adjoining the De Winton Hotel and staying a week or longer, but these posed no threat to school attendance as they probably operated outside school hours.

Epidemics A much more serious threat – to chilcren's health and the continuation of their schooling – were the periodic epidemics which swept through the village during a period when sanitation was still primitive by modern standards. The school had flush toilets but only a cesspool which had to be emptied at intervals. In April 1904 scarlet fever was on the increase and the school was closed down, on medical orders, for five weeks, during which time the premises were disinfected. In October 1907 an epidemic of measles closed

18

the school for three weeks. In January 1909 the school managed to stay open despite scarlet fever, mumps, typhoid and ringworm, but closed for three weeks a year later when measles spread among the children. During the closure the teachers were temporarily transferred to other schools in Caerphilly, Abertridwr, Taffs Well and Radyr. Glamorgan County Council had a regulation that teachers must obtain lodgings if an infectious desease broke out in the house where they were living; if the doctor attending the infected person advised the teacher to stay away from school this advice had to be confirmed by the School Medical Officer before it was acceptable.

The Education Committees concern in 1905 about health and hygiene is demonstrated by the recommended adoption of a syllabus for schools which included teaching the following:-

Cleanliness, hair, skin, teeth, eyesight, hearing
Erect carriage, posture
Good and bad personal habits
Breathing, perspiration, change of clothing and bedding
Signs of good health
Quiet speech, restraint, self respect

It was further stated that "formal teaching should not be given to young children on the laws of health, but a few simple rules of health may well be impressed upon young scholars, and illustrated by the school discipline or by the practice of their homes – if the latter is significantly good to be appealed to with advantage".

The demon drink   Alcoholism, or excessive drinking, was another serious health hazard of this time. The local newspapers frequently reported men and women being dealt with in the Police Courts for offences of drunkenness and fighting in the streets. Many children would have suffered indirectly from the abuse of alcohol and the Education Committee was concerned to warn them of the dangers to themselves if they followed the example of their elders. In 1907 the committee commissioned the County Medical Officer to produce a placard for distribution in all the schools :

"The Education Committee of glamorgan County Council desires
to call the attention of school children to the following facts :-
a)   The abuse of alcoholic drinks produces physical degradation.
b)   Alcohol is not a food, but a drug.
c)   It is not a source of physical or mental vigour, and when taken in excess dulls the nerves, weakens self–control, excites the passions, ending in muscular weakness and prostration.
d)   Its habitual use impairs the productive power of the skilled artisan.
e)   Its habitual use in any form (even though never to the extent of drunkenness) results in chronic poisoning.
f)   It weakens the general health, greatly increases the risk of contracting Consumption and other Inflammatory Disorders,

and delays recovery.

g) It perverts the mental nature, affects the judgement and impairs the memory.
h) It deadens sensibility to surroundings, and destroys all desire for improvement.
i) It shortens life.
j) Intemperance in parents brings suffering on children.
k) It produces Physical and sometimes Mental Weakness in them. If they escape death in infancy, Permanent Disablement may still result from Paralysis, Epilepsy.
m) The death rate among the infants of inebriate mothers is 2½ times greater than among children of sober mothers.
n) Undoubtedly, alcoholism is the most terrible enemy to personal health, family happiness, national prosperity and even to the future of the Race.

Perhaps one or two of these statements might be disputed nowadays but the Education Committee's concern for children's health arose from the social conditions of the day rather than a chapel morality. At about the same time the anonymous Llanbradqch correspondent of the Caerphilly Journal used his weekly column to make a sharp comment on the local drinkers :

"There are three large hotels, two clubs and a grocer's shop from which intoxicants can be had in our neighbourhood, and yet there are some sober men and women here.
What earthly excuse can they have?
Surely they are not afraid of the police. What policeman in his right mind would trouble them with no police station or lockup within two and a half miles?
They can't say they are afraid of the law.
Possibly they have an idea that to get drunk is degrading".

On another occasion he wrote :–

"Is it not a pity that some folks' idea of a holiday is a severe drinking bout interspersed with bouts of fisticuffs?"

Ladies choir However, drinking and fighting were by no means the only recreational activities enjoyed in the village. In 1902 the Llanbradach Ladies Choir had been formed under the direction of Mrs Sarah Moses, the Coedybrain head teacher's wife who herself taught in the school for a while. She recruited members from among the women of Llanbradach, including several of her teaching colleagues, and found an accompanist for the choir in one of the pupil teachers, young Willie Davies. In 1904 the choir achieved a double success in a matter of weeks, winning first prize at the Aberdare Eisteddfod and then sharing first prize with the Manx Ladics Choir at the Rhyl National Eisteddfod. On

Llanbradach Glee Society, July 1918, photographed outside the old public hall, home of the Workmen's Social Club at this time. Among those pictured are Mrs Annie Jarvis, Coedybrain Infants teacher (centre, second left), Mrs Louisa Moses, former Coedybrain teacher and conductress of Llanbradach Ladies Choir (centre, fifth left), and Tommy Williams, grandfather of J P R Williams, Welsh rugby star (front row).

returning overnight from Rhyl the choir was greeted by a crowd at the railway station, men and boys drew Mr & Mrs Moses and Willie Davies in a trap to the Workmen's Hall where breakfast had been prepared for everyone. According to the Caerphilly Journal Mr T P Davies, headteacher of the Llanbradach School, who had lived in the Isle of Man for three years, "gave an impromptu address". On 28 September a concert was held during which the choir sang its Eisteddfod pieces. Mrs Moses was presented with an inscribed gold medal, the choir members with silver brooches, and the accompanist with a pendant.

The ladies' high spirits did not always win them an appreciative audience – in September 1905 they gave a concert in aid of Blackwood Cricket Club and the following week a comment appeared in the Caerphilly Journal: "Much as we appreciate the good work of the Ladies Choir it certainly does not add to their dignity to awaken the inhabitants in the late hours of the night with their singing when returning from a concert".

The choir achieved even greater success at the 1906 Caernarfon National Eisteddfod, beating off competition from the ladies' choirs of Blackpool, Cardiff, Pontypridd, Swansea, and Bangor to win the first prize outright. The choir was honoured by having Madame Clara Novello Davies (Ivor Novello's mother) as their accompanist, winning the £30 prize and a baton for Mrs Moses. The Caerphilly Journal expressed the local sense of pride : "Well done! You are a credit to Wales and have added dignity to the little pit village of Llanbradach." The choir remained active for a number of years, giving concerts to raise funds for charity.

Running to stand still The considerable enlargement of the Mixed School, completed by the end of 1904, provided room for a maximum of 350 children as compared with the 150 planned for on its opening in 1900. By the autumn of 1907 the numbers on the register had risen to 380 with an average attendance of 344; a year later the register contained 434 names with an attendance which rapidly rose from 381 to 414 by December 1908 as more children were registered. A temporary building was erected in the school–yard :

9 December 1908   Ald. E H Davies, Cllr. Charles, and the County Architect visited the premises for the purpose of choosing site for new school. Although the temporary school is ready, we are unable to start work there. Our number is rapidly increasing.

Two temporary classrooms provided space for another 100 children, but less than a year later Mr Tom Moses noted:

13 September 1909   For the first time in the history of the school the number present has reached 500.

His staff consisted of nine teachers, a student teacher and a pupil teacher.

5 November 1909   Attendance : 454 out of 508. We are going through one of those periods where many people leave the place and many new families enter.

The County Inspector of Schools reported in July 1910 :

"The school is uncomfortably full, and the admission of a large draft from the Infants Department after the summer holidays will cause great over-crowding. General condition of discipline and instruction reflects much credit on the Master and Staff. A special difficulty to be contended with is the migratory character of the population".

The County Council had decided in 1908 that the way to deal with the constantly growing child population was to build a new school which would allow the boys and girls, after the Infants stage, to be accommodated separately. Negotiations were opened with representatives of the De Winton Estate for about an acre of land adjacent to the existing Coedybrain Schools. The builder who was leasing the land agreed to give it up on payment of £150, and the land was purchased, freehold, for £1008 in February 1910. In November 1910 the plans for Coedybrain New Boys School, to accommodate 326 scholars, were approved and forwarded to the Board of Education.

It is interesting to note that only a month previously the Board of Education, in returning the plans of the proposed Cwmaber (Abertridwr) Boys School, made the following observations :-

"The enclosed plans are satisfactory, except for the arrangement of the Hall .... I am to point out that it has been brought to the notice of the Board repeatedly that with an arrangement such as is proposed the Hall cannot be, and is not, used for the purposes for which it was primarily intended. If singing lessons, drill, etc., are taken in the Hall, it is found that the noise distracts the attention of those at work in the classrooms and as a consequence such lessons are not given as often as they should be. The Board do not by any means wish to discourage the building of Halls, but they feel from the actual experience they have gained, and as the methods of teaching have progressed, that a school is more usefully planned with a Hall so arranged that the classrooms do not open directly out of it; by this plan, moreover, cross ventilation of the classrooms and the Hall itself is more easily attained".

The plans for Coedybrain Boys School, amended in March 1911, evidently complied with the Board of Education's thinking, as can be seen from the building as it is today. The plans, specification, and quantities were fully prepared by the end of the year and tenders were advertised for; in January 1912 the tender of Hamilton and Millard at £5850 was accepted; these were the Caerphilly contractors who had built the original Coedybrain Schools. The Clerk of Works, appointed by the County Council, was required to live in Llanbradach during the

23

construction of the new school. Determined, no doubt, not to be overtaken by another unforeseen surge in the population, the final plans increased the accommodation of pupils from 326 to 364. It was decided that "Nid dysg heb ei dilyn" should be the school's motto. (translation: "There's no education without continuity".)

In February 1913 the Education Committee requisitioned the items with which to furnish the school : dual desks, chairs and tables, cupboards for books, maps and inkwells, seven attendance boards and a hand bell, two museum cases and a globe, eight Darlington blackboards on stands and casters, log book and punishment book, one clock and two scraper mats, a rug, set of fire irons and a coal vase for the teachers' room, £8 worth of pictures and a portable boiler (for cleaners use). And what, I wonder, were a Conscience Clause and a Gunters Chain?

Punishment   The inclusion of a punishment book in the requisition is a reminder that even in an age when the general attitude towards the disciplining of children was less tender or circumspect than it has become towards the end of this century there were, nevertheless, official constraints on the punishments allowed to be exercised within schools, even if they were not always strictly observed! In 1906 the Glamorgan Education Committee had already issued the following instructions :–

"It is desirable that Teachers should try to reduce punishments to a minimum. Corporal punishment should be resorted to only where other methods have failed, excepting in cases of most serious offences. In each Department corporal punishment may be inflicted by the Head Teacher only, except that the Head may delegate the power to any Assistant holding a parchment certificate whom he selects for the purpose, the delegation and punishment on every occasion to be recorded in a book provided for that purpose. With regard to girls and infants this method of punishment ought in practice to be dispensed with.

In cases where it is found necessary to detain children after the ordinary school hours for the purpose of discipline or punishment, the period of detention should not exceed 15 minutes in the morning and 30 minutes in the afternoon. The time of detention should be spent under the immediate supervision of a responsible Teacher. Children must on no account be detained or otherwise punished for dulness".

In March 1913 Mrs Margaret Watts was appointed school cleaner, to be paid 5/– per week for oversight of the school until open, and then £35 per annum with an extra £6 allowance for cleaning the central hall.

The syllabus extended   The completion and opening of the new school was approaching but, retracing our steps to 1910, the teachers and children were still having to make the best of the cramped conditions in the "old" buildings. An indication of the positive attitude towards education among at least some of the children and their parents is to be seen in this entry in Tom Moses' logbook :

19 October 1910   A new library of 79 volumes has been added to the school through the subscriptions of some of the first class children who took it upon themselves to replenish the library.

As well as the traditional three Rs, the syllabus had been gradually widened to include Welsh – made compulsory in 1905 at 30 minutes a day in all classes, although before the end of the year the headteacher commented, "Welsh is not making the progress anticipated. There are far more English children living here than Welsh owing it is believed to the fact that the management of the local industries are chiefly English people". History was added in September 1906 – "Tuesday morning's reading lesson has been given up to it". In February 1909 girls in the upper classes started attending cookery lessons in Caerphilly. Also Nurse Vaughan, the school nurse, gave the older girls a talk on "Baby Feeding", while Dr Evans, school medical officer, spoke about "Ventilation of Houses".

Monarchy, Miners and Minimum Wage   1911 was marked by two Royal events:

16 June 1911   Closed for one week to commemorate the Coronation of H.M. King George V. On Coronation Day, 22 June, the children of these schools and those of Llanbradach schools will be entertained to a tea and mugs will be presented to them by Caerphilly Urban District Council. A procession will be formed from these premises to parade the village.

12 July 1911   Closed this afternoon (Wednesday) until Friday to celebrate the Investiture of the Prince of Wales at Caernarfon.

21 July 1911   Investiture books given out this afternoon.

A national strike in support of a minimum wage for coalminers brought production to a halt in March and April 1912, during which period many of the children were fed on the school premises, the cost borne in part by the local canteen committee and partly by authorization of the Education (Provision of Meals) Act 1906 which allowed the County Council to provide breakfasts for 1½d and dinners for 2d. The feeding continued throughout the Easter holidays and ceased three weeks after the strike ended.

Halfway through the six weeks' strike a report in the Caerphilly Journal gave a vivid picture of conditions in the Rhymney Valley :

"Collieries are still idle, men are lounging about, women scolding, children hungry more often than not, and tradesmen are handling but little money .. rents are falling in arrears, people running into debt, the cost of food is on the increase and famine is threatened in bread in about a week. Soup kitchens have been established ..... numerous calls on the distress funds which have been opened ..... furniture has been pawned ..... hundreds of fowls have been stolen in all parts of the valley ..... coal pickers are selling coal around Bargoed at 8d per bag, much cheaper than in prosperous times".

The Asquith government quickly passed the Minimum Wage Act to bring the dispute to an end.

During the year contracts were made for the chimneys to be cleaned (George Hyman, 27 Gough Street, Cardiff) the clocks to be maintained and repaired (A G Mabbett, 2 Market Street, Caerphilly) and the pianos and harmonium to be tuned (Messrs Dale Forty and Co Ltd., High Street, Cardiff).

Chapter's end   On 22 and 26 November 1912 the school was inspected by HMI William Edwards. He reported as follows:

1.   At present the work of this large Mixed School is conducted under very arduous conditions, all the rooms, permanent and temporary, being quite full, but the new boys School is expected to be ready in the course of a few months. The school is liberally staffed with capable Certificated Teachers. The periodical reports to parents and the criticism lessons for the benefit of the Pupil Teachers are commendable features of this school.
2.   A varied supply of literature has been provided and silent reading has been fostered. Owing to the size of the classes the amount of individual practice in reading aloud is limited.
3.   The predominant home language of the children appears to be English here. It is gratifying to note the earnest efforts of the English teachers to improve themselves in Welsh.
4.   The teaching of Geography and History is satisfactory, and of Mathematics good.
5.   Voice production receives great attention and the singing is excellent, while the marching and physical exercises are executed with precision and promptitude.

During June and July 1913 delivery was taken of most of the desks and other items requisitioned for the new school and by the end of July five classes, of boys only, had moved into the new building. The summer holidays began and a chapter in the story of Coedybrain Schools ended.

Chapter Two

LLANBRADACH MIXED SCHOOL 1900 – 1927

The handover   The Education Act, 1902, legislated the demise of the School Boards throughout England and Wales. Consequently, in September 1903, the Eglwysilan School Board went out of existence, handing over responsibility for its schools at Coedybrain to Glamorgan County Council. By virtue of the same legislation, the County Council became responsible for the National (or Church) Schools situated in Llanfabon parish at the Wingfield end of the village, renaming them the Llanbradach Mixed and Infants Schools. This administrative change meant that the County Council was to pay the teachers' salaries while the Managers retained responsibility for the fabric of the buildings; the Managers (one third of whom were henceforth nominated by the County Council) had the right to hire and fire the teachers, subject to the approval of the County Council. The schools retained their close links with the Church of England as the Foundation Managers and Trustees, including Colonel Morgan Lindsay of Ystrad Fawr, remained in office and the incumbent of All Saints, at this time the Rev. Edwin Edwards, was always one of the Managers. And, of course, the headteacher, Mr T P Davies, appointed in 1896 under the old dispensation was a churchman.

Anything but   In these early years, Mr Davies had a complement of three untrained teachers – Lucy Adams, Nana Evans and Mary Evans. In addition there was Rebecca Jane Jones who, aged 15 years, had been taken on as a pupil teacher. Being a firm disciplinarian he found it galling to have on his staff some-one like Miss Mary Evans, who had been appointed in April, 1900 and had charge of Standard II :

11 May 1900	I cannot trust Standard II from my sight. The new teacher is of little (if any) assistance to me. She is undoubtedly a weak disciplinarian; and a poor teacher, even when I have secured the necessary discipline for her.
18 June 1900	Miss M Evans is without doubt careless of school materials – slate pencils in particular – and is a poor disciplinarian.
8 July 1900	Standard II have been transferred from their usual place in the Main Room to a classroom where their bad discipline will have little chance of being contagious. I cannot be held responsible for their welfare when such a poor teacher has been provided for them.

| 16 July 1900 | Miss M Evans is more of a hindrance than otherwise to the progress of her class. I am seriously thinking of giving her no class. |

Despite his severe early criticisms of her, Mary Evans remained on the staff for five years without further mention in the head teacher's logbook until the day of her departure. He experienced difficulties of a different order with one of the other teachers :

| 4 May 1900 | Miss Nana Evans is absent. She complains of nervousness. I cannot excuse her absence on this account, as she was anything but nervous in speaking to me yesterday morning. |

In June 1901, he had occasion to call out two children from Nana Evans' class for talking. She contradicted him in front of everyone. He resented her interference and "a sharp altercation followed". She was told to go on with her work, but she refused. Miss Evans and her class were kept in detention for 25 minutes after school! Having reflected on the incident overnight, she apologised to Mr Davies the next day. Despite their propensity to clash (I suspect this was the only "altercation" sufficiently serious to be recorded in the logbook) T P Davies and Nana Evans remained colleagues until she left her post in September 1910.

Lessons and cold comfort   The HMI Report in July 1903 says :

"The school is very intelligently conducted. The syllabus is well drawn out, especially in Drawing. In some subjects, as Arithmetic and English, the work is somewhat uneven, but considerable allowance is due on account of the fact that many of the children in this unsettled district are newcomers. The lowest class is too large for the teacher. The Clock is out of order. Better apparatus should be provided for the teaching of Geography".

This reference to an "unsettled district" is a reminder that in 1903 Llanbradach, the pit village, was still a very recent creation. The first coal was brought up ten years earlier from the shallowest seam (house coal) and the deep steam coal seams came into production only progressively during 1894, 1895 and 1896.

The HMI Report for 1904 says :

"This school maintains its high character for efficient work. The Drawing is excellent and the syllabus of work, system of conduct marks, and Singing, deserve special praise".

The syllabus at this time consisted of English (which included reading, recitation, reproduction of anecdotes, essays, letter writing, word building, spelling, penmanship), Arithmetic, Elementary Science (suitable to the needs of the district, including first aid to the injured), Geography (with special reference to British

Possessions), History, Drawing (boys), Needlework (girls), Music, Drill, Manual Training (modelling in plasticine) and General Conduct.

An idea of the physical conditions in which the teachers and pupils had to work may be gained from these entries in the logbook :

| 10 October 1904 | Fires for the winter set this morning – very miserable failures all of them. |
| 19 October 1904 | Since the beginning of this month the school has been very badly swept and dusted. The fires have been but meagre apologies for heating the rooms. Indeed, every day two or more teachers have had to light their own fires and dust their own desks. The WCs and urinals are filthy. |

Between 15th and 29th November, the headteacher recorded the morning temperature in the school. It fell progressively from 41F (5C) to 29F (-2C). He made a formal complaint to the Managers. Three teachers developed severe colds and on 1st December the school was closed that afternoon and the next day due to staff sickness.

The HMI Report for 1904 further states :

"It would be as well to have at least one male assistant on the staff. The success of the teaching is still hampered by the frequency of fresh admissions, although this drawback is less acute than it has been in former years".

Another two and a half years were to lapse before a male teacher was appointed to the staff. Richard Jones, aged 23 and untrained, taught at the Llanbradach Mixed School until he left for St Luke's College, Exeter, in 1913. His salary on appointment in 1907 was £60 per annum. Meanwhile, in August 1905, at the start of another school year T P Davies comments :

It is next to impossible even to fairly conduct this school, for the following reasons :

1. Master is tied to a class of over 50.
2. Insufficient stationery, books etc.
3. The staff too weak to cope with the attendance which is over 220.

Welsh in the syllabus Welsh was introduced in to the syllabus in 1905. Mr Davies was proficient in the language since he later gave instruction in Welsh and Drawing at the Hengoed Pupil Teacher Centre. In September 1919 he noted the difficulty the school had with this element of the syllabus as he was the only member of staff who was able to teach the subject. Before the influx of men and their families from the English counties, Welsh had been predominant among the farming and market-town folk of East Glamorgan. The Welsh–

speaking immigrants from other parts of Wales had for a time helped to strengthen the local people in their old ways, but the tide of Anglicisation, aided by English-language newspapers, was flowing fast. An additional factor operating in Llanbradach was the colliery company's decision to engage English managers, who, in turn had a natural tendency to employ their fellow countrymen.

There was an increasing awareness on the part of the local Education Authority, reflecting an anxiety among some sections of the community, that the Welsh language and culture were under threat in the coalmining districts of Glamorgan. The Caerphilly Group of Managers (responsible for all the schools in the district) in June 1919 discussed the teaching of Welsh and found it to be unsatisfactory. They felt that teachers should be required to attend Welsh classes at Barry Training College and that at least one day a week should be set aside for Welsh education in the schools. They returned to the issue in October 1920, recommending to the Glamorgan Education Committee that Welsh be made a special subject and that teachers with special qualifications be appointed and paid £10 extra per annum.

In November, 1925 the Education Committee adopted the policy that teachers who were appointed without being proficient in the Welsh language were appointed on the condition that they attend the classes provided by the Education Committee in order to qualify themselves as teachers in Welsh; and that "as from 1928 no teacher whatsoever is to be appointed who has not already shown himself (or herself) to be qualified as a teacher of the Welsh language". One of the leading proponents of this policy was a Caerphilly woman, one of the local Managers, who before marriage was headteacher of Senghenydd Infants School. Mrs Catherine John (nee James), often referred to by her bardic name Megfam, was an ardent Welsh Nationalist who advocated the teaching of Welsh in schools on the same lines as English, both languages receiving the same amount of time and attention. She had been admitted to the Gorsedd in 1906 and was a pioneer of Welsh drama for children, winning two prizes at the Swansea National Eisteddfod in 1926.

The first mention of St David's Day in the school logbook occurs in 1904 when a half-holiday was given, but there seem to have been no special activities in the morning. In 1906 the children were given a lesson on Patriotic History before the half-holiday, and this seems to have been the token observance every year until T P Davies' retirement in 1927.

Preparation for life The inevitable fate of the majority of the boys and girls in 1906 – working down the pit for the former, going into "service" and later caring for their own husbands and children for the latter – is made brutally plain in the scheme of work for Elementary Science as taught to Standards 6 and 7 (12 and 13 years of age) :

Girls : care of the home; ventilation; sick room; clothing; washing; earnings etc. and other suitable subjects of "home hygiene".
Boys : mining; ventilation; coal gas; fire damp; principle of the safety lamp; timbering; methods of working etc.

These young children were already aware of the realities of life and death in Llanbradach. In September 1904 William England, a collier boy aged 14 of Wingfield Crescent, was stowing rubbish in the gob when a piece of coal measuring 6 feet 6 inches by 19 inches by 18 inches thick fell on him and he died of severe head injuries two days later. On 12th January 1905 John Lane, a 16 year old collier boy who lived with his parents in Cardiff, was crushed to death by a piece of coal measuring 10 feet 3 inches by 18 inches by 3 feet thick. Working on the surface of the colliery was no guarantee of personal safety. Isaac Powell, aged 16, employed as a cleaner in the winding–engine house, was struck on the head by the crank of the winding–engine in December 1906. His body was found outside the crank–pit fence while the head of his brush was in the crank–pit. He had evidently attempted to sweep it out. In August 1907 Richard Thomas, 15, of Pencerrig Street, the son of a local builder, was at work on the screens as a slag–picker. When the screen engine was started at the commencement of the shift, screams were heard coming from the end of one of the picking belts; the machinery was stopped and Richard's body was found twisted around the shaft of a sprocket wheel.

Woodwork and metal work were added to the syllabus for the boys in October 1913 when an equipped Manual Centre was incorporated in the newly opened Coedybrain Boys School. Mr F S Way was appointed to teach boys from Coedybrain and Llanbradach Mixed School in this centre. The older building which had until then accommodated boys and girls became Coedybrain Girls School and the reduced numbers allowed a cookery room to be set up, although it was May 1918 before the facilities were good enough for the Llanbradach girls to use them on a weekly basis. The Education Committee laid down a fairly detailed sewing curriculum for all girls in the County: they were to spend two or three hours per week learning how to cut from paper patterns,sew buttons, mend hooks and eyes, make and mend garments, knit stockings, and, later, how to use and care for the sewing machine. The Singer Sewing Company was able to supply machines at £2-15-0 each.

Boots and breakfasts   Between 10th September and 2nd November 1908, as a result of a dispute with the local management, the Llanbradach miners were out on strike. The effects on the children and their families were soon apparent in the schools. T P Davies noted a drop in the number of children registered due to parents seeking work elsewhere. On 6th October he recorded that in the last quarter 43 children were admitted and 42 removed, a total change of 85 children from an average number on the register of 266. But he also noted :

Notwithstanding the local strike the attendance is very satisfactory – in fact,generally speaking, so far, it is better than in times of prosperity, being now over 92%.

26 October 1908   Through the kindness of Mrs Lindsay, Miss Thomas, Llwynmadoc, and Mrs J S Corbett, the Master has been able to distribute garments, boots etc., to the children

31

most in need of them. Mr Jones of Llanishen National School also kindly sent a large quantity of second-hand clothing.

Oakfield Workmen's Social Club & Institute,
LLANBRADACH.
Catering Committee, Coal Strike, 1912.

Oakfield Workmen's Social Club Catering Committee, Coal Strike, 1912
T Fordham	W T Jones	E Morgan	F Langdon	W White
Chairman	Secretary	Vice-Chairman	Committee	Steward

The Oakfield Club, predecessor of the Old Comrades Club, helped to feed its members and their families during hard times.

Courtesy of R. Handford

30 October 1908   Breakfasts, the cost of which is borne by the Workmen's Committee, have been dispensed by the staff to 30 children this morning. These breakfasts will likely continue daily until the first pay after the strike will have been settled.

Local girls (and boy) make good   Generally speaking, it was only academic success which moved the headteacher to record the names of individual pupils. Ann Allsopp, aged 13, won a scholarship to Hengoed Girls County School in September 1905. Other records show that she passed her Senior Certificate of the Central Welsh Board in 1910. She was appointed to the staff of Coedybrain Infants in September 1913 as an uncertificated teacher, and then Coedybrain Boys before transferring three years later to the Twyn Mixed School in Caerphilly. Ellen (Nellie) Westhead went to Hengoed in the same year as Ann Allsopp. She later taught in Llanbradach Infants, and on marriage became Mrs Smith. Roy Meyrick Evans won a scholarship to Pengam Boys County School in 1907 and gained his Higher Certificate in English, History and Latin (equivalent to today's A levels) in 1912. He was then taken on as a student teacher at Coedybrain Mixed School just before his 18th birthday, at an annual salary of £30, leaving a year later to do a teacher–training course in Cardiff. He returned to his old school for a month's temporary work during the college summer vacation of 1914, and was due to go to Coedybrain Boys in September 1915 in another temporary engagement but he opted instead to work in a munitions factory, and this is the last we hear of him. Mabel Griffin went to the Hengoed County School in 1910. Having obtained her CWB Certificate, she went as a student teacher to Coedybrain Infants on a salary of £25 in August 1916. She stayed on as an uncertificated teacher, on £45 per annum, and remained in the post until the early 1920s when she transferred to Twyn Girls School, Caerphilly.

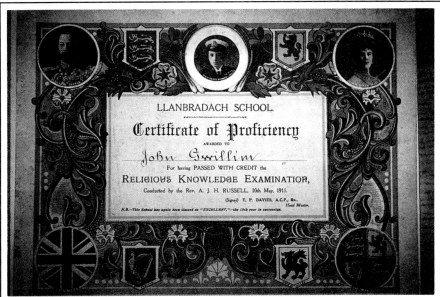

As a "Church School" Llanbradach Mixed received an annual Diocesan visitor who examined the Anglican pupils in their knowledge of the Scriptures. John Gwillim was presented with this certificate in 1911.

Courtesy of Les Gwillim

A name which first crops up in the logbook in 1898 is that of Gertrude Fuell. She appears, then aged 9 years, in a list of scholars who distinguished themselves in the annual religious inspection conducted by the Rev. Holme Russell. In 1901 she passed the entrance examination for Hengoed Girls County School. She next appears in the logbook in December 1906 when she was appointed to the staff of Llanbradach Mixed as a supplementary teacher. At the age of 18 years, with no teaching experience, she was put in charge of Standard I, a class with 53 pupils on the register. She survived this daunting start to her career, remaining in the post until July 1913, on a final salary of £45 per annum, when she obtained a place at Fishponds Training College, Bristol. Along with Roy Evans she taught for a month at her old school in September 1914 at a rate £10 less per annum than he was paid, the usual differential between men's and women's pay – and she already had six more years of teaching experience than he had!

On completing her training, Miss Fuell returned to Llanbradach Mixed in September 1915, but moved to Coedybrain Boys School in March 1916 on a salary of £85 per annum. Her name is recorded in the Coedybrain logbook on three occasions :

18 September 1916	Miss Gertrude Fuell absent, attending her sister's wedding.
13 February 1917	Miss Fuell away on account of the death at the Front of Captain Nicholls, her brother–in–law. (Captain Wm. Harold Nicholls of the 15th Battalion, Australian Imperial Force, was killed in France on 26th January, aged 29 years. His widow presented a lectern to All Saints Church in his memory).
5 March 1919	Miss Fuell absent, attending her grandmother's funeral.

She transferred to Coedybrain Girls School in December 1919 and was given charge of the top two standards (VI and VII). She left Coedybrain in February 1923 having been appointed Headteacher of Oxwich National School. Ill-health forced her to relinquish this post and in October 1923 she returned to Coedybrain Girls, taking Form I and then Standard IV. her good health must have been completely restored as she taught in Coedybrain for another six years, when the final logbook entry reads :

30 September 1929	Miss A G Fuell leaves today to take up duties as head-teacher of the Church of England School at Stanton St Bernard, Wiltshire, where married women are allowed to teach. Miss Fuell is leaving here to be married.

A happy ending to her life in Llanbradach and a happy beginning to a new life in the rural depths of Wiltshire, where she lived with her Welsh husband (known locally as "Taffy" Payne) until her retirement in 1949. The contrast was great between Llanbradach with its large industrial population, associated disputes and economic depression, and the tiny hamlet with its handful of houses, its church, and its two–class school serving an agricultural district.

Fairy tales and play sheds The HMI inspected the school in September 1910 and reported :

"The school continues to suffer from the presence in the district of a some-what large migratory element. It must be discouraging. The general

management is marked by much intelligence, and the headteacher deserves credit
for his success in maintaining the efficiency of the school in difficult circumstances. His assistants give him zealous support according to the measure of their abilities and experience. Perhaps the distinguishing merit of the school lies in the skill and thoroughness with which drawing is taught. The time devoted to Arithmetic is a little in excess of the needs, and some of it might be spared for other subjects. The teaching in English is careful and conscientious but might advantageously be on more elastic lines. At present the children have not quite enough practice in expressing their own thoughts on what they read or hear and more matter of the fairy tale description should be used for the younger children".

As for the buildings, the HMI recommended better ventilation and a sliding partition in the main room; the playground should be levelled or asphalted, and he thought playsheds would be useful. T P Davies had noted in June :

It is found impossible to conduct lessons in Physical Exercises, as a rule, if outdoors, as the yard is either too dusty in dry weather or too wet and muddy in wet weather.

Cabbages and Kings   School life was interrupted and enlivened from time to time by a variety of events :

8 May 1903	Poor attendance – circus in adjoining field
1 July 1903	Holiday – All Saints Church Consecration
7 September 1903	Half holiday – free tea to children of Co–opertive Society
13 April 1904	Circus in village at 3.30pm – school closed at 3.45pm
22 June 1904	Half holiday this afternoon – opening of New Parish Rooms, Teaparty, etc.
7&8 Deceember 1904	No school. Bazaar in aid of School Building Fund.
13 February 1905	Half holiday this afternoon. Religious "Revival" Meetings in the town.
28 June 1904	At the request of J P Charles, school manager, a holiday was given at "assembly time" in honour of the Visit of the Prince of Wales to Cardiff.
11 September 1905	No school. Miners Demonstration.
12 July 1907	Medals provided by Mr W Spickett, were presented to the children in honour of the King's Visit to Caerphilly in the afternoon. Holiday granted.
24 May 1909	"Empire Day" observed here. Col. Lindsay has presented a huge flag, and Mr Gregory (pit manager) a flagstaff for the school. The flag was saluted by the whole school at noon, and a half holiday given for the afternoon.
1 November 1909	Half holiday. Opening (after completion) of the Parish Church.

16 June 1911	School closed for "Coronation Week".
13 July 1911	Holiday. Investiture of Prince of Wales.
25-27 June 1912	Closed on account of George V's visit to South Wales.

Old money, new money   The school's connection with the Church of England and the squirearchy remained close during the early decades of this century. The Rev. Edwin Edwards, first vicar of the Parish of Llanbradach, was Chairman of the Governors. Miss Clara Thomas and Colonel and Mrs Lindsay maintained their interest in the schools, Mixed and Infants. Clara Thomas visited the village on special occasions connected with All Saints Church and sometimes called at the school, making her last recorded visit on 2 November 1909. In March 1913: "Three young trees planted to beautify the southern aspect of the school – the gift of Mrs Lindsay". When the Lindsays died in the 1930s it was the end of an era. The school and the village had lost their last link with the beneficient but outmoded patronage of the land owning families which had played a vital role in the early years of their history. The "National" Schools owed their very existence to the Thomas, Lindsay and Wingfield families.

They were now, since 1903, at least partly in the hands of the elected, hostile, members of Glamorgan County Council. The Local Education Authority disliked being in the position of having to support these Anglican semi-independent schools which had the power to choose two thirds of the managers and appoint teachers (albeit with the LEA's approval). There had been fierce opposition in Nonconformist Wales, led by Lloyd George, to the provisions of the Education Act, 1902, which compelled LEAs to give rate-support to the Church of England Schools. The County Councils paid the teachers' salaries and general running costs while the Foundation Managers remained responsible for the maintenance of the buildings which had to comply with the County Councils' requirements. In Caerphilly a serious dispute between the Managers and the LEA over the lack of repairs to the National School buildings in Park Lane resulted in the school closing permanently in 1906 after the Council refused to pay the teachers' salaries from June 1905.

During the early years of this new regime there are signs in the Llanbradach Schools' logbook that the teachers felt themselves to be unfairly treated, salary-wise, compared with their colleagues in the Council Schools, and the County Council occasionally cracked the whip over the condition of the school buildings.

When one of his teachers, Miss Lilian Prentice, left Llanbradach Mixed to take up a similar post in Bargoed in January 1912 the headteacher commented: "£95 there – £75 here, same LEA!". The disparity in salaries had been taken up with the County Council in June and December 1911 and again in January 1912 by the Rev. Edwin Edwards, chairman of the Llanbradach managers. His letters had merely been acknowledged, no satisfaction, or even justification, had been offered. He claimed that teachers were leaving the school for higher salaries in the Council schools. How he managed it is not known, but the Rev. Edwards got the question of his unanswered correspondence raised in the House of Lords on 20 March 1912. The report in the Caerphilly Journal states that the Earl of Portsmouth, the Archbishop of Canterbury and the Marquis of Londonderry between them raised the matter. Earl Beauchamp and Lord Haldane replied on behalf of the Government. It is clear that in anticipation of the questions being raised the Board of Education had communicated with Glamorgan Education Committee expressing concern about the issue and had received assurances that the Committee would comply with the provisions of the 1902 Act in the matter of equitable salaries.

When T P Davies' salary was considered by the LEA in April 1912 it was decided that as "The headteacher has and will have no pupil teachers or student teachers to supervise, an increase in salary is not recommended". However, an Inquiry by the Board of Education held in August resulted in the LEA agreeing to increase both headteachers' salaries :-

T P Davies, headteacher, Mixed, £170 (from £168)
Miss Louisa Moses, headteacher, Infants, £100 (from £95)

Also two of Miss Moses' staff received an increase :-

Miss Harriott Hilditch, certificated teacher, £95 (from £85)
Miss Doris Harrison, certificated teacher, £85 (from £80)

The Board of Education had earlier in the year reported on the improvements deemed necessary in the buildings of Llanbradach School and confirmed the LEA's assessment of the state of the premises. The Board called upon the Foundation Managers for an assurance that the improvements would be carried out within a reasonable period, failing which the support of the school by the County Council would be discontinued. There is no record of how the School Building Fund succeeded in warding off this threat; probably by a combination of fund–raising activities in the village and an appeal to the school's original benefactors.

Fever and Floods   The work of the school was severely disrupted on many occasions by what might be termed "natural causes" which the authorities were unable to remedy : disease and flooding. These are detailed in the log book :-

21 April 1904	School closed for three weeks by M.O.H. on account of Scarlet Fever being prevalent, but which did not affect this school (The Coedybrain Schools were also closed).
16 April 1907	There are several cases of typhoid fever in the vicinity of the school. One of the school boys is being buried today, having contracted the fever just a week or ten days ago.
18 September 1907	An epidemic of Measles has greatly reduced the attendance this week.
21 October 1907	Telegraph from Chief Education Official : close school today for three weeks; inform Infants' Mistress. To re-open 11 November. (Codeybrain schools too).
20 December 1909	Closed for three weeks (this includes Christmas Holiday)

37

owing to epidemic of measles and fever.

13 January 1910	Closed another three weeks on account of measles.
16 December 1910	Street and school road flooded. No school.
18–20 December 1911	Floods (P.C. Osborne advised headteacher to dismiss the children).
4 March 1912	Heavy rain storm. Flood. No School.
26,29 August 1912	Flood. Closed.

The Caerphilly Journal (22 December 1910) reported that recent floods in the district had been at their worst in Llanbradach. Victoria Street and Charles Street had water in the houses up to the third stair; the milkman handed up the milk to people reaching out of their bedroom windows; the National Schools had closed and the cellar of the Wingfield Hotel was flooded, the contents destroyed. The report added that "floods do not occur frequently but a wall or embankment should be constructed".

Victoria Street in 1912, one of the several occasions
when the river Rhymney flooded the neighbourhood.

Courtesy of Ellis Stanbury

The Merthyr Express (4 January 1913) carried this report : "Cottages Flooded. For several days last week, owing to the incessant rain, the Rhymney River was in a swollen state and as invariably is the case at such times one part of Llanbradach – the northern part – was flooded with most uncomfortable results to numbers of the inhabitants whose cottages were invaded by the water. The

Caerphilly District Council have at various times tried to come to terms with landowners with a view to cutting an additional course for the river, as its circuitous course at Llanbradach is considered to be the primary cause of the flooding. Nothing, however, has yet been done to mitigate matters, despite the various proposals made by the Council".

Teachers and scholars The headteacher and his staff were coming under increasing pressure from the greater number of children entering the school in 1913, probably related to the peak in numbers employed in the colliery that year, about 3,000 :

20 October 1913   320 on register. Accommodation for 264. Staff of five assistants.

Of the five teachers mentioned at this time, the name of only one is known : Miss Gladys Sarah McCarthy who joined in 1910 and left to get married in 1919.

24 November 1913   A class of 39 children from the bottom of the school have been transferred this day to the Infants Department, at the instruction of the LEA for (1) want of accommodation, (2) want of a teacher.

31 July 1914   The classes have been too big and unwieldy. One class had 6 teachers during the year!!!!

4 March 1915   The strain of working here with but one permanent (uncertificated) teacher for a school of this size has become intolerable and nerve–wrecking.

31 March 1915   24 teachers have worked in the Department last year – 18 came 19 went.

A degree of relief for the hard–pressed headteacher and his staff came shortly afterwards from the welcome return of Mrs Rebecca Jane Thomas (nee Jones) in May 1915. Rebecca, who began her career at the school as a pupil teacher had stayed on as an untrained teacher until she resigned in December 1912 to get married to T L Thomas the local builder and make her home at 31 Tynygraig Road. T P Davies described her then as "an excellent teacher". Further relief came as the result of an unexpected (and for those concerned surely a distressing) happening:

4 June 1915   The average has been reduced to 210 this week owing to all the tenants of Victoria Street having had notice to leave. Many of the families moved away during the week.

This situation arose from serious flooding several months earlier which caused Caerphilly Urban District Council to declare the whole street unfit for human habitation and to take steps to place a Closing Order on all the properties. However, the Council did not pursue this course of action to its end, although further flooding in November 1916 caused fresh concern.

More examples of academic success are proudly recorded in the logbook:

15 September 1913 Hilda Davies (12 years) has secured the first place in the Day Scholarship Examination for Howell's (Llandaff) County School – open to girls from the Glamorgan Elementary Schools.

Howell's School, Llandaff funded by an ancient charity, opened in 1860 in order to train young orphan girls to earn a living as governesses. By the 1890s it provided a secondary education for girls, as boarders or day–pupils, who went there on scholarships or as fee–payers. I wonder how well young Hilda coped with the transition from life in a pit village to the academic surroundings of a middle–class establishment? Probably better than most of her peers would have done as she was the daughter of T P Davies, the headteacher. The school continues to flourish to this day.

30 July 1915 Claude K Davies (11) and Edward T Williams sat the County Council Scholarship Exam at Pengam School and came 2nd and 3rd in the list.

The official scholarship list confirms that Edward Williams, 12 years, was 2nd on the list, but shows Claude Davies, 16 months younger, was 18th on the list. Claude was T P Davies' son who became a teacher and joined the staff of his old school only a week after his father's retirement in 1927.

30 June 1916 It should be recorded that on 25 January 1915 a little Belgian Refugee, Francois Van De Velde, 10 years of age, was admitted to this school knowing nothing of the English Language or its system of calculations. After but 12 months instruction he was promoted to the Seventh Standard and has become, without a doubt, the top boy of the school – not only in English (including written and oral composition) but also in Arithmetic with its various systems of tables, so unlike the metric he had used previously on the Continent. He leaves this week for a Belgian School at Cardiff.

The Belgian School referred to, provided on a voluntary basis, was housed in Richmond Road, Cardiff, and catered for the locality's share of the 119,000 refugees who fled to this country after the German invasion of their country in 1914.

A hint of war His reference to little Francois is the first indication in T P Davies' log book entries that the country had been at war since August, 1914.

The day after this entry the Battle of the Somme opened, a day in which 19,000 British were killed. With well over a hundred men from the village lost during the war – a higher rate of killing than even the colliery achieved – the impact of the European conflict must have been very great, yet the log book merely hints at what was going on :

5 June 1917	Mrs Evans absent – giving her husband a "send off" to the army.
4 October 1917	Miss Lloyd absent owing to the death of her fiancé in Salonika, "killed in action".
7 March 1918	Miss McCarthy has 1½ days leave of absence to meet her fiancé home from the War.

The local press carried frequent reports of war-wounded who were convalescing in the Red Cross hospital which had been set up in Bronrhiw House, Caerphilly: entertainment provided for the men by local organisations and fund-raising activities on behalf of the hospital. Miss Sybil Corbett of Pwllypant House was commandant of the Red Cross Society and many local women were active in the organisation. In December 1915 Llanbradach Social Club (Chairman, Rowland Tucker, secretary, William Selby) organised a competitive carnival and rugby football match to raise funds towards the extension of the hospital. A procession headed by Llanbradach and Caerphilly Silver Bands – made up of the Voluntary Training Corps, Red Cross Corps, St Johns Ambulance Brigade, Church Lads Brigade, Boy Scouts, competitors in fancy dress, and the football teams – walked from Station Road through the village to the Wingfield football field. The Wounded Soldiers beat the Llanbradach XV by one try to nil. A silver cup (given by the Workmen's Club) was presented to the winners by Councillor J F Gregory, manager of Llanbradach colliery.

The Armistice was signed on Monday 11th November, 1918. All schools closed for the remainder of the week. T P Davies had been, from the outbreak of the war, the local honorary representative of S.S.A.F.A. In October 1919, as Chairman of Caerphilly Local War Pensions Committee, he headed a deputation to the Minister of Pensions.

Unsympathetic magistrates and mine-owners   A matter of concern, as always, was the non-attendance of an often large percentage of the pupils:

13 December 1918	The attendance has been exceedingly bad for the past three weeks in particular, partly owing to influenza epidemic, and partly owing to local magistrates' lack of sympathy with the education of the masses.
20 December 1918	Without fear of contradiction it would be difficult to find magistrates, as a body, discharging their duties so inefficiently as those of Caerphilly judging by the cases sent before them from this school, by the results as reported by the Attendance Officer.

41

A perennial cause of large-scale absenteeism in many schools during the first half of the century is first mentioned at Llanbradach on :

10 September 1919   A large number of children, 33, have gone away with their parents hop-picking.

The School Attendance Officers were kitted out by the County Council with a standard wardrobe of clothing; a suit costing £2-13-6d. and extra pair of trousers (15/-), a cloth cap (8/6d), straw hat (2/6d), mackintosh coat (£1-3-6d) and a pair of leggings (9/6d)

The national lockout of miners between 1 April and 1 July 1921 resulted in hardship for the families and once again the feeding of children in school was resumed :

18 April 1921   The Provision of Meals to Schoolchildren Act was put into operation this morning - owing to miners' protracted strike.
13 May 1921   Meals to be provided during the holidays.
18 July 1921   Meals ceased yesterday after 13 weeks of daily feeding of two meals per day, 41,541 meals served in this period. Attendance improved, exceptionally good - probably owing to the feeding, but discipline suffered because the Head Master had extra work and outside helpers were frequently on the premises.

Not surprisingly, it was generally found, on all such occacions, that the children's attendance markedly improved when nourishing meals were made available on school premises!

The miners, returning to work on the coal-owners' terms, found their wages cut by half. Before the lockout a collier, the top earner of the labour force, might have been paid £5 or £6 per week, whereas a labourer's wages would have been barely half that sum. The weekly output at Llanbradach had varied between 4,500 tons and 6,000 tons before the dispute; for a few weeks afterwards the men pushed the production up to 8,000 tons and 9,500 tons in an effort, no doubt, to make up for lost wages in the previous three months. As many as 500 men (according to the Caerphilly Journal) had not been re-employed at Llanbradach by September and had little prospect of returning to work.

Improved attendance figures, apart from those resulting inadvertently from industrial unrest, were traditionally sought on the "carrot and stick" principle. The "stick" was wielded by the L.E.A. through the efforts of the Attendance Officer and the local magistrates, albeit with little effect as far as Mr T P Davies was concerned. The "carrot" came in two shapes - a half day holiday (which the school gained only once in the 1920s) or a presentation to individual pupils :

19 December 1924   Before closing for the Christmas holidays County Councillor J Phillips of Nelson attended for the special

Llanbradach Junior Mixed, 14 November 1922. Mrs Myra Harding (née Jones), aged 5½ years then, is first from the left in the second row up. Others identified are Bessie Jones, Gwladys James, Cassie Meyrick, Wilf Drane, Harold Jones. Courtesy of Kevin Williams

Llanbradach Mixed School, c. 1922. Mr T P Davies and another teacher (probably Mrs L A Evans or Mrs G M Wilson). Among the children are: Queenie Williams, Gwen Kinch, Dolly Williams, Tom Evans. Courtesy of Mrs Marion Linder

43

purpose of distributing 40 certificates for good attendance, 17 books for one year's perfect attendance, 4 books
for two years perfect continuous attendance, and eight
silver medals for three years. The latter were earned by
Kenneth Evans, Gilbert Morse, Thomas Yeo, Evelyn
Kinch, Cecil Neale, Mary Westhead, Alice Ferris and
Nancy Westhead.

In 1926 six of the eight medallists achieved four years perfect attendance and for
this were rewarded with mathematical and drawing instruments (the boys) and
a workbasket (the girls).

Turmoil and steam   The coal-owners' national lockout of 1926, from 1 May to
30 November, inflicted the greatest damage yet on the families of Llanbradach.
The full story of those seven months is beyond the scope of this book, but the
following log book entries afford a sidelong glance at the picture through the
harassed eyes of a headteacher grappling with his professional responsibilities
in the midst of social upheaval :

3 May 1926	Only 88% of children present owing presumably to the local miners strike which has begun.
17 May 1926	Feeding of necessitous school children was commenced this morning when 165 out of 252 breakfasted. Both breakfasts (at 8.30am) and dinners (at 3.40pm) are supplied.
21 May 1926	Education Committee has decided that the Schools be closed for Whit Monday only – not the whole week as announced previously – owing to the continued strike of the miners.
25 May 1926	School meals, 3 per day, were provided during non-school days.
29 July 1926	Work done in term quite satisfactory especially considering that since 17 May the feeding of necessitous children – two thirds of the whole school – had occupied much of the Head Master's time, while the six classes had to be housed in five rooms, owing to one classroom being used as food store and meals preparation room.
30 July –	Summer holidays.
5 September 1926	Feeding continued throughout
8 October 1926	The discipline is suffering much from the fact that the school is being used for feeding – manned by voluntary helpers who are on and about the premises almost throughout the day. Feeding at 8.30am, 2.15 and 4pm.
15 October 1926	The attendance has been good for many weeks, but the discipline and work suffer much through my inability – on account of the feeding arrangements – to give the

necessary supervision and usual help. For some time past boots and "daps" have been provided for the barefooted to the number of several dozens, and already some 250 pairs of boots and shoes have been repaired on the premises by voluntary "cobblers".

22 October 1926   I find as the cold, and particularly the wet, weather comes the limited space or accommodation here for both school-work and feeding purposes militates sadly with the efficiency of the teachers' work. My own room, which is ordinarily used for Class F (Standard VII) and for Music, is now almost exclusively used to store and prepare the meals, and I have consequently to do much of my own school work in the turmoil and steam.

Llanbradach Mixed School, Class E6, c. 1926–7. Mr. A E Morgan on the left, Mr T P Davies on the right. Among the children are: Joe Williams, Billy Drane, Catherine Meyrick, Anita Handford, Gwyneth Williams, Billy Evans, Jimmy Young, Bessie Jones, Mary Pratley, Doris Williams, Gladys James.   Courtesy of Kevin Williams

5 November 1926   This morning by 9am the school was completely surrounded by the flooding of the local river. No water, however, came into the school itself. At midday the children could not possibly reach their homes owing to the depths of the waters. I, therefore, took upon myself to give all the children – the "necessitious" and the others – a "midday lunch" of bread and butter and bread and jam and kept them all on the premises for the afternoon school.

Llanbradach Mixed School, class F7/8 c. 1926–7. Mr T P Davies on the left, Mr Lewis Conibear on the right. Among the children are: Eric Williams, Claude Evans, Dorothy Smith, Gladys Tudor, Maida Smith, Doris Brice, Ethel Williams, Jim Summers, Vic Stone, Teddy O'Shea.   Courtesy of Kevin Williams

Llanbradach Mixed football team, 1926–27. Teachers: Mr E A Morgan, Mr T P Davies (head), Mr Lewis Conibear. Among the boys are thought to be: George Walker, Eric Williams, Bobby Davies and Claude Evans.   Courtesy of Ellis Stanbury

23 November 1926	The attendance for at least a fortnight has showed considerable decrease owing to the epidemic of whooping cough coupled with colds caught during inclement weather chiefly by children possessing poor footgear. The barefooted children appear to be suffering less than the others in health. Many of the barefooted children remain absent because the school arrangements fail to provide a second pair during the industrial strife – a rather unique way of showing their gratitude to those whose money and voluntary work has catered for them for some months past.
24 November 1926	Received two "bends" of leather from the Pontypridd Board of Guardians to mend the boots of the schoolchildren.
29 November 1926	Most of my Voluntary Workers (men) have returned to work after the coalmining dispute; but the provision of meals for necessitous children is well carried on by deputies – chiefly women and youths.
16 December 1926	Owing to the parents restarting their work after the "strike" only about 80 children now attend for their meals at school.
23 December 1926	Only 33 children made application for meals during the past week. No applications have been received for the continuation of the meals further than today.
10 January 1927	It may be of interest to record that during the period of 32 weeks when necessitous schoolchildren were fed upon these premises, 130,318 meals were served at a cost of £1525–14–5d. During the same period nearly 500 pairs of boots were mended free of cost to the wearer, and 3 dozen new pairs of various footgears were also distributed. The figures given here refer to both departments of this school. The average cost per meal per child works out at 2.8 pence.

The improved attendance brought about by the feeding arrangements of the previous months is reflected in the following entry :

23 December 1926	Yesterday afternoon Colonel and Mrs Lindsay of Ystrad Fawr presented the following awards to the children – 72 Certificates for Regularity of Attendance 20 Book Awards for One Complete Year 4 Book Awards for Two Complete Years 1 Book Award for Three Complete Years 2 Silver Medal Awards for Four Complete Years 2 Solid Silver Watches for Five Complete Years

There were also presentations of 12 Silver Medals as "Runners Up" in A.F. Cup

Matches and a large silver cup gained in the Sports held on Bank Holiday against Coedybrain School.

Some children's dedication to obtaining one of these attendance awards must have been sorely tried the following summer :

7 July 1927   "Seion" Sunday School Monstre Outing to Barry. Attendance today 58% – lowest on record during the last 31 years. Hitherto, holidays have been granted for this annual treat but this year – although correctly warned of the expected bad attendance – the Education Office did not close the school.

It is a little surprising that in a nominally Anglican School there were so many children participating in a Nonconformist trip to the seaside. But then, I suppose, as we are discovering in these oecumenical times there is really only one God – and for sure, there was only one Barry Island!

Respect for authority   In the 33 years (1894–1927) after the school moved into its permanent premises at the Wingfield end of the village there were only four recorded instances of illegal entry :

20 April 1903   Re-opened after Easter holidays. Desks and door damaged wilfully.

15 June 1903   School broken into yesterday (Sunday) by Rayfiel Haines and Wm. Geo. Yemm – both of Charles Street (present day Oakfield Street).

14 November 1913   Headmaster attended Bargoed Police court to give evidence as to breaking and entering into this school on Saturday, 8th inst., and stealing moneys. Phillip Gardner (12) and his brother James (18) being charged.

28January 1914   School broken into again.

After 1908 Llanbradach police station was manned by Sergeant David Davies and three constables. Probably this police presence, the influence of church and chapel, the constraints of living in a tightly-knit community, and the greater heed paid to authority all contributed towards a respect for property in those earlier times.

Farewell Mr Davies   T P Davies, himself, was a figure of awesome authority to the children who passed through his hands. His former pupils, many years afterwards, recalled him as a "terror with the stick" which he carried behind his back when he stood at the door of a classroom. He used the cane to discourage left-handed pupils and anyone who came late, and to punish any boy who failed to raise his cap when greeting an adult in the street. He was a formidable man. One suspects that even his staff would have hesitated to arouse his displeasure! Yet he must also have inspired a more benign kind of respect as a man who expected as much of himself as he did of others and whose sternness was softened by his love of music and art, and probably of nature, too, as he sometimes walked to Pwllypant and back along the river before school started. On retirement he gave up his home in Llanbradach – 9 Central Terrace (now Park View), "Iona House", where he had lived since March 1900 – and moved to Pentyrch.

His final entry in the log book is characteristic of the man –

25 October 1927   As I am retiring from the Scholastic profession on 31 October, it may be of value to record the following:-

A   My experience for many years has been that the parents of children attending the school do not desire, as a rule, secondary or higher education for their children. Although I invariably counsel them to change their mind in this matter, they tell me – over and over again – that they are quite satisfied with the education offered at this school. They say it is more fitted to their purpose than what they find children getting at Secondary Schools, especially during the first year or so there. Besides, although children may gain so-called Scholarships, parents complain that they are called upon to pay for books and railfare (in the past), caps, badges, gym-dresses, games, etc., –and this upon parents in poor circumstances is rather more than they can reasonably bear. I may prove, roughly, the above, by the following figures :-

	1926	1927
No. children eligible to sit Scholarship Exam	20	15
No. children who went to, and sat, the Exam	3	3

B.   For upward of 20 years the school has opened for morning sessions at 9.10 because, from previous experience, it was found that the majority of the children were not sent from their homes until the local colliery time-signal went at 9am. For the same reason the afternoon session starts at 1.10pm, as well as the fact that artificial light has never been installed for school purposes. Hence, if the afternoon school started at 1.30 or 2.0pm there would be no light to carry on during several of the darker months of the year.

C.   Respecting the Curriculum appropriate to this locality it has been considered wise to emphasise the following subjects :

1.   Private reading, not only for acquiring knowledge, but also a means of using up long leisure hours in the coal industry in which most of the scholars will, in various ways, be attached after leaving school.
2.   Correspondence.
3.   Music – so that interest may be taken after they leave school.
4.   Drawing.
5.   Science : Mining and First Aid.

It is with the deepest regret I sever my connection with this school after 31⅓ years; and when looking back upon the work done here – often under extreme difficulties – I cannot help thinking that the results which have over and over again manifested themselves have been nothing short of miraculous, thanks chiefly to a loyal staff.

In conclusion, I have the honour to put on record my heartfelt gratitude to the school managers for their sympathetic dealings, particularly to the Chairman (Rev. Edwin Edwards) for invaluable help at all times.

T.P. Davies
Headmaster
1st July 1896 to 31st October 1927

The phrase "long leisure hours in the coal industry" refers, of course, to the enforced periods of inactivity resulting from unemployment, short working weeks, and industrial strife.

Chapter Three

COEDYBRAIN BOYS 1913 – 1931

Jobs and journeys   The colliery in 1913 reached a peak of production (646,520 tons) exceeded only in 1928 and 1929. The company's importance as the main source of employment for the children's fathers (and for the children ultimately) is evident in the occupations listed in the Coedybrain admission registers : miner, collier, timberman, haulier, fireman, overman, ostler, hitcher, pumpsman, roadman, repairer, coker, stoker, checkweigher, storekeeper, winder, manager, tipper, rider, splicer, lampman, fitter, carpenter, electrician. The local railway companies are represented too : railwayman, engine–driver, platelayer, signal-man, station master. The village tradesmen are well represented : butcher, baker, grocer, greengrocer, fishmonger, fruiterer, bootmaker, draper, newsagent, barber, chemist, club steward and hotel proprietor. The population was approaching 5,500 and beginning to stabilise, although the tag of "tramp–pit" was still applied to the colliery due to the coming and going of men in search of work. During 1913 and 1914 children entering the Coedybrain Schools had moved from Birkenhead, Sale, Todmorden, Swindon, Bishopsgate, Hereford, Exeter and Williton, as well as many more from within Wales – Shotton, Cardigan, Pontycymmer, Aberfan, Treorchy, Trealaw, Rhydyfelin, Abertysswg, Bargoed, Bettws–y–Coed, Swansea, Brynmawr, Llanhilleth and Ystradgynlais among others.

When the new school reopened on 1 September 1913 there were 300 boys' names on the register and an attendance of 272, a figure which was rarely exceeded thereafter; as the building had been designed to accommodate 364 there was no longer a problem of overcrowding, nor would there ever again be a problem, even when the evacuees arrived during World War Two.

The Teachers   Tom Moses, headmaster of the Mixed School since its opening in 1900, became the head of the new Boys School and remained in post until his retirement in 1931. He began his teaching career in Blaina, Monmouthshire, in November 1889; then taught in Caerphilly for several years before being appointed headteacher of the Taffs Well Boys School in 1897 where he remained until he came to Llanbradach. He and his wife, Sarah Moses, lived in 54 High Street. Mrs Moses taught at the Coedybrain Mixed until December 1904 when Glamorgan County Council's policy of not employing married women teachers obliged her to give up her career; she continued to conduct the Llanbradach Ladies Choir which had won first prize at the Rhyl National Eisteddfod in June 1904. Mr Moses was a prominent member of Bethel, the English Congregational Chapel, and a keen member of Llanbradach Bowling Club, on one occasion absenting himself from school in order to compete in an important match!

The all-male teaching staff in 1913 consisted of:

Edmund Morgan who was appointed to the Mixed School in October 1908 at a starting salary of £95 p.a. after training at Bangor Normal College. He enlisted in the Welsh University Corps in October 1914 and no more is heard of him. Did he, I wonder, survive the war? Cledwyn Watkins started at the Mixed School in November 1909. Being a member of the Territorial Army he was given leave of absence to attend training camp in July 1910 and he enlisted in November 1915, serving with the Welch Regiment at Salonika. He returned to Coedybrain Boys in March 1919 remaining there until, in June 1922, he became headteacher at

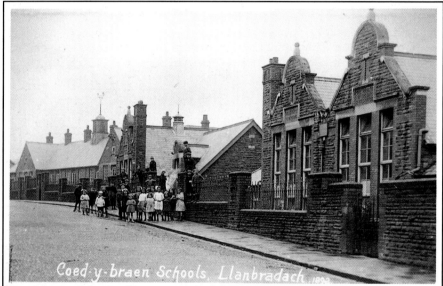

Coedybrain Schools. The nearest building accommodated the original Mixed School in September 1900 and, from 1913, the Girls School; the second building was the Infants School; the Boys School, at the far end, opened in 1913.

Courtesy of Kevin Williams

St. Ishmael's, Pembrokeshire. William Jones took his B.A. and teacher training at Aberystwyth before coming to Llanbradach in October 1910 at the age of 22 years. Within less than two years he was Mr Moses' senior assistant and in October 1912 he applied, unsuccessfully, for the post of English master at the soon-to-be-opened Caerphilly Higher Elementary School. He left Coedybrain Boys in December 1914, having obtained a post near his home. George R A Wilson had been a pupil teacher in County Durham before training at Carmarthen. He came to Coedybrain in May 1911 and transferred to the Gwyndy School, Caerphilly, in September 1915. Thomas Lewis started in

August 1912. He was given leave of absence in 1914–15 in order to attend Caerleon Training College. On his return as a trained and certificated teacher his salary was £105 p.a. In November 1916 the Military Medical Board classed him as fit only for home service and he remained at Coedybrain Boys, one of the longest serving members of staff, until May 1929 when he transferred to Rhiwbina Junior Mixed School. Another teacher who remained at Coedybrain nearly as long was Edmund Evans. He joined the staff in January 1914, shortly after his fiftieth birthday, certificated but untrained, on an annual salary of £120. He retired from teaching on 31 October 1928, aged 65 years. Mr Evans had a degree of local fame as a writer of Welsh poetry and was known by his bardic name of Elfryn. He lived in Pwllypant Cottage.

A woman's place   The effect of the 1914–18 War on the staffing of Coedybrain Boys was very striking: of eleven new appointments made in these years only two were men, neither of whom stayed for longer than a year. Three of the women were forced to resign on getting married, the longest serving of those being Lilian Stamforth who stayed for seven years. Despite the shortage of male teachers during and after the war, Glamorgan County Council (along with many other employers) stuck to its policy of not employing married women. One of the Education Subcommittees recommended, in the first months of the war, that "during the continuance of the war married women teachers whose husbands are serving with the Colours be eligible for re–appointment to any authorised vacancy on condition that their service cease immediately on the husband's return". This was adopted as a temporary exception to the general bar on married women, although the wives of merchant seamen were not allowed to benefit from it.

In October 1915 the Caerphilly Group Managers tried to go a step further when they 'resolved to recommend to the Education Committee that the regulation of the Committee against employment or appointment of married female teachers be relaxed during the present crisis and that Managers be authorised to appoint suitable married women teachers whose husbands are not members of H.M. Forces". This suggestion was not accepted by the Education Committee. The old policy was re–imposed after 1918 and rigidly enforced until Westminster legislation outlawed it throughout the country in 1945. The view that "a woman's place is in the home", that a married woman's duty was to care for her husband and children, was fortified by the corollary that it was the man's duty to be the family breadwinner, a status which might be threatened if his wife had an income of her own. Another aspect of the current attitude is reflected in the inequality of salaries between men and women. In 1917 the Glamorgan Education Committee fixed the following scales :

		Minimum	Maximum
Men	Trained	£90 x £5 to £130 x £10 to £170	
	Untrained	£80 x £5 to £130 x £10 to £170	

		Minimum	Maximum
Women	Trained	£80 x £5 to £100	x £10 to £130
	Untrained	£70 x £5 to £130	x £10 to £130
Uncertificated Teachers	Men	£55 x £3	to £85
	Women	£45 x £3	to £75

Exemptions A new regulation brought in by the Education Committee during the war years allowed a number of boys and girls to leave school before the statutory age of 14 years in order to take up employment, or in the girls' case, to assist in the home. Edward Payne, 93 Coedybrain Road, was allowed to leave in March 1917 on the application of his father, described as "a cripple for 18 years", whose two older sons had joined the Army, and who required the boy's assistance in cultivating three plots of ground. Albert Keirle, 27 Thomas Street, whose father was serving in France, left school at the same time, on his mother's application, to work for T M James, a local coal merchant and haulier. Thomas Seabourne left in February 1918 to work for Joseph Fry, the newsagent in High

Llanbradach Prisoners of War Committee, 1914–1918. It claimed to be one of the first formed in the country, parcels were sent to "local boys" as early as November 1914. About 800 men from the village served during the war. Among those in the photograph are: Griff Williams, colliery winder; Dan Llewellyn, colliery official and, later, licensee of Llanbradach Hotel; D J Williams, licensee of Wingfield Hotel, Tom Moses, headteacher of Coedybrain Boys; John Bassett, chairman of Llanbradach Lodge of SWMF ("The Fed"); James Prout, shopkeeper, grandfather of Miss Kitty Hughes.

Courtesy of Miss Kitty Hughes

Street. In June 1918 three boys left early to take up employment, George Preece of 6 Lewis Terrace (Central Stores, High Street), Benjamin Smart of 15 Richmond Terrace (Mr Coppage, butcher) and John C Hodge of 29 Garden Street (Mr Pennington, Cardiff Collieries). Another six boys left Coedybrain to work with village butchers, grocers and a hairdresser before the Education Committee scrapped the regulation early in 1919.

Ripples of war For the most part, whatever the effects of the war on families (husbands, fathers, brothers serving in the Armed Forces, many of them never to return to the village) it had little direct impact on school life apart from the shortage of men teachers. The logbook contains only a few entries which indicate that (to use a phrase from another time) "There's a war on" :

9 June 1916 School closed on Whit Monday only. This is done in accordance with the general opinion that the holiday spirit should be broken to conform with the national exigencies of the moment.

11 December 1916 Miss Henderson away. Unable to catch train from seeing her friend who was ill with malaria and who had just returned from France.

A card sent from France to W H Selby, secretary of the Llanbradach Social Club, dated 20 December 1916. The message reads : Wishing you a jolly time at Xmas and all the boys of the Club and please to accept this little Card showing the engagements our Division has been in.
                                                                    from Pte E Handford

13 February 1917	Miss Fuell away on account of the death at the Front of Captain Nicholls, her brother-in-law.
6 March 1917	Miss Henderson sent to say that she would be unable to attend again owing to her marriage taking place this week. Her future husband obtained short leave from the Military Authorities, before leaving for France, to get married.
8 March 1918	"Business Week" in connection with the War Savings Association. The three departments of this school subscribed £210-10-0 in War Certificates.
26 April 1918	Gardening affects attendance a little. The number of allotment gardens has increased considerably this year. Parents are anxious, owing to critical times, to take advantage of the fine weather to finish setting and sowing.
21 June 1918	Closed this Friday afternoon – visit of "Tank" to Caerphilly.
29 June 1918	Result of the "Tank" week for the school was £725, the largest sum realised in the Caerphilly Group of Schools. Total of War Savings since its inception has reached £1250.
12 November 1918	School closed owing to General Holiday granted to miners on the occasion of armistice signed. It was found impossible to get children to school.
13 November 1918	Received notice from Chief Education Official that schools were to be closed for the remainder of the week in view of the excellent news.

Allotments, blackberry jam, and savings   The increase in allotment gardens to which the headteacher refers was one of the results of the Cultivation of Lands Order, issued by the government in 1917. The aim was to counteract the German submarine menace and increase the acreage of cultivated land in order to feed the civilian population. Farmers were encouraged, or if necessary directed, to put more land under the plough; the Caerphilly district was expected to find another 1500 acres during 1918. Farm workers were increasingly exempted from military service and as many soldiers as could be spared from military duties were posted to assist the farmers. The County Council's War Agricultural Committee also had the power to take possession of land for allotments.

In August 1918 LEAs were asked by the Ministry of Food to arrange for the systematic picking of blackberries by older children for jam making "in view of the urgent national importance of increasing supplies of jam for the Army and Navy", and the Board of Education was prepared for three half-days holiday a week to be granted for this purpose. Glamorgan Education Committee decided to take no action in the matter, perhaps deeming the children's schooling to be more important than the military requirement for blackberry jam.

Most, if not all, schools in the County took part in the War Savings movement. As well as regular weekly savings by the pupils there were, from time to time, special weeks, such as the "Tank" week in June 1918, when large sums of money were raised. In July 1917 the LEA directed that money collected should not be kept "on school premises as there had been several cases in the County of breaking and entering with the evident intent of stealing money".

In February 1918 Mr Moses had noted in his logbook that several boys were absent one afternoon owing to "the presence of huntsmen and hounds in the neighbourhood". In the same month he wrote to the Caerphilly Group Managers seeking permission "to send upper standard boys, in the charge of a teacher, to a Ploughing Match to take the form of a lesson in Nature Work". As Llanbradach was "not an agricultural district", the Managers did not think it desirable to give permission. Yet, in August 1919 the school closed on a Thursday afternoon because of the East Glamorgan Agricultural Show in Ystrad Mynach.

Spanish 'flu In 1918 there was a world-wide epidemic known as "Spanish Flu" which killed more people than the fighting in the war. Although no deaths appear to have occurred among the children of Llanbradach, the school logbook demonstrates the epidemic's effect on the locality :

12 July 1918	Attendance has dropped to 54 per cent. Influenza is spreading and is the chief cause.
19 July 1918	Attendance 59.8 per cent. The disease attacks with great suddenness ..... teachers are suffering too.
22 July 1918	Influenza still raging. Children and adults are taken very suddenly, in some cases standing or walking in the streets. It seems to affect patients in different ways. Some lose the use of their legs. Others suffer severe headaches and others severe back and abdominal pains. Children showing the least symptoms are advised to go home and take to bed and keep warm.
24 October 1918	Attendance for last fortnight has been more satisfactory than for some considerable time. This can scarcely be accounted for when it is noted that the neighbouring schools are very low on account of the epidemic of influenza. In many cases schools have been closed on account of the serious outbreak which proves fatal in quite a large number of cases.

None of the village's schools had to be closed and the effects varied from one to another : Coedybrain Girls was still suffering from the epidemic in February and March 1919, whereas the Llanbradach Mixed logbook refers to it only in November and December 1918, which suggests that the Wingfield end of the village came off relatively lightly.

Lost in France A year after the end of the war, Mr Moses made a list of the old Coedybrain boys who died as a result of the war, adding that "it may not be complete owing to the one time floating population of the district" :

| David Stanley James | Brothers | Parents living at 8 Garden Avenue. Stanley, serving as a private in the 1st Battalion, Australian Imperial Force, was killed in action at Pozieres in France on 25 July 1916 aged 25. Tom Stoker 1st Class, Royal Navy, was killed in action while serving in Royal Naval Division, Anson Battalion, at Gallipoli on 4 June 1915 aged 20 years. |
| Thomas Treharne James | | |

| David Williams | Brothers | Parents living in School Street. |
| Edwin Williams | | |

| Idris Lewis | Brothers | Parents living at 2 Tynygraig Terrace. |
| Hubert Lewis | | |

Emrys Lewis

| Charles Warren | | Parents deceased. This boy died at home from effects of gas. |

| Walter Bassett | | Parents living at 5 Morgan Street, son of John and Julia Bassett. Died in Egypt. |

| Albert Greenway | | Parents in Ystrad Mynach. Albert, serving in the Royal Artillery, died in France on 17 September 1916 aged 25 years. |

Douglas Tudor		Parents in Ynysddu
George W May		Parents living at 16 Tynygraig Road
Frank Burnett (born 20/8/1901)		Parents living at 6 Richmond Terrace
John Collister (born 18/10/1897)		Parents living at 19 Richmond Terrace
Edward Shaddick		Parents in De Winton Terrace
Tom Churches		Parents at 24 Coedybrain Road
Reggie Cooper		Parents in Machen

The three young men named on the list whose parents were living outside the village when Mr Moses compiled it do not appear on the Llanbradach War Memorial; perhaps their names are honoured elsewhere.

Dumplings in May? The coal mines, which had been under government control during the war, were handed back to the owners on 31 March 1921. The owners offered a greatly reduced rate of pay to the miners; when they refused this offer they were locked out of the collieries. The men stayed out for three months but were forced to return to work on 1 July 1921 on wages which were less than half their previous level. As in all the other schools in the village the Coedybrain Boys were fed on the premises during this period.

15 April 1921	Necessitous school feeding was carried out this morning as a case of emergency – 33 boys were fed bread and butter and cocoa. Voluntary help was profuse. It is hoped the local Canteen Committee will take over the matter of feeding thus relieving the teachers of the responsibility.
13 May 1921	Closed for Whitsun Holiday – feeding to continue. Mr Edmund Evans has been made Acting Supervisor during my absence over the weekend.
24 May 1921	Mr Bryn Davies, County Inspector, visited to examine the food and utensils .... he thought dumplings should be supplied but it is the general opinion of the Canteen Committee helpers that these are out of place during this warm weather when soup is also provided. Children get sufficient food and good food.
3 June 1921	Average attendance for this week is 278 (91.6 per cent). School meals have had a decided influence on attendance.
21 June 1921	During the time children have been fed at the school we have been fortunate in having the weather fine and sunny throughout the whole period so that the feeding has been done outside in the yard and the school kept clean for children to enter.

After the men had been back to work for a fortnight, the feeding arrangements discontinued. To provide for the feeding of children under and over school age during the lock-out a committee of local people was set up, under the chairmanship of the Rev. R J Jarman, to raise money and organise the arrangements. Meals were supplied at the All Saints rooms, the English Baptist Chapel (Ebenezer) and the English Congregational Chapel (Bethel); a total of 36,840 meals were provided at a cost of 3.28 pence per meal. The funds of a little over £500 were raised in a variety of ways: regular takings at the Workmen's Hall on Wednesday and Thursday evenings, substantial contributions from the Colliery Company and the Colliery officials, concerts given by the Male Voice Party and collections made by the Silver Band in Llanishen and Weston–super–Mare, as well as donations from the Workmen's Social Club, the Constitutional Club, and the R.A.O.B. The Constitutional Club also gave each of its own members a joint of meat and potatoes every week, while the Workmen's Club expended £25 a week on its members.

The circumstances of the miners and their families in the aftermath of the 1921 lock-out are illustrated by the following logbook entries:

22 September 1922	Attendance far from satisfactory. There are a few reasons for this such as the efflux for the hop fields, the inability of parents of large families to buy boots for children owing to the low rate of wages. There are several children attending school at present without boots or shoes.
3 November 1922	Attendance has suffered from bad weather. Children,

owing to the bad times, are fairly poorly shod and are kept at home during such weather as we are experiencing lately.

More Teachers   the scarcity of men teachers which occurred during the war years continued into the immediate post-war period so that of five new appointments made in 1921-22 only one was a man, Mr Uri de La Haye-Davies, aged 22 years, who began his three years of military service before his 17th birthday. After being demobilised in February 1919 he did two years of teacher training at Goldsmiths College, London, and joined the Coedybrain staff in July 1921 at a salary of £175 per annum. Despite the exotic flavour to his name it is likely he was a local man as for two or three months before the Army got him he was in a temporary junior position on the teaching staff of Gwyndy Boys, Caerphilly. He left Coedybrain Boys in November 1925 for another appointment at Ely School, Cardiff.

On 24 April 1922 two young women came to Coedybrain Boys. Miss Gwendoline Margaret Morrisey, just a month short of her 22nd birthday, trained at Barry College and began her teaching career at Hengoed Mixed. Her starting salary was £189-3-6d. In October 1925 she transferred to Coedybrain Girls but left in May 1926 to teach in Cardiff where her home was. Miss Elizabeth Lorna Jenkins had taught in Coedybrain Infants for a few months before joining the Boys department. She was 19 years old and unqualified and so commenced on a salary of £98. Although she was living at The Manse, Mountain Road, Caerphilly, her home address was in Lanon, Cardiganshire. She left in August 1924 to enter Bangor Normal College.

On 28 August 1922 another two young women joined the staff. Miss Doris Hall, aged 23 years, trained at Cheltenham, and transferred from Pengam Junior on a salary of £189. She left Coedybrain in December 1925 for a post in Taffs Well. Miss Elizabeth Grace Black arrived in Llanbradach on the day of her 26th birthday. She had taken her degree and teaching qualification at University College, Cardiff between 1914 and 1918; her starting salary was £221. She, along with a few of her male colleagues, formed the mainstay on the teaching staff through the 1920s and 1930s, leaving Coedybrain in 1941 for a post at Whitchurch Junior Girls School.

An inspector calls   Mr H Price, HMI, visited the school in September 1922 and reported as follows:

"This school continues to be conducted with great success. Although the staff has been considerably changed during the past year, yet (owing to the inspiring direction of the headmaster) there is no break in the continuity of his aims and methods. The Authority's Advanced Instruction Scheme is taken in the top section of the school, and these classes are in very good hands.

The senior course in English has for its aim not only the securing of correct expression (both oral and written) in simple language, but also the formation of taste for good books – thereby enabling the children to obtain pleasure in after life from pure literature. A careful selection of poems is made and the senior boys helped to note such points as beauty of diction and the general structure of the poem under consideration. Arithmetic is very well taught in the upper classes by means of models made by the children from careful measurements.

The singing is excellent. Particular attention is paid to the selection of songs, to voice training, and to cultivating a taste for good music. Rural lore is also emphasised in the curriculum, and means are taken to familiarise the children with the Geography, History, Antiquities and Place Names of the locality.

The drawing and written work generally are very creditable in the two top classes, but more attention might be given to these in the lower classes. There appears to be some laxity in enforcing the attendance to the end of term of those boys who attain their 14th birthday in the middle of the term".

The emphasis in the report is very much on the Three Rs, other subjects seemingly regarded as rather peripheral. There is no mention of the teaching of Welsh which had been in the curriculum since 1905 and was a matter of increasing concern among the Caerphilly Group of Managers. The Advanced Instruction Scheme to which the HMI refers was introduced into Glamorgan Elementary Schools at the beginning of 1922. These schools had traditionally been organised into seven classes, Standards I – VII, each class being in the charge of one teacher who had responsibility for all the subjects taught. The new scheme renamed the top classes Forms I and II and grouped children aged 12 and over into them, where they received instruction in subjects by the teachers best qualified in those subjects. This was in line with progressive educational thinking at the time.

Middle schools During 1918 parliament debated the Education Bill, which aimed to make schooling compulsory, without any exemption, to 14 years, and to provide Day Continuation Schools which young people aged 14 to 18 would have to attend for 8 hours per week. Glamorgan Education Committee, on the other hand, formulated its own policy of wishing to establish about forty entirely new schools throughout the County (including Ystrad Mynach, Abertridwr and Caerphilly) which would be called Middle Schools. It was proposed that all children (except those who passed the entrance examination for the more academic Intermediate or County Schools) would transfer from the Elementary to the Middle Schools at 12 years and be offered a free four year course at a secondary level, possibly of a technical, commercial or trade nature. The Education Committee sought to ensure that the parliamentary bill would be framed so as to allow its own policy to be implemented locally, and began immediately to identify suitable sites on which the Middle Schools would be built. This bold and visionary policy did not, however, come to fruition (nor did the Education Act's provision for Day Continuation Schools) as a consequence of the drastic reduction in public expenditure which followed the post-war boom.

Higher Elementary school In December 1912 the Caerphilly Higher Elementary School had opened its doors in the building, in Crescent Road, which later housed the Girls Secondary School and is now a Welsh Language Primary School. The Higher Elementary offered boys and girls from Elementary Schools in the Caerphilly District a three year course supposedly of a vocational character different from the academic education provided in the older County Schools at Pengam (boys) and Hengoed (girls), Pontypridd (boys) and Treforest (girls). On 1 January 1921 it was re-designated as a Secondary School, still taking boys and girls, but now offering a four year course until the age of 16 years and, increasingly during the 1920s, more geared towards examination success in the CWB School and Higher Certificates (which equated with present-day O and A Levels).

Burglary and vandalism Another element of the curriculum which receives no mention in the HMI's report is Manual Instruction which was provided by Mr Archibald T Williams, of 23 Ludlow Street, Caerphilly, between 1914 and 1938. The new Boys School had been designed to include a large workshop and storeroom, alongside the boiler room and coal house, underneath the classrooms. Boys from Coedybrain and Llanbradach Mixed had lessons in woodwork and metalwork here. Just as the expensive equipment used in present day schools is a prime target for thieves, so the tools stored at Coedybrain occasionally attracted unwelcome attention:

21 July 1915	Cleaner reported that the Manual Instruction room has been broken into and two cupboard locks forced. Material stolen from school premises some years ago has been recovered from a cave in the Quarry and handed over to us by the Police.
9 January 1928	School was broken into during the latter end of the vacation. Damage and list of articles taken sent to Dr James (Chief Education Officer) and Architect.
16 January 1928	Two arrests have been made by the Police in connection with the illegal entry last week. Police request my evidence tomorrow at the Police Court to identify certain articles.
17 February 1928	Headteacher attended Glamorgan Assizes at Cardiff concerning illegal entry of school premises. E T Williams sent to prison for eight months, Ernest Green for six months.
4 June 1928	Reported attempt at forced entry into Manual Room – broken window fastener and strained door lock.

That the "good old days" were not as free of thieving and vandalism as we would like to believe is evidenced by a report in the Caerphilly Journal on 17 April 1926: a 14 year old boy from Llanbradach appeared before the Caerphilly Magistrates charged with damaging an electric lamp and reflector near

Llanbradach station; the prosecutor said that in the last year over 300 lamps were broken in Llanbradach alone by children throwing stones; the boy was fined ten shillings and ordered to pay the cost of the damage.

The normal school routine and the depressed economic conditions were interrupted and lightened by a variety of holidays and events :

9 June 1921	Closed on account of Prince of Wales visit to Cardiff. The local Boys Brigade have been asked to form part of a guard of honour.
30 August 1921	Attendance affected by local outing to seaside.
28 February 1922	Closed on account of Princess Mary's marriage.
12 May 1922	School closed this afternoon by managers' permission due to visit of Sanger's Circus to Caerphilly.
3 October 1922	Prize Day. Prizes distributed by Alderman Howells, Caerphilly, accompanied by Cllr. J Phillips, Nelson.
26 April 1923	Closed on account of Duke of York's wedding.
20 July 1928	Welsh Baptist Sunday School outing – 28 boys absent.
23 July 1923	Closed this afternoon for School Sports.
29 February 1924	This morning given to St Davids Day programme. Several playlets were given by Standards 1 – 5.
2 May 1924	Closed on Monday by order of the managers on account of Labour Day.
10 July 1924	Closed on account of Welsh Baptist and Welsh Independent Sunday Schools outing.
29 October 1924	Closed for General Election.
16 January 1925	Prizes distributed by County Councillor Phillips for perfect attendance.
6 April 1925	Closed on account of Guardians and District Council elections.
30 April 1925	Closed this afternoon by managers – Singing Festival at Caerphilly.

"Was it for this the clay grew tall?   Another logbook entry refers to a significant event taking place in the village :–

2 February 1925	Yesterday the War Memorial was unveiled by Mrs Lindsay, Ystrad Mynach. The schoolchildren took a prominent part in the ceremony especially in singing the selected hymns.

A committee had been set up after the war with the object of providing a memorial, holding events such as an eisteddfod and a dance in the Workmen's Hall in order to raise funds. The Rev. Edwin Edwards of All Saints Church had wanted the memorial to be placed within the church grounds, but its present, more neutral, site was eventually chosen. Although the inscription refers to "110 Gallant Men" there are, in fact, 121 names of those who fell in the 1914–

1918 War. The Merthyr Express described the memorial, which cost £1,150, as consisting of a "flight of marble steps, granite pillar, Sicilian marble figure symbolic of victory". the contractor was T J Durbin, sculptor, of Caerphilly. Several thousand people attended the ceremony, the procession was made up of representatives of Caerphilly Urban District Council, the Buffs, Fire Brigade, St John Ambulance, Girl Guides, Boys Brigade, fifty men from the Welsh Regiment and a large body of ex-servicemen under the command of Lient. Col. K D Murchison, DSO (Llanbradach G.P.). Master Willie Llewellyn, son of the licen see of the Llanbradach Hotel, laid a wreath on behalf of absent relatives.

Llanbradach War Memorial Committee, 1925.
Among the members are: County Councillor William Bowen (back row, first left); Dr. Charles Robertson (second left; Emrys Jones, chairman of Social Club (back row, extreme right; V C Hardacre, civil servant, photographer, local historian (centre, second left); D J Williams, licensee, Wingfield Hotel (centre, fourth left); Miss Louisa Moses, headteacher, Llanbradach Infants (front, second left); John Bassett, SWMF (third left); District Councillor John Bassett, nephew of the other John Bassett (fourth left); Tom Reynolds, teacher at Cardiff High (fifth left); Mrs Mary Stainer (extreme right).

Courtesy of Mrs Irene Bassett

Make way for men   The employment of women teachers in Coedybrain Boys, brought about by wartime circumstances, came to a virtual end in the mid 1920s. Of the fourteen women who had been on the staff for various periods of time since 1914 only one, Miss Black, survived the return to the old practice of appointing men only, until war conditions after 1939 once again made the services of women teachers indispensable to the running of a boys school.

The second man to be appointed after the end of the war, in September 1924, was Mr Harold Vernon Williams who had received his own schooling in Taffs Well and Pontypridd County School, and still lived in Taffs Well. He was uncertificated, untrained, and had no teaching experience when, aged 24 years, he arrived at Coedybrain boys. His starting salary was £104-10-0. The logbook notes, in June 1932, that he had a week's leave of absence to sit a Law Degree examination but there is no mention of whether or not he was successful.

Mr Thomas Reece, aged 27 years, had done military service 1917 – 1919 before setting out on his teaching career. After a few months in Abertridwr he studied and trained at University College, Cardiff from 1919 – 1925, graduating with degrees in mathematics and physics. He was appointed in October 1925 on a salary of £204. He commuted from his address at 28 Station Terrace, Caerphilly, until he obtained a post in Durham in January 1927.

Mr Edmund R Evans aged 23 years, was appointed in December 1925 transferring from Nelson Mixed where he had gone in 1923 after completing his two year training at Bangor Normal College. He was already familiar with Coedybrain Boys having been a student teacher here in 1920 – 21. Now living at The Cottage, Pwllypant, he received a salary of £183-10-0. He was the son of the Edmund Evans who had been teaching at Coedybrain Boys since 1914; father and son were colleagues for three years before the older man retired. The young Eddie Evans merited two mentions in the headteacher's logbook :-

12 September 1932   Mr E R Evans was out of his room for 20 minutes leaving his class to be noisy and disturbing to the general work.

On 21 November 1934 Mr Evans, along with two of his colleagues, was transferred from Coedybrain on the instructions of the Education Office. There is no reason given for this sudden removal of nearly half of the teaching strength, but it follows an unexplained "occurrence" on 9 October which warranted the personal investigation of Captain I J Evans, County Inspector, in the same week. The three young men were transferred to three different schools, Mr Evans going to Cwmaber.

Mr Thomas Ieaun James Watkins, aged 22 years, trained at Caerleon College and worked briefly at the Industrial School, Quakers Yard, before joining the Coedybrain staff in February 1926. His salary was fixed at £180 and he lived at 36 Cardiff Road, Caerphilly. He left Wales in April 1933 to take up a new post at St John's School, Sparkhill, Birmingham.

Seasons, sickness and snow   Various seasonal factors affected attendance; bilberrying in July, blackberrying in August and September, hop-picking in September. Even the colliery company unintentionally introduced a weekly blip in the attendance figures:

| 16 January 1920 | Attendance on Friday afternoon has fallen considerably owing to workmen receiving their pay on Fridays in place of Saturdays. Men working on the "two o'clock shift" take their children with them to the offices and send the pay with them to their homes. They are kept away until close upon two o'clock, too late for their attendance marks. |

A more serious matter was the epidemic of scarlet fever and measles which broke out towards the end of 1920 and led to all the village schools being closed for three weeks during January 1921. Deaths were reported among the pre-school infants.

A spell of bad weather affected attendance during the winter of 1926 :-

8 January 1926	Weather has been severe this week – snow and frost. This has affected attendance particularly where families are unable to buy boots for children. Several families who lived in the huts at Energlyn have removed to houses built for them at Caerphilly so that about eight boys have been marked as having left the district.
20 January 1926	Snow fell at the beginning of the week. This was followed by rain and the roads made it impossible for children badly shod to attend. Reported that the tall chimney is tilting at a dangerous angle.
25 January 1926	Weather exceedingly stormy with floods.

Huts, houses, and bungalows   The reference to "huts at Energlyn" is slightly puzzling, as the only "huts" which are remembered among Llanbradach folk are the "Quarry Huts" which backed onto the railway line close to the Pwllypant Quarry and adjoined the Quarry Mission Church. These dwellings, which had stone walls, had been built by the Bute Trustees to accommodate the masons and labourers employed in the quarry, together with some of their families. In 1871 there were single men and a few families living in what are described in Kelly's Directory as "model lodgings" for a small weekly rental. In 1881 the overall number of residents had reduced from 40 to 35 but now consisted entirely of seven families which included 8 children attending school and 6 not yet old enough to do so.

These so called "huts" were gradually abandoned after the quarry ceased operating before 1914. Mr & Mrs Albert Crumb and their six children were the last family to live in what became known as Quarry Cottage. They moved there from Stanley Row in 1926 and gave up the property in the 1950s. The cottage, made out of two of the original dwellings, no longer exists, nor does the church building to which it was joined.

It is possible that the "huts at Energlyn" were the wooden dwellings situated in the field behind Wilkins Terrace, Pwllypant, which remained in use for many years after 1926, sometimes entered in the admission register as "Van Field".

The Coedybrain registers show that between 1908 and 1919 at least 19 children lived in various houses in Energlyn Row, whose fathers' occupations were mostly given as railwayman and platelayer, although one was a quarryman and another a collier. The connection with the railway industry suggests that Energlyn Row was an earlier name for the terrace of houses which was later known as Barry Cottages due to the Barry Railway Company housing its employees in them. This is confirmed by the fact that the registers, from 1919 to 1940, contain the names of 27 children who resided in Barry Cottages and whose fathers' occupations were mainly signalman, railwayman, platelayer, repairer, boilermaker and railway porter. The 1881 Census reveals that this row of thirteen cottages had been built to accommodate the colliers, and their families, who were employed in the adjacent Eneu'r-glyn Colliery, and at that time were known as Coedleddyn Cottages.

It appears that the Barry Railway Company, having completed the construction of Llanbradach Viaduct by the end of 1904, acquired the cottages, terminated the tenancies of the families already living in them, some of whom had been there for nearly thirty years, and put their own employees in. The cottages, now demolished, once stood above Pwllypant between the railway and the northern by-pass.

The Coedybrain registers reveal another set of dwellings, no longer standing, which were occupied from the 1920s to the 1950s. These were the bungalows grouped on the hillside above the railway line looking down onto De Winton Terrace and Coedybrain Road. There were ten of them, prefabricated in wood and asbestos with corrugated iron roofs (except one which was a railway carriage), erected by individual families on plots of land rented from the Bute or De Winton estates. Mrs Joyce Bishop (nee Chinn) and Mr Danny Seabourne, who still live in the village, remember their childhood years in this little, slightly isolated, community overlooking the valley with a small disused quarry on either side and two mountain streams. There were no mains sewerage, water or electricity so the families used chemical toilets or cesspits, oil lamps and candles, and fetched water from the streams. Each dwelling had its own plot of land, made into a vegetable garden, marked off by walls or privet hedges. Mr Seabourne believes most of the bungalow-dwellers disliked living in the terraced streets of the village and were, perhaps, of farming stock, as his parents were. They were neighbourly but independent, and all the men worked in the colliery. Although a good many children were successfully raised in these semi-rural surroundings the local authority condemned the bungalows as unfit on the grounds of inadequate sanitation in the 1950s.

1926 Strike   When the miners were locked out on 1 May 1926 much of the trade union movement came out on strike in support of negotiations over the miners' grievances. But the General Strike collapsed after ten days, leaving the miners to hold out for seven months on their own, when hunger and desperation forced them to return to work on the coal-owners terms – longer hours, lower wages.

As in all the other schools in Llanbradach, and all the pit villages in Glamorgan, "necessitous" children were fed on the premises throughout the seven months and beyond. The headteacher's logbook bears mute testimony to the burden placed on the running of a school in these exceptional circumstances. Whereas, normally, the headteacher would have taken time to record a variety of events and concerns inherent in the daily life of the school, Tom Moses falls almost silent between May and October, finding time only to note the high level of attendance during these months, fluctuating between 92 and 95 per cent, and some information about the feeding arrangements which commenced on 17 May and ended on 23 December :

Week ending 21 May	No. of meals in three departments 7054 (Coedybrain Boys Girls and Infants). Amount expended £88–13–6d. Cost per head 3d.
Week ending 28 May	No. of meals 9811. Amount expended £97–2–9d. Cost per head 2⅔d.
Week ending 4 June	No. of meals 10606. Amount expended £118–0–2d. Cost per head 2½d.
11 June 1926	No. of meals given since commencement – 37698.
30 July 1926	School closed for summer vacation – five weeks. Children will be fed, three meals per day, throughout the vacation.
19 November 1926	Heavy rains have interfered with attendance. Several children are without boots and several are also badly clad owing to the industrial dispute. Average attendance this week – 232 (89.6 per cent).

Llanbradach Colliery, showing the two large water coolers in the background and the pithead gear and winding – engine house for the newly sunk No. 3 pit. To reach the House Coal Seam the shaft was sunk to a depth of 260 yards by May 1925 and the first coal was brought up in July.

Courtesy of Alan Morgan

It is worth remarking here that the number of boys on the roll had fallen from 298 in May 1925 to 258 in November 1926, perhaps an indication of some families having moved out of the village during the industrial dispute, but more likely the result of a drop in the birth rate between 1916 and 1919 when a large number of men were absent from the village due to their military service. By 1928 the roll had risen to above 300 again. The improved attendance figures achieved during 1926 were rewarded at the Prize Day the following February when 41 boys received recognition for perfect attendance during the year and another 45 for near-perfection. One boy, Stanley Towell of 62 School Street, had evidently not needed the encouragement of being fed on the premises to achieve his personal record of six years perfect attendance.

More teachers   During the next two years another four teachers were appointed to the staff :

Mr Howell J Thomas transferred from Heol y Cyw in March 1927 shortly before his 27th birthday on a salary of £223 p.a. He had trained at Carmarthen College. He receives little mention in the logbook, except in November 1941 when it was recorded that he was "exempt from fire-watching duties in the school as he does them at Rhiwbina". His home was in Rhiwbina with his actress wife, the well known Rachel Thomas who became typecast in films and television dramas as the archetypal Welsh "Mam". Mrs Thomas wrote to me not long before her own death, saying that Mr Thomas died in November 1964 and had been ill for ten years before that. She wrote "I can tell you that he was very happy teaching the boys there; he always said that no other boys could touch them for singing!".

Mr Percival Meecham Davies arrived at Coedybrain in May 1928, aged 25 years. He had trained at Cardiff and taught previously at Nantymoel Boys. His salary on appointment was £221. After his arrival there is no record of him until his sudden departure, along with two of his colleagues, in November 1934, when he was transferred to Llanfabon School.

Mr Glanffrwd Thomas, aged 25 years, was appointed in November 1928, on a salary of £190. He had, unusually, split his two year teacher training between Cheltenham and Carmarthen, and had taught at a boys school in Stourbridge, Worcs., before coming to Coedybrain. His home was in Taffs Well where, like his colleague from Rhiwbina, his fire-watching duties in 1941 allowed him to be excluded from the schools rota. After sixteen years service in Coedybrain he went to teach in Taffs Well in January 1945.

Mr Ernest Cecil Jenkins came to Coedybrain in July 1929. He completed his training at Brighton Municipal College in the summer of 1914 and probably did military service before resuming his teaching career in 1919. He had gained ten years experience in Glynneath Boys School by the time he was appointed to the Coedybrain staff, hence his salary of £340. When Mr Tom Moses, the head-teacher, retired in 1931 Mr Jenkins, as senior assistant, took temporary charge of the school for several weeks until the new head was appointed. In May 1932 he transferred to Victoria Boys, Penarth.

Boots limited   Although production in the colliery in 1928 (679,753 tons) and 1929 (690,701 tons) surpassed the earlier peak of 1913 it did not bring full employment and prosperity to the village, as the following logbook entries show :-

14 May 1929   21 pairs of boots supplied (from a fund for relieving people of little means or unemployed). Four times this number would hardly suffice the applications made. The most deserving cases were selected but in choosing these it was felt that many others would have been glad to obtain a pair. There are still boys who attend without shoes and stockings. Those supplied are inspected daily to watch that they are being cared for.

12 October 1928   Weather has been very boisterous but attendance has kept up fairly good. Owing to the impoverished state of the coal industry many boys are bootless while many others are wearing "daps" which are useless during rainy weather.

12 November 1928   Weather very wet. Attendance much affected. So many children are badly shod. Parents will not send them to school in such weather.

The winter of 1928–29 gave these children a hard time. High winds and rain in November damaged the school's weather vane and broke slates, a tree was blown down in the school yard; there were severe snow storms in February which, together with measles and chicken pox, affected attendance, a situation somewhat improved by a slow thaw and the distribution of another 20 pairs of boots. Mr Moses recorded the fact that the average temperature of classrooms during the winter was 59.3 Fahrenheit.

The following winter was equally inclement, the headteacher noting severe gales and floods through November, and several children attending without boots, those from Pwllypant being more irregular in their attendance on account of the distance they had to walk in bad weather. However, by November 1930 there was a measure of relief for at least some :

"Weather very severe and changeable. Owing to number of unemployed men many children attend school badly shod. During the last fortnight several children take advantage of the low bus fare to travel from Pwllypant. These children do not arrive in school until about 9.30am. They thus lose the Scripture lesson".

There had been concern about the children's inadequate footwear since the industrial dispute of 1926, a situation which was not noticeably affected by return to high productivity in 1927. The Wall Street Crash of 24 October 1929 heralded the Depression of the 1930s when unemployment reached 2½ million in December 1930 and its peak of nearly 3 million in January 1933.

Llanbradach, along with the rest of South Wales and other industrial areas far removed from London, bore more than its fair share of the next decade of social deprivation.

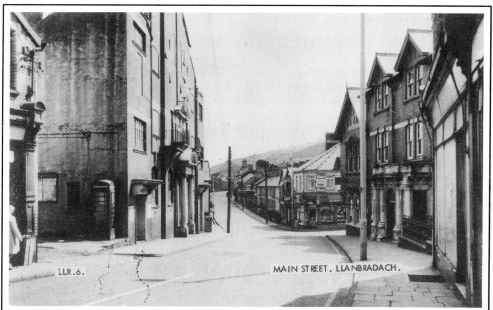

MAIN STREET, LLANBRADACH.

LLR.6.

Workmen's Hall on the left, Co-op Drapery and Llanbradach Hotel on the right. As a result of a campaign, including a petition, mounted by the Llanbradach Chamber of Trade, the village was given its first telephone kiosk in 1929 on a site rented from the Workmen's Institute at five shillings per annum.

End of an era   It was at this time, June 1931, that Tom Moses who had been the first headteacher of the Coedybrain Schools, now took his retirement after spending 31 years of his working life in the village. The Caerphilly Group Managers placed on record their appreciation of his faithful and efficient services and conveyed their best wishes on his retirement.

Chapter Four

LLANBRADACH MIXED AND INFANTS 1927-1952

A young team   On the retirement of Mr T P Davies another chapter in the schools' development opened with the appointment of a new headteacher, Mr George Lewis Evans, on 1 November, 1927. He began his career as a pupil teacher and uncertificated teacher before entering Carmarthen Training College in 1911 where he obtained the Board of Education Certificate in 1915 with merits in Welsh, Music and Physical Training. He taught at Ynyscedwen and Godre'rgraig in the Swansea valley until he came to Llanbradach at the age of 38 years. This was his first and only headship as he remained here until he, too, retired in 1951.

Llanbradach Mixed School, unidentified class c. 1928. Mr Geo L Evans (headteacher), Miss N J Rees and Miss Rosemary Davies.

Two young teachers joined the staff in the same month as G L Evans. Miss Rosemary Davies, just 19 years, a former pupil of the school, was appointed as an uncertificated teacher having completed her secondary education in

Caerphilly only a year earlier. She taught here for the next 20 years before obtaining a qualification under the post-war Emergency Training Scheme in 1947–48, finally transferring to Coedybrain Girls School in 1952. Claude Kenneth Davies, aged 23, also a former pupil of the Llanbradach school, had been educated at Lewis Boys County School; he remained on the staff until June 1939 when he was transferred to Dinas Powis. He was the son of T P Davies.

There were another four teachers already on the staff. Mr Lewis Conibear had been a student teacher at Penarth C of E School before starting at Llanbradach Mixed in October 1923, then aged only 18 years; when he transferred to Whitchurch Junior Boys School in July 1947 he was described by Mr Evans as "a very loyal, conscientious member of staff and will be greatly missed". Mr Albert Morgan, aged 25 at the time of Mr Evans' arrival, had come to the school as a trained graduate teacher in 1925; he left in June 1933 to become headteacher of the Anglican School at Wick and Monknash. And finally, Miss Dorothy Price who taught at Llanbradach between July 1927 and April 1932 before obtaining a post at Pencoed Junior School.

Another trained graduate teacher, Miss Beatrice Ann Martinson, 22, fresh from college, was appointed in January 1928. She had been a pupil at the Caerphilly Higher Elementary School from 1917 to 1923 before going on to University College, Cardiff, to take a degree and complete her teacher training in 1927. She was a Caerphilly girl, living at 7 Celyn Grove, a member of St Catherine's Church where she sometimes played the organ while still at university. The school logbook records that she was absent on 4 February 1930, attending a medical examination at the American Consulate in Southampton, following which she had six months leave of absence to visit her parents in Kingston in the United States of America. On 21 May 1931, she had the day off in order to attend the enthronement of the new Bishop of Llandaff. While teaching at Llanbradach she studied in her own time to obtain a second degree, a B.Sc., in 1933. In September 1936 Miss Martinson gave up teaching to marry the Rev. Edmunds, Vicar of St Catherine's Church, Caerphilly.

For the next four or five years there was little change to this youthful group of seven teachers, with little or no experience, headed by a young but experienced colleague.

Gone to Pwllypant Although the Mixed School was authorised to accommodate 264 pupils, the number on the register fluctuated around the 200 mark, so that class sizes must have been more manageable than in the earlier years. A circumstance which contributed to, or may even have been the main cause of, the decline in numbers is described in a logbook entry made by T P Davies :-

1 April 1927   Only 29 were received from Standard I of the Infants Department. this is the smallest number on record here transferred from the Infants Department. The new houses erected at Pwllypant give accommodation to many families which formerly lived in the neighbourhood of this school. Hence, with the exception of a small

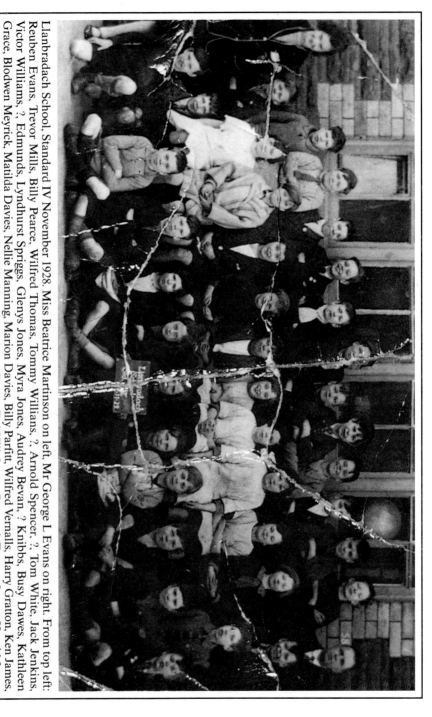

Llanbradach School, Standard IV November 1928. Miss Beatrice Martinson on left, Mr George L Evans on right. From top left: Reuben Evans, Trevor Mills, Billy Pearce, Wilfred Thomas, Tommy Willians, ?, Arnold Spencer, ?, Tom White, Jack Jenkins, Victor Williams, ?, Edmunds, Lyndhurst Spriggs, Glenys Jones, Myra Jones, Audrey Bevan, ? Knibbs, Busy Dawes, Kathleen Grace, Blodwen Meyrick, Matilda Davies, Nellie Manning, Marion Davies, Billy Parfitt, Wilfred Vernalls, Harry Gratton, Ken James, ?. Ivy Jones, Madge Donovan, Adeline Davies, Lily Shannon, Nancy Evans, Ted Hill, Lenny Barnard, Tommy James, Harold Jones.

Courtesy of Mrs Kathleen Russell

74

percentage, those children do not now attend here, as the distance is considered too great.

In February 1926 Caerphilly Urban District Council had accepted a tender from T.R. Jones of Abertridwr to build 50 new houses at £380 per house. These had been completed by June 1927 and another 10 were under construction before the end of the year. The CUDC's request to the Education Authority to provide transport for the Pwllypant children attending Llanbradach school was turned down.

Team spirit and sports Although a new broom, in succession to (professionally speaking) a very old one, George Evans seems to have wisely bided his time before introducing any changes into the organisation of the school:

16 July 1928   A new system of forming lines at assembly was today introduced by the headmaster. The system which is worked in "Teams" is an attempt to combine the Team Spirit with Physical Training and Assembly and also to improve the attendance. The whole school has been divided into four teams, each team in charge of a captain who keeps a daily record of the marks gained by his team for smartness in assembly. Marks are deducted for unpunctuality and absences except in the case of illness. These marks together with the Physical Training marks are totalled weekly and recorded on the charts kept for the purpose. So far there is a distinct improvement in assembly and attendance, and the Team Spirit is taken up enthusiastically.

In keeping with the headteacher's special interest in physical training it is not surprising that, apparently for the first time in the school's history, a Sports Day was organised later the same month. The logbook contains a full list of events and winners:-

1.	80 yds Flat Race. Boys (under 10)	R Williams
2.	80 yds Flat Race. Girls (under 10)	K Brice
3.	80 yds Three–legged Race. Boys	T Payne & E Jones
4.	80 yds Three–legged Race. Girls	K McCarthy & M Allen
5.	Egg and Spoon Race. Boys (over 10)	R Parsons
6.	Egg and Spoon Race. Girls (over 10)	D Evans
7.	40 yds Three–legged Race. Girls (under 10)	K Brice & M Amos
8.	Potato Race. Boys (over 10)	E Neale
9.	Potato Race. Girls (over 10)	G Tudor
10.	Wheelbarrow Race. Boys (over 12)	E Neale & G Williams
11.	Thread Needle Race. Girls (over 12)	G Tudor
12.	100 yds Flat Race. Boys (10–12)	T Payne

13.	100 yds Flat Race. Girls (10–12)	K McCarthy
14.	Potato Race. Girls (under 10)	K Brice
15.	Pick–a–back Race. Boys (over 10)	D Davies & R Morse
16.	Skipping Race. Girls (under 10)	T Jones
17.	Skipping Race. Girls (over 10)	K McCarthy
18.	Sack Race. Boys	J Hill
19.	Sack Race. Girls	D Evans
20.	120 yds Flat Race. Boys (over 12)	L Jones
21.	120 yds Flat Race. Girls (over 12)	D Evans
22.	Throwing Cricket Ball. Boys	J Goldsworthy
23.	220 yds Flat Race. Boys (over 12)	R Donovan
24.	220 yds Flat Race. Girls (over 12)	G Tudor
25.	Obstacle Race. Boys	J Davies
26.	Fancy Dress. Girls	E Barber
27.	Flat Race (1½ miles). Boys	R Donovan
28.	Relay Race Teams. Boys	Yellow (G Williams, Captain)
29.	Relay Race Teams. Girls	Yellow (G James, Captain)
30.	Chariot Race Teams. Boys	Red (G Piper, Captain)
31.	Team Dodgeball Competition. Boys	Yellow (G Williams, Captain)
32.	Team Tunnel–ball Competition. Boys	Yellow (G Williams, Captain)

Mr Evans added the following remarks :

"The Sports were held at the Wingfield Ground near the school. Although the crowd was rather disappointing the sports proved to be of the first order. The various events were contested with exceptional keeness, especially the competitions between the various teams of the school. Team marks were awarded to each successful team and also to the teams to which the various individual event winners belonged. Unfortunately, owing to the rain coming on about 6pm, the following items had to be abandoned :-
Spoke Relay, High Jump, Long Jump, Hop Skip and Jump, Dodge Ball and Tug-of-war.

The school having organised such a comprehensive and successful Sports Day it is surprising that the logbook reveals no other event of a similar nature in all the succeeding years.

Dydd Dewi Sant   Another change which the new headteacher introduced was a greater observance of St David's Day. Throughout T P Davies' headship the occasion was marked by a half-day holiday but there is no reference to any celebrations within the school, despite the fact that he was himself competent in the Welsh language – in 1919 he referred to the difficulty of teaching Welsh to the pupils as, among his staff, only he was able to do so. G L Evans from the Swansea Valley (Ystradgynlais), probably a native Welsh speaker, had gained a credit in the language whilst studying at Carmarthen.
On St David's Day 1928 he and his staff prepared the children in a full

Llanbradach Mixed School, Form 1, 1930

Back row: Irvine Dawes, Dai Pugh, ?, Tom Payne, Roy Tudor, Ron Pook, Eddie Evans, Cromwell Hurlow, Francis Manning, Tom White, Roy Spencer. Second row: Wilfred Vernalls, Victor Williams, Tom Williams, Lyndhurst Spriggs, Trevor Mills, Jack Jenkins, Harry Gratton, Wally Hill, Ken James, Arnold Spencer, Reuben Evans. Third row: Betty Pearce, Florrie Ferris, Evelyn Snook, Elsie Pratley, Joy Lawley, Eliz. Hurlow, Beryl Meredith, Ruby Price, Emily Barber. Front row: Blodwen Meyrick, Tilley ?, ?, Violet Shaw, Kathleen Grace, Myra Jones, Marion Davies, Busy Dawes, Ivy Jones, Nellie Manning, Audrey Bevan. Also: Mr G L Evans (headteacher), Miss Beatrice Martinson, Mr A E Morgan.

Courtesy of Mrs Joyce Marshall

77

programme of music, recitations and sketches. Mr Evans opened the proceedings with a patriotic address on St David, Owen Glyndwr and Sir Thomas Picton (whose statue stands in Carmarthen Town). The children sang a hymn in Welsh ("Grugybar"), then Edith Rowlands played a piano solo and Betty Pearce and Nellie Allen recited; there were songs by Winnie Bird and Katie Jones; another piano solo by Robert Davies and recitations by Lorna Mason and Gladys Davies; an Action Song in Welsh ("Doli") by Standard 2; songs by Winnie Townsend and H Spencer; a sketch ("Caradoc") by Standard 3; more recitations from John O'Shea and Gilbert Strong; Standard 7 performed a sketch ("Llew") and Victor Stone played the piano; Standards 6 and 7 combined to sing "Cyfr'r Geifr" and "Dydd Gwyl Dewi". The concert was brought to a conclusion with a hymn and the National Anthem.

The next year's concert opened, again, with short lectures on Welsh notabilities – William Pantycelyn, Henry Richards, Dr Morgan – but delivered this time by Vera Silk, Ernest Piper and Joseph Davies, all Standard 3 pupils. Other items of music and recitation were contributed by Audrey Bevan, Harold Jones, Daisy Evans, Marion Davies, Gladys Camplin, William Howells, Lily and Cissy Shannon and James Hill.

In 1930 the morning concert was held in the All Saints Rooms in order to accommodate more people and it was "attended by a very large and appreciative audience of parents and friends". The programme was varied by the inclusion of the Trial Scene from Shakespeare's "Merchant of Venice" performed by Standards 6 and 7. The cast list was as follows :-

Antonio	—	E Hurlow	Duke	—	J Gratton
Bassanio	—	T Payne	Portia	—	I Wise
Gratiano	—	G Hurlow	Shylock	—	T Brice
Salerio	—	R Pook	Nerissa	—	E Barber
Judges	—	R Parsons and R Tudor	Clerks	—	I Barnard and M Preece

The celebration remained in the form of a concert, mostly held in the All Saints Rooms, on one occasion presided over by Mrs Ellen Lindsay, until 1935 when it became an Eisteddfod with local people acting as adjudicators, usually the Vicar and his wife, the headteacher's wife, and Mr Henry May or his son, Arthur. In 1935 the successful competitiors were :-

1.	Essay – Dewi Sant	Ruth Poole
2.	Recitation – Robin Goch	Joseph Gater
3.	Handwork – Welsh Dragon	Raymond Odey
4.	Song – Tra Bo Dau	Betty Thomas & M Davies
5.	Recitation – Y Briallu	Billy Powell
6.	Painting – Daffodil or Leek	Alfred Perrett, Mervyn Turner
7.	Solo – Y Fwyalchen	Sibyl Davies, Clive Lucas
8.	Recitation – Mawrch a Dewi	Olive Lucas
9.	Stencil Work – Daffodil	Arthur Hayter, R Furze
10.	Canu Pennillion	Marion Davies

11.	Girls' Choirs – Ymdaeth Capten Llwyd		
		1.	Irene Greenhouse's Choir
		2.	Hilda Williams' Choir
12.	Boys' Choirs – Cyfri'r Geifr	1.	Walter Hill's Choir
		2.	Dennis Linehan's Choir
13.	Country Dances	1.	Irene Greenhouse's Team
		2.	Glenys Jones' Team
		3.	Norma Drane's Team
14.	Swimming Certificates presented.		

Amalgamation   When George Evans was appointed headteacher in 1927 he was put in charge of the Senior Mixed Department only, the Infants Department having as its head Miss Louisa Moses, who had held the post since November 1900. When she retired in 1928, Mr Evans took provisional charge of the Infants Department pending consideration of whether the Mixed and Infants Departments should be amalgamated, which they subsequently were under his permanent headship.

Prizes and Scholarships   A highlight early in the 1929 school calendar was the presentation, for regular attendance, of certificates, books, medals and watches, which were handed out by Colonel Lindsay, the Rev. D J Wills (recently arrived in the parish after the death of the Rev. Edwin Edwards the previous August), and Mr Daniel Davies, a Caerphilly Group Manager, who lived in Manchester House, Llanbradach.

   Another cause for satisfaction that year was that three boys passed the Entrance Scholarship Examination : James Hill, Leonard Carter and Donald James. Presumably they enrolled at the newly built Caerphilly Boys Secondary School where Mr Evans and his colleagues were invited to attend the official opening ceremonies on 18 September. The following year eight pupils passed the examination and Thomas Payne secured 4th position on the list for the Caerphilly area, a result which Mr Evans found gratifying. The logbook contains no further information about Scholarship successes until :–

18 June 1935   Thomas Phillips, Marion Davies, Mary Price, Joyce Dyer passed County Entrance Scholarship Exam. This makes a total of 36 scholarships gained in the school since 1928.

   As eight of these scholarships were won in 1930 the average for the other years is four or five. It is interesting to note that during the period 1931–36 the County Education Committee adopted a policy that every child over 10 years and under 12 years 9 months must take the County Entrance Examination. This commendable attempt to bring a secondary education to the maximum number of children was brought to an end when it became evident that, whether due to the parents' financial straits or the difficulty the children had in adjusting to the social and educational ethos of the secondary schools, many of those who passed dropped out as soon as they could. In 1937 the former policy was revived

The children's playground shortly after the official opening on 31 May 1930

Courtesy of Miss Kitty Hughes

of allowing headteachers and parents to decide which children should be entered for the examination.

Road Safety A matter of increasing concern to the Education Authority was the safety of children on the main road through the village. Even before motor vehicles became more numerous, horse–drawn traffic created its own hazards – in 1913 all headteachers were asked to impress upon children from time to time the necessity of being careful and observant when entering or travelling on the roads so as to avoid undue risk from the traffic "and in particular to refrain from hanging on to carts". At that time there were very few motor cars and no motor buses (the first application to run a public motor bus service between Caerphilly and Ystrad Mynach was made in June 1914). The number of cars and other vehicles on the roads increased during the 1920s and in May 1930 the County organised a "Safety Week" when each class was taken as far as the main road and practical demonstrations given on how to cross the road safely. In October 1936 a Belisha Beacon was installed on the main road opposite the exit from the school and all the classes were instructed on the correct use of it.

Cause for pride The month of May 1930 marked an important development in the village, one which had significance for children and adults alike, and not only benefited everyone who lived in the village but also added to the communal self–esteem, giving cause for pride when the stigma of unemployment and poverty was almost at its worst. The event which heralded this milestone in Llanbradach's history receives only an oblique reference in the school logbook:

27 May 1930   28 boys and 33 girls were taken this afternoon for a school journey to the Welfare Park for instruction and observation, accompanied by the headteacher and Mr A E Morgan.

On the same day pupils from Coedybrain Boys and Girls schools were also taken there for "instruction in shrubs and flowers and general care of grounds and plants" and in preparation for the opening of the Park "on Saturday next when senior children will demonstrate use of new playing apparatus etc."

The Caerphilly Journal (24 May 1930) reported the forthcoming event:–

To the mining village of Llanbradach at the entrance to the Rhymney Valley has fallen the distinction of having the first Children's Playground under the Miners Welfare Fund, and which is regarded as the model for Wales. Thanks to the energetic local Miners' Welfare Committee, of which Mr R.C. Wright is the "live wire" and secretary, the village is in possession of a beautifully situated recreation ground containing provision for all kinds of outdoor games for the adult population. The new children's playground covering over 2½ acres is adjacent thereto. The whole presents a picturesque scene. The cost is about £2700 ..... The grounds will be opened to the public on Saturday 31 May, the ceremony to be performed by the

Rt. Hon. the Earl of Chelmsford, supported by the Rt. Hon. Thomas Richards (President of the Miners Federation of Great Britain), Ald. Hubert Jenkins J.P. (Chairman of Glamorgan County Council), Col. D. Watts Morgan, M.P. Morgan Jones M.P., and Will John M.P.

The local Miners Welfare Association, under its dedicated committee, had been working since 1925 to develop the multiplicity of leisure facilities which now reached final fruition. In addition to the hardworking secretary the chairman was Dai Carlick and among other members were H. Thomas, Emrys Jones, Cllr John Bassett, Tom Moses, George L Evans and Dr. R C Robertson. Funds were raised locally by means of a levy on the colliery workmen, and substantial grants were received from the Miners Welfare Fund of Great Briatin.

Another view of the children's playground,
in which the tennis pavilion can also be seen.

Prior to the opening ceremony the school children marched through the streets, headed by Llanbradach Silver Band under the conductorship of Dan Hughes. the children then assembled near the gates and sang "Land of Hope and Glory", assisted by the Band.

Lord Chelmsford, former viceroy of India and governor of New South Wales and Queensland, as chairman of the national fund, said in his opening speech that he had come down from London that day because he wished to impress on everyone that a great responsibility rested on them to see that the apparatus in this model playground was well looked after : "Unfortunately, in some places boys and girls over school age used the apparatus and ruined it and no-one wanted that to happen in Llanbradach" ... "Llanbradach would give a lead to the rest of England and Wales, and it would depend on them to a large extent how far recreation grounds would be developed in other centres" (Merthyr Express, 7 June 1930).

The idea of providing a "Recreation Ground" had been actively considered as far back as 1910 by Clara Thomas and Caerphilly Urban District Council. The Council applied to Lord Tredegar to buy a piece of land on the Monmouthshire side of the river and Miss Clara Thomas offered to give part of her land on the village side. These combined portions amounted to 15 acres with the river running through the middle. For some, as yet undiscovered reason, these negotiations and plans came to nothing and Llanbradach had to wait nearly another 20 years before the desired recreation ground came into being through the efforts of the villagers themselves. It was the Llanbradach Welfare Association which eventually, in 1925, bought nine acres of market garden land from Mr William Amos for £624 and made the dream a reality. For several generations of village children the reality was a dream, a hugely enjoyed fantasy playground: ships and horses, lullaby, swings and slides, box and umbrella, spider's web and monkey puzzle, leap-frog and tadpoles, sand pit, cascade and paddling water, bushy dens, Disneyland on our doorstep. For the grown-ups there were tennis courts and a pavilion, football pitch, putting green, and colourful flowerbeds, all of which had been laid out since 1927.

When the Public Welfare Association, in June 1931, placed advertisements for a groundsman-gardener in the Daily Herald, the South Wales Echo and the South Wales Argus, a total of 208 applications were received from all parts of Wales, England, Scotland and even the Channel Islands.

Would you be so kind   The applications sent to the secretary (Cuthbert Wright of 14 Grove Street) are, in their number and nature, vivid testimony to the tragedy of the huge unemployment problem of the early 1930s. Ben Charles from Ton Pentre, aged 26, wrote that he "took a delight in caring and attending flowers and plants, a keen tennis player, would be glad to teach young players in tennis, bowls or cricket .... Brought up in a good Christian home". Sydney Harding from Haverfordwest had worked five years on a private estate living in a tied cottage with his wife and three children on a wage of £2-7-6. Alfred Brett from Ewelme, Oxfordshire, aged 40 with two children, wrote from a private estate : "I have
served here two years, the place has been sold. My wife is a very nice woman to have about, keeps her cottage beautifully....children very quiet, well behaved and would never be any trouble". George Lewis from Caerphilly wrote; "I have only had experience doing my own gardening. I am able to turn by hand to any kind of work. Last worked at Llanbradach. P.S. Shall be very much obliged if you will be so kind as to do your best as I am unemployed. Have wife and three children. Also a heavy rent of 11/- per week to pay out of 30/- unemployment". John Lewis from Machynlleth provided references from the head gardeners of

the Earl of Lisburne's estate near Aberystwyth and of Chirk Castle in addition to one from the hotelier in Devil's Bridge who, after six years, had made him redundant due to "the acute depression in trade". William Turner from New Tredegar wrote: "I am thoroughly acquainted with your village as I assisted my father, Charles Wm. Turner, in the making of your bowling green". Several applications were from soldiers about to leave the Army who were undergoing vocational training at Chiseldon Camp, Wiltshire. One man had just returned from New Zealand, another from Australia, and two from Canada – one of whom wrote, from Sheffield, that he had served four years in the Army during the war, now had a family of five children, and had returned from Canada after four years when his "farm failed through frozen and hailed crops".

The references accompanying the applications reveal a large number of potentially suitable candidates for the post. A short list of six appears to have been made and the post was finally given to Mr Charles Offa who lived at 9 Grove Street! In the Coedybrain Infants admission register, when his son Douglas started at the school in April 1927 Mr Offa's occupation is given as "gardener"; when Douglas transferred to Coedybrain Boys in April 1929 the father's occupation is "Welfare Groundsman". It seems that having bought the land in 1925 the Welfare Association may have already been employing Mr Offa as groundsman two years before the official opening of the park.

The Public Welfare Association advertised at the same time for a pavilion attendant to run the kiosk in the park. There were ten applicants, all young girls from the village:

> Gladys Tudor, 17, of 3 Graddfa Road
> Olive Beale, 23, of 7 Oak Terrace
> Winifred Dobbins, 22, of 7 Ffrwd Terrace
> Gladys Bassett, 16, of 14 Rees Terrace
> Daisy Morgan of 23 De Winton Terrace
> Doris Wright, 29, of 15 Rees Terrace
> Violet Kitt, 15, of 48 School Street,
> R Melloy Evans of 14 Wingfield Crescent
> J.E. Griffiths, 16, of 4 Station Road
> Violet Morris, 16, of 3 De Winton Terrace

I have been unable to discover which of these was appointed.

Break-ins In September 1932 the school was broken into, nothing was taken but several cupboards and teachers' desks were tampered with. There had been a similar incident a few years earlier:

8 April 1928	The headteacher visited the school on Sunday and found that an illegal entry had been made by some person or persons unknown. The new padlocks placed on the six teachers' desks had been forced open with a poker and the contents strewn all over the floors of the classrooms.

The matter was immediately reported to the police, and Sergeant Rowe, the headteacher and the cleaner spent nearly two hours investigating the burglary. Footprints and a deposit of clay were found on one of the window ledges, showing that entrance had probably been made through the window by removing one of the ventilators. Nothing of value was taken by the burglars.

There were only two more minor break-ins recorded in 1946 and 1951. Whatever the burglars hoped to find the only items they ever succeeded in taking were two soccer balls from the games cupboard.

Barry Island and the Queen Mum   The daily routine of school life was, as ever, subject to pleasant interruptions :-

4 June 1929	Closed for GWR excursion for schoolchildren to Stratford-on-Avon.
4 July 1929	Closed for Sunday Schools trip to Barry Island.
5 July 1929	Attendance considerably lower than usual – very heavy rain and 45 absent who went to Barry Island yesterday.
4 September 1930	Closed at 3.15pm so children could attend the Combined Sunday Schools Festival at the Childrens Playground.
12 December 1930	Closed in afternoon for Attendance half-day holiday – first for this school since 29 June 1923.
14 May 1931	Closed – Ascension Day Celebrations.
17 March 1932	The children were this morning lined up along the side of the main road to watch the Duke and Duchess of York (the present Queen Mother) passing through Llanbradach on their way from Cardiff to Merthyr.
1 July 1932	Closed – trip to Clifton (Bristol) Zoo.
7 July 1932	Closed for Sunday Schools Outing to Barry.
8 July 1932	50-60 children absent – too tired to get up, so most of the parents told me.
24 Febraury 1933	Severe snow blizzard raged through the night. The school approach is almost impassable, only 81 children present. At 9.55am the Director of Education ordered the school to be closed.
28 March 1933	Closed for Scholarship Examination.
26 May 1933	Closed for Urdd Gobaith Cymru Eisteddfod at Caerphilly.
29 June 1933	Closed for London Trip organised by G.W.R.
19 October 1933	Closed early for Seion's Gymanfa Ganu.
7 May 1934	Closed for May Day celebrations.
29 November 1934	Closed all day – wedding of Princess Marina and the Duke of Kent.
6 May 1935	Closed for Jubilee Day.
6 November 1935	Closed for Duke of Gloucester's Wedding.

14 November 1935   Closed for Parliamentary Election.

LLANBRADACH BATHS
Having obtained a 99 year lease from 1 November 1933, at £6 p.a., on a piece of land running down to the river, Hughie Jones, the local builder, opened the baths to the public at the end of May 1934. School pupils from Llanbradach, Caerphilly and Ystrad Mynach were soon enjoying the new facility as part of their Summer curriculum.

Courtesy of Miss Elsie Davies

The Baths   On the 29 November 1933 Mr Hugh Jones of 1 School Street, Llanbradach obtained from the Trustees of the Thomas Estate a 99 year lease on "a piece of land part of Tynygraig Farm" at an annual rent of £6. The conditions of the lease were that he should "securely fence in the said land before building operations are commenced" and "erect Swimming Bath, Dressing Boxes etc., at a cost of at least £500". The pool, whose sides were built up, not excavated, was 100 feet long, 35 feet wide, 3 feet deep at the shallow end and 8ft. 6ins at the deep end; the engineer was Wallace Evans, Cardiff. Hughie Jones, as he was known, had been a builder in the village for many years and was a member of the Workmen's Institute Committee in 1910–12 which found the money and made all the arrangements for the building of the new Hall. He now provided Llanbradach, as a private venture, with a leisure facility which, like the park it adjoined, served the community well for more than forty years. Schoolchildren were among the first to benefit when it opened to the public in May 1934 :

30 May 1934   Large number of children in Standards 5, 6 and 7 attended
                     at the Swimming Bath.

Classes from Caerphilly and Ystrad Mynach Schools soon began using the pool and there was talk in the village of starting a swimming club and a polo team (Merthyr Express, 23 June 1934)

26 February 1935   Welsh Amateur Swimming Association certificates for children who passed the Pupils' Elementary Test during 1934 season :-
Glenys Jones, Arthur Smith, Ronald Furze, William Mills, Clarence Williams, Freda James.

Dydd Gwyl Dewi   The 1936 St David's Day Eisteddfod produced another large crop of successful competitors:-

Recitation	1. Eva Poole	2. Hilda Collier
Song	1. Tony Preece	2. Kenneth Smith
Song	1. Maisie Meredith	2. Glyn Griffiths
Pastel	Margaret Owen	
Pianoforte	Hilda Williams	
Recitation	1. Glenys Lewis	2. Thelma Garaway
Junior Choirs	divided between Ralph Jones' and Kenneth White's Choirs.	
Song	1. Marion Jenkins	2. Margaret Taylor
Drawing	1. Edward Turner	2. Clarence Williams
Piano Solo	Joan Martin	
Recitation	1. Ruth Poole	2. Marion Jenkins
Junior Choirs	1. Peggy O'Shea's	2. Gladys Hole's
Lino Cutting	"Programme Cover Design"	
	1. Edward Turner	2. Clarence Williams
Canu Penillion	1. Kitty O'Shea	2. Blodwen Allen
Recitation	1. David Evans	2. Irene Greenhouse
Song	1. Kitty O'Shea	2. Ida Tovey
Chief Choral	divided between Irene Greenhouse's and Hilda Williams' Choirs	
Senior Dances –	1. Ida Lloyd's Team	2. Hilda Williams' Team

Miscellany of 1937   the logbook entries for 1937 record a brief snowstorm in January, the St David's Day concert, the Coronation Tea on 11 May and the Royal Visit to Cardiff in July. In December Mr Evans attended the funeral of Mr T P Davies, the late headteacher. A glimpse of the social conditions in the village is afforded by the following entry :-

23 December 1937   Ten sacks of clothing, books, toys etc., were received from Upton House Central School, Urswick Road, London E9 and distributed amongst the children. £3 also received from the same school to be used by the headteacher for

providing a tea for the children. The tea will be given after the Christmas holidays.

Also in 1937, one of the pupils, Audrey Drane, had a letter from the Caerphilly Group Managers congratulating her on 8½ years unbroken attendance; another girl, Marion Jenkins was later praised for her 7 years perfect attendance.

Let there be light In April 1938 the school was inspected by HMI Mr A G Prys-Jones whose report was, on the whole, pleasingly satisfactory :-

"The number of children enrolled is 224; in February 1933 this was 269. The headteacher was appointed in 1927, and he has carried out his duties with unfailing energy and zeal .... He deserves commendation for the general quality of the results which are achieved.

The number of assistant teachers is eight, four being certificated. They all devote themselves industriously to their tasks. Several of the teachers have special aptitudes for the teaching of particular subjects and they are encouraged to give full scope to their abilities.

The written work in arithmetic reaches a creditably good standard throughout the school; it is neatly set out and well marked. But greater care should be exercised in the use of the conventional mathematical symbols denoting multiplication, division, equality etc., and clear statements should be insisted upon in working out mathematical problems.

Reading and writing are well taught throughout. But despite this there is some weakness in these subjects. The older children show commendably good powers of expression in writing. All through the school, however, stress should be laid upon the importance of clear and correct speech. This should be done not only during English lessons, but also during other lessons.

The two Infant Groups are under the care of two young teachers. One of these is a good pianist and has recently made a good beginning with percussion band work, instruments for which were acquired a short time ago out of funds raised privately by the school.

In the "baby" room, the children appear to derive pleasure and interest from their activities. They are accommodated at dual desks of the usual type. A couple of cots, with steel frames, are available for use during rest period. In the creation of a homelike atmosphere here, it should be borne in mind that a scrupulously clean floor is one of the first conditions.

This building originally housed two departments, Mixed and Infants, which were amalgamated in 1929. It comprises ten classrooms, one of which is used as a medical inspection room and another as a store room. As little seems to have been done in recent years to maintain the premises in good condition, a thorough overhaul is now necessary. Among the repairs and alterations which should be carried out are the following :-

1. Installation of electric light
2. Redecoration of the interior
3. Extension and modernisation of the offices
4. Re-plastering of the ceiling in one of the classrooms
5. Repairing of floorboards
6. Reconstruction of the windows in north classrooms in order to obtain improved ventilation.

Expert examination by an architect may well reveal further defects no less urgently in need of attention".

The number of children on the register had fallen from 300 (Mixed and Infants) in 1928 to 224 ten years later. It is likely that smaller families and emigration to England in the search for employment were factors in this decline in numbers. Llanbradach colliery, although in production through the depressed market conditions of the 1930s, employed only about 1500 men and boys at this time, compared with twice that number at its peak.

Staff Changes   There had been several changes of staff since Mr Evans' arrival. Miss Gwenllian Jones had come straight from Barry Training College in 1929 and remained until 1943. Miss Mona Frances Gill came in September 1932, aged 17 years, having passed the CWB Senior with credit in History, Welsh, Arithmetic, Drawing, Cookery, Needlework and distinction in Botany; she left in 1945 after her marriage to Mr Douglas Clinch of Caerphilly. Miss Martha Jane Thomas trained at Swansea and was appointed to teach one of the Infant classes in 1932; she transferred to Whitchurch Girls School in 1940 but later married Mr Lewis Conibear, one of her Llanbradach colleagues. Miss Violet May Davies, who received her schooling at Aberdare Girls Secondary School, trained at Bangor and held teaching posts in Wolverhampton and Cheshire before coming to Llanbradach in 1933; she moved to a new post in St Albans, Hertfordshire, just after the outbreak of the Second World War. Mr William (Bill) Williams graduated at Swansea University College and did his teacher training there before he arrived in 1933, leaving in 1951 on being promoted to be head-teacher of Ystrad Mynach Junior Mixed School; in 1941 he had taken a day off work to marry Miss Ida Griffiths who taught at Coedybrain Girls, and in the late 1940s was elected to Caerphilly Urban District Council.

And there was light   The HMI's recommendation that electric light should be installed was acted on fairly promptly. When the staff and children returned from the midsummer holidays on 1 September 1938, they were able to enjoy for the first time in the school's history, a form of artificial light. Although TP Davies mentioned the lack of lighting on a number of occasions, usually in the darkening days of November, George Evans had never referred to it since his appointment in 1927, which suggests that it did not strike him as being an unusual circumstance. An immediate result of the innovation was a directive from County Hall that the afternoon session should begin at 1.20pm (instead of

1.10pm) and close at 3.50pm (instead of 3.40pm). During the holidays, the lavatories were also modernised and extended.

The wireless   Another sign of the times was the Caerphilly Group teachers having to attend an address on "Broadcasting for Schools" given at Caerphilly Senior Boys School in February 1939. The wireless set, like the television set of today, was universally present in homes throughout the country – nine million sets had been licensed by the end of the 1930s. Listening to the wireless was the paramount form of entertainment at this time and during the war years which were to follow. Vastly popular though "the pictures" were, the wireless was cheaper and even more readily available. Broadcasting for schools had been started by the BBC in the 1920s, but its use in many schools spread very gradually. There is no mention of its installation or use in Llanbradach Mixed, but the Coedybrain Boys' logbook records one instance of Form II listening to a 50 minute programme on "East Anglia" and "The Industrial Revolution" in February 1936, which suggests it was a novelty at the time; the Coedybrain Girls were not provided with wireless equipment until 1953, the beginning of the television age!

Eisteddfod   The St Davids Day celebrations in 1939 began with special lessons on "Dewi Sant and other Great Welshmen" and concluded with an eisteddfod which was adjudicated by the Rev. Handel Thomas (the new incumbent of All Saints), Mrs G L Evans, Mr Henry May, Mr T Jones, and the headteacher. Councillors John Roach and Tomkinson represented Caerphilly District Council and the school was "overcrowded with parents". The successful competitors were :–

> Rose Smith, Leslie Townsend, Hilda Bird, Ethel Griffiths,
> C Payne, Jean Glass, Rosie Griffiths, Dorothy Linehan,
> Florrie Sheppard, Kitty Williams, M Meredith, Violet Bird,
> Rachel Evans, Glenys Lewis, Thelma Garaway, James Smith,
> Marie Bumford and J Lewis Davies.

Also Tony Preece (Standard 4) played the accordion, some of the older boys played bamboo pipes and the school's percussion band was encored.

World War Two

11 September 1939   School coloured and painted internally during holidays. Reopened after one extra week's closure due to the outbreak of War on 3 September.

This entry in the logbook nicely sets the tone for the next six years. The greatest conflict in human history exploded at points all over the globe, many millions of civilians and servicemen were to die in those years, men and women left Llanbradach to perform their military service, some never to return, yet the ordinary daily life of the village, with its mundane concerns went on, albeit restricted by the "Black-out", rationing of food and clothes and other shortages, the occasional excitement of an incendiary bomb falling in the vicinity or an aeroplane overhead (usually one of "ours").

24 September 1939	Gas Mask and Air Raid Drill given this morning.
1 November 1939	School hours in "Black-out"
	From today until 29 February 1940 times of assembly will be 9am and 1pm, dismissal 12 noon and 3.30pm. .... this is to enable the children to reach their homes before the "Black-out" hour during the war.

St David's Day 1940 was celebrated in the customary way and the school closed for Ascension Day and May Day, but the Whitsun holidays, usually a full week, were curtailed by order of the Government to Whit-Monday only.

14 May 1940	Gas Mask Drill given today. A.R.P. wardens present.
20 May 1940	Air Raid practice given this afternoon under the supervision of staff, police and wardens. All the children were under cover at their homes or places provided for them within 4½ minutes.
5 June 1940	Folkestone Evacuees : 24 admitted today and 1 teacher
6 June 1940	Folkestone Evacuees : 19 admitted plus one teacher.

This first wave of evacuees followed the German invasion of Holland and Belgium in May and the evacuation of British and French soldiers from Dunkirk completed on 3 June 1940. The Battle of Britain began on 10 July and on 13 August the German Luftwaffe began its all-out attack on south-east England.

The admission registers for this period are unavailable, but the Coedybrain registers would suggest that these 43 children and their teachers were from the Mundella Infants and Girls Schools and the George Spurgeon (Boys) School in Folkestone. Large numbers of children from these schools accompanied by their teachers were also accommodated in the Cwm Aber Schools, Abertridwr. The two teachers who came to Llanbradach Mixed and Infants, Miss Frances Quested and Miss Winifred Turley, returned to Folkestone in, respectively, October 1941 and February 1942, so it is likely that most of the Folkestone evacuees had returned to their homes by the end of the year.

Although Llanbradach was never bombed, it was subject to periodical air raid warnings which became a familiar feature of wartime life and disrupted school routine, sometimes to the annoyance of the headteacher :

15 November 1940	The Alert Siren was blown this morning at 9.50 and owing to the failure of the Cardiff Collieries to blow the "All Clear" all the morning, the parents did not send their children to school, and the registers were therfore not

marked for the morning session.

Since July "owing to the serious war conditions" the morning session in all Glamorgan schools had started an hour later than usual, i.e. 10.10am. Otherwise, despite accommodating two classes of evacuee children, school life appears to have proceeded quite smoothly: one or two teachers came and went, Mr Bill Williams had a day off to get married in March 1941, St David's Day was celebrated (though not recorded in the usual lengthy detail in order to save paper), all the children who sat the County Entrance School Exam ("The Scholarship") were successful.

In December 1941, as the Folkestone children were leaving the village, an influx of evacuees arrived from a number of Birmingham schools. Those who were accommodated in Llanbradach Mixed brought their own teacher, Miss Dilys Jones, who returned to Birmingham in April 1942 and was replaced by Mrs Winifred Hughes. Mrs Hughes began her career at Rhoose in 1931 after graduating with honours and training as a teacher at Swansea University College. She had been obliged, under Glamorgan Education Committee regulations, to give up teaching when she married in 1941; in 1942 she was directed back into teaching as war work. By September, with a few exceptions, the Birmingham children had returned home. Mrs Hughes, whose original post had been temporary and paid for by the Birmingham Education Authority, became a permanent member of staff, remaining in Llanbradach until she transferred to Caerphilly Girls Secondary Modern School in July, 1951. A year after Mrs Hughes joined the Llanbradach staff, Miss Gwenllian Jones transferred to Maesmarchog Junior School; Miss Jones had taught in the village since 1929.

During 1943 and 1944, the school had to contend with a much older, more immediately worrying, enemy than Adolf Hitler. In May and June 1943 heavy rains flooded the playgrounds and lavatories to depths of up to 9 inches. The Director of Education, the Chief Primary Inspector and the County Architect visited the school to investigate the problem – to no effect, as in September and October 1944 the playground and South Lane were flooded to a depth of 12 inches, making it impossible to use the boys' and girls' entrances :-

20 November 1944   Boys' playground and south side of the school flooded. Attendance this morning was 23.4% due to the flooding of the main road between Wingfield Crescent and Plasturtwyn Terrace to a depth of at least 2 feet 6 inches. The houses in Wingfield Crescent, Plasturtwyn Terrace, Oakfield Street and Victoria Street were marooned and it was impossible for the inhabitants to leave their homes, hence attendance was very adversely affected.

During the summer months of 1944, London was attacked by "flying bombs" (or "doodle-bugs"), a pilotless aeroplane carrying a ton of explosive in the nose which flew for 150 miles before diving into the ground. They killed about 6000 people and injured many more. In September the V1, as it was also known, was succeeded by the even more deadly V2, a 12 ton rocket which was launched 60 miles high and travelled at 3000 miles an hour. Unlike its predecessor the approach of the V2 could not be heard and there was no defence against it; before the launch sites were over-run by the Allied Forces after D-Day another 2700 people died in London and its environs.

A group of Llanbradach Mixed children who took part in a fund-raising event for Caerphilly Miners Hospital c. 1949.

Back row: Betty Gater, Joan Pellandine, Dorothy Glass, Margaret McCarthy, Bella Davies, Shirley Davies, June Maizey, Pat Evans, Marina Yorath.
Middle row: Pat Price, John Yorath, Graham Davies, Lucy Davies, Marion Davies, Betty Jones, Irene Preece.
Front row: Betty Lane, Tommy Turner, Jennifer McDowell, Angela McDowell, Thelma Davies.

It was at this stage of the war that the village received its final in-flow of evacuees, this time from schools in London (mainly Islington) and Maidstone, Kent. An LCC teacher, Miss Page, was appointed to the staff of Llanbradach Mixed and Infants in September 1944 and remained until June 1945, by which time most of the children had returned to their families. The records relating to the evacuees are very incomplete, but these show that at least four children remained in the village for a year or two after the end of the war in Europe; two young brothers, Robert and William Semon, admitted to the Infants in 1941 and 1943, lived at 35 Wingfield Crescent until they returned to London during 1946; in April 1944 ten year old Pearl Parsons came from London and lived at 76 Garden Street until at least May 1946; in September 1944 Rosemary Morris, aged 5 years, who must also have been already living with her mother at 28 Church Street, was admitted to the Infants; she moved to London in March 1947.

In September 1944 Miss Elizabeth M Thomas, who had joined the staff in April 1941, departed for a post at Three Crosses Mixed School and was replaced by a young woman who was born and brought up in the village, whose father and grandfather had been family butchers in Llanbradach since the 1890s. Miss Joan Coppage had qualified as a teacher at St Katherine's College, Tottenham, in 1943. She remained on the staff until the closure of the school in 1952, by which time she had married Mr Desmond Lewis. One of her colleagues recalls her bringing in sausages etc., from her father, Mr Les Coppage, which were consumed around an open coal fire in the staff-room – a welcome addition to the meat ration, no doubt! She taught at Coedybrain Infants before leaving in October 1953 to start a family.

More floods, fewer pupils   The running of the school was plagued by floods throughout the winter of 1946– 47 and the building seems not to have been properly maintained. Cllr. W H Westhead, a school manager, made this entry in the logbook when he visited :–

20 October 1947   the roof of the building is in a very bad state, and as a result of water coming through, the ceilings are cracking up and falling.

On a later occasion he wrote :–

28 June 1948   The School appears to be kept in a very clean condition under adverse conditions.

The eventual fate of the school was foreshadowed two years later when, as a consequence of the Education Act 1944, the secondary modern schools were created in Caerphilly. When the school re-opened after the summer holidays of 1950 all the children aged 13 plus had been transferred to the Twyn (boys) and Gwyndy (girls). The fall in pupil numbers resulted in the school being organised into five classes instead of six. In fact, the LEA had already decided in March 1950 that it wished to cease maintaining the school and transfer all the pupils to the Coedybrain Schools and gave public notice of the proposal. When Caerphilly Urban District Council asked the County Council in July 1950 to share the cost of making up the un-made approach road to the school the County declined to do so on the grounds that the school would probably be closed by the end of the year.

Retirement   At the end of July 1951 Mr George Evans retired from the teaching profession after 21 years as headteacher, years which despite the various difficulties he felt had been very happy ones. During his early years in the village he lodged at 1 De Winton Terrce until he and his wife made their home in the house called "Tarran" on the corner of Grove Street and Tynygraig Road, which they re-named "Heddfan". He had been a loyal member of the congregation at All Saints Church, where he served as choirmaster, and during the war he conducted a mixed choir at occasional Sunday concerts to raise money for the Forces Benefit Fund. He was one of the very few villagers who owned a small car in the 1930s and 1940s. He died in October 1957, whereupon Mrs Lilian Evans went to live with her sister at Sketty, Swansea.

Two other members of the staff also left in July 1951 : Mrs Winifred Hughes transferred to Caerphilly Girls Secondary Modern School, and Mr Bill Williams was promoted to the headship of Ystrad Mynach Junior Mixed School. When the new school year opened in September 1951 there were only four teachers and a temporary headteacher on the staff.

The teaching staff 1947–48, Llanbradach Mixed
Standing : Cllr. Bill Williams, Mrs. Prydwen Whatley, Miss Joan Coppage,
Mr. ? (temporary replacement for Miss Rosemary Davies)
Sitting : Mrs A E Owen, Mr George Evans, Mrs Winifred Hughes.

Courtesy of Mrs Winifred Hughes

The end   The final entries in the logbook made a sad ending to the story of the school :-

3 March 1952	Headteacher reported leaks in roof and burst pipes.
5 March 1952	Excessive leakage from roof. Police Sergeant Jones and the headteacher ascended to the roof to investigate the damage and found that three pieces of lead sheeting 3'x8½' and six pieces of 6¾'x2¼' had been removed.
28 April 1952	Headteacher arrived at 9.10am and was met by Mr D W Davies, Divisional Education Officer, and the Vicar of Llanbradach, Rev. C J Edwards. The D.E.O. told the headteacher the school was to be closed without delay. The staff and children assembled. Mr T J Evans, Chief Primary Inspector, Mr Shepherd, Primary Inspector, and Mr Jenkins, County Architect's Department, arrived. Headteacher informed children the school was to be closed immediately and they should attend at Coedybrain Boys, Girls and Infants Schools from tomorrow.

Later that same day the Director of Education reported to the appropriate subcommittee that "The Ministry had now declared in favour of the representations made some time ago that this school which had fallen into a bad state of repair was redundant to the needs of the area and should be closed". The subcommittee confirmed the action of the Director in arranging for the transfer of all the children on the next day – 44 boys, 25 girls from the Mixed Department, 53 boys and girls from the Infants.

In this traumatic fashion the first school in the village – the National, the Church, the Llanbradach Mixed and Infants as it was variously known during its 60 years – finally closed its doors. It had originally accommodated its pupils in the old Public Hall in 1892, moving into the purpose-built building on the Wingfield Estate two years later. For 55 years of its existence, it was guided by only two headteachers, T P Davies and G L Evans.

Chapter Five

COEDYBRAIN BOYS 1931-1945

Discord among the teachers   The new headteacher arrived in time for the beginning of the Autumn Term in 1931. He was Mr David Daniel, who until then had been headteacher of Bedlinog Boys School. Of the three male headteachers who between them served the Coedybrain Schools for 64 years, his tenure of the post was to be the shortest, as he died after only 8½ years. His entries in the logbook are less frequent and less interesting than those of his predecessor and somehow give the impression of a man who was more detached from the community in which he worked, although he complied with the County Council regulation by living in the village, at 33 High Street.

Mr Daniel, in his early years at Coedybrain, experienced difficulties in his relations with some of his colleagues as several logbook entries indicate :-

23 June 1932	Mr A T Williams, Manual Instructor, was in three classes this morning session for what reason I cannot imagine. I found him addressing Standard 4 on the care of tools in the Manual Department. It apparently is one of the many little acts which cannot but be harmful to the general discipline of any school.
	During the week a spirit level was found in the drawer of my desk. The drawer is kept locked except when I am on the premises. Several months ago following a general talk following an attempted entry of the school a master key was found in the same drawer. After repeated efforts to bring co-operation in the work of the school and after eight months constant attention to bringing co-operation amongst the staff I am of the opinion that some members have no intention of 'fitting in'.
30 June 1932	After many requests to teachers to do their part in keeping out of classrooms such papers as the 'Marvel', 'Gem' and similar publications, I find the practice allowed in the forms.

During July 1932 as a result of unspecified 'complaints made by the headteacher' the school received four visits from the County Primary Inspector, the Director of Education and the HMI. Mr Daniel gives no indication of the nature of the complaints he had made or what the outcome was of the officials' investigation of them.

Coedybrain Boys, 1932 – Teacher Miss E G Black.

Top row: ?, ?, Jimmy Edwards, Kenny Keirle, Jackie Holland, ?, Idris Minton, ?, ?, Ronnie Edwards, ?
Second row: Cliff Jones, Bert Taylor, Jack Elson, Maldwyn Fleming, Billy Shannon, ?, ?, Glyn John, Dewi Ashdown, Tom Shannon.
Third row: Stanley Piper, ?, Philip White, Billy Eynon, Eddie Lewis, Tommy Mitchell, ?, Leslie Thomas, Norman Carter, Edgar Butt.
Fourth row: ?, Hadyn Rudge, ?, George Saysell, Billy Thorne, ?, ?, ? Frank Brimble, Ron Thomas.
Bottom row: Stan Stride, Graham Shannon, ?, ?, Ivor Wiltshire, Trevor Windmill, ?, Norman Lewis, Ken Jones, Harry Coles.

Courtesy of Graham Shannon

| 3 July 1933 | A request made on the 19th that classes should not be left unattended has not been followed, hence this special entry. |
| 10 July 1934 | Mr A J Richards (Standard 1) behaved badly, giving an unseemly exhibition in his classroom before the class. Owing to a note Mr Richards sent to the headteacher concerning 'Real Lives', the headteacher told Mr Richards he could not have these books and he shouted quite aloud 'I will have them' several times. |

In October 1934 the County Primary Inspector visited the school to investigate an "occurrence" (again Mr Daniel provides no details) which was followed in November by the sudden and unexplained transfer of three teachers to other schools. Two of these were mentioned in Chapter 3, the remaining member of the trio was Mr Leslie George Crook, aged 27 years, who had joined the staff in July 1932 and merited no mention in the logbook before his abrupt departure, after little more than two years, to one of the Senghenydd schools. Whether coincidentally or not, Mr Daniel appears to have had no more cause to complain of his staff from this time onwards.

The transferred teachers were soon replaced. Mr Richard Bryn Rees, by way of a straight swap, was drafted in from Senghenydd Boys the very next day; he remained on the staff for more than six years but received only one mention in the logbook – in September 1938 when he and several boys attended the Gileston Camp – before transferring to Dolau Mixed. In January 1935 Mr Glynne Walters, M.Sc., took up his first teaching appointment at Coedybrain; in July he and twenty boys went to Pembrey Camp (another five went to Pendine); in July 1937 he applied unsuccessfully for the post of Chemistry Master in Whitchurch Secondary School and in March 1938 moved to Bargoed Boys Senior School.

In February 1935 Mr Frank Phillips, B.A., came to Llanbradach from a teaching post in Shrewsbury. In the summer of 1936 he was in charge of twenty five boys who attended the Gileston Camp. In September 1941 he appeared before a Military Medical Board but was not accepted for Military Service. He then embarked on a series of job interviews – French master at Walsall Grammar School, at Coleshill Grammar School, Birmingham, and at a secondary school also in Birmingham – none of which brought him the desired progress in his teaching career. The last of these interviews occurred in the early part of June 1942; possibly the disappointment and stress arising from his frustrated ambition contributed to the behaviour which resulted in the following logbook entry by the then headmaster, Mr Tom Jones :

| 25 June 1942 | After school this morning, I called four members of my staff together just before their lunch. These teachers travel by bus from Caerphilly daily, and I wished to discuss with them in order to arrange whether we would confer with the teachers on Girls' Staff with a view to altering school times in order to facilitate the travelling of teachers and children. |

Llanbradach Chamber of Trade Ratepayers Association, 1930, on their annual outing, Builth Wells. The photograph includes :
Mary Smith, Rebecca Thomas (former teacher at Llanbradach Mixed), Les and Gladys Coppage (butcher), Tom Lane, Olga Griffiths,
Evan Davies (butcher), Trevor James (baker), Mrs Stainer, Margaret Garaway, Kate Coppage, Mrs Trevor James, Annie Wells, Walter
Garaway, Fred Coppage (electrician), Henry T Lewis (grocer), W H Wells (Co-op), Wil Griffiths, Bob Hopkins, Southey and Phyllis
Parrish (ironmonger), Winnie Lane, Horace Griffiths, Maida Smith, Winnie Dobbins, Walter Lewis (Co-op), Nellie Lane.

Before commencing our talk Mr F T Phillips burst into the room, and spoke to me in the presence of these teachers in a very impudent and disrespectful manner. His grievance was that he had not been consulted to attend our meeting. When it was pointed out to him that this was not a staff conference and did not concern him (he lived in the village), he continued to adopt an over-bearing manner, and showed an outburst of temper, not only towards me, but to other members of the staff. Have had reason to complain of insolence and insubordination on his part before, but after his outburst of temper, he apologised.

There is no further mention of Mr Phillips in the logbook until the following cryptic entries :–

11 June 1945   This morning before I left home, Mr Phillips, B.A., called at my house (the headteacher lived at 54 High Street) and stated he would not be on duty at school today as he intended attending the County Hall to have an interview with the Director of Education regarding a transfer to another school as a result of what had happened in the village over the weekend.

12 June 1945   I was informed by the Director this morning that Mr F T Phillips had been transferred to Caerau Boys School.

Hard times   The headteacher's logbook offers only glimpses of what life was like in the village during the 1930s. There were outbreaks of scarlet fever and diphtheria during 1933, many children having to spend time in the Isolation Hospital at Energlyn. Numbers of malnourished children, selected after medical examination, received free milk during term time and through the school holidays; the distribution of milk during the holidays was supervised by local school managers – County Councillor William Bowen (or occasionally by Mrs Bowen) of 9 Garden Avenue, Mr Dai Carlick of 10 Grove Street, or Mrs Ionwy Davies of 18 Glenview Terrace. There was still mention of poor footwear on occasions. The colliery records show that in the early 1930s many shifts were lost through bad trade, so that even the men who had jobs were often unable to bring home a full week's wages; production of coal fell steadily during the decade and in 1935 the colliery employed 1535 men and boys instead of the 3000 who worked there in 1914. The restless, constantly changing population of the village's early years had gradually, to a large extent, stabilised or stagnated into a population in which those who were fortunate enough to still have a livelihood through the colliery stayed put; others survived on the dole; while yet others took themselves and their families to start a new life in the London area and the Midlands, parts of the country which the Depression hardly touched.

The Llanbradach Chamber of Trade in its July 1930 newsletter apostrophised:

"What is wrong with Llanbradach? We have 14 empty shops in our village for which rates are not paid and our shopkeepers one by one are leaving. Others are only staying on because they cannot possibly leave". In February 1940 the Chamber was still bemoaning the depressing sight of empty shops and the loss of contributions to the rates.

However, all was not doom and gloom for the children (or even for the adults). The park had opened in 1930, the swimming pool in 1934, both facilities greatly enjoyed by many villagers. There were annual church, chapel and club outings to the seaside by train or charabanc. Some families, even in those impoverished days, managed to take a holiday in places such as Weston–super–Mare (a short paddle steamer trip away) or by visiting relatives in other parts of the country. In November 1935 the Caerphilly Group Managers received a report from the Attendance Officers that 328 children were absent from schools in the Group (which included Caerphilly, Llanbradach, the Aber Valley, Nantgarw and Taffs Well) in June, July and September when they were away on holiday with their parents, in the light of which they decided not to take proceedings against the parents of 49 children absent for hop picking. Mr Daniel, the headteacher, noted in September 1938 that 16 boys were away in the Herefordshire hop–fields and would be away for at least four weeks. The annual exodus to the hop–fields of Herefordshire and Kent was a regular feature of some children's lives through the 1920s (or earlier) into the 1950s.

A royal celebration in Church Street, probably for the coronation of King George VI in May 1937. In the evening there was a carnival procession through the streets to the park where there were illuminations, a fireworks display and a bonfire erected by the Boys Brigade.

Other diversions from the mundane were provided, more frequently than today, by royalty. In November 1934 a holiday was granted on the occasion of the Duke of Kent's marriage to Princess Marina of Greece; on 6 May 1935 there was a holiday and a tea in the school to celebrate the King's Silver Jubilee; in November another for the wedding of the Duke of Gloucester and Lady Alice Montague Scott. Not an occasion for rejoicing but at least a day off school when King George V was buried at Windsor in January 1936. Having been cheated of a coronation holiday for Edward VIII there was perhaps even more occasion to enjoy the celebrations which marked George VI's coronation on 12 May 1937 – tea in school, a mug and a packet of sweets, and three days holiday, plus another day off when the King and Queen visited Cardiff in July.

Hollywood comes to Llanbradach   Of course, one of the principal delights for children and their parents, and as far removed from reality as royalty, was the "Pictures". Llanbradach was generously provided for in that respect, having two cinemas, the first one being the Empire Cinema (known simply as "The Cinema") which was built and operated as a private commercial venture in 1913 and remained in private hands throughout its existence. It stood on the corner of Thomas Street on the site now occupied by the flats. The other was incorporated into the Workmen's Hall and opened towards the end of 1913. By the 1930s "The Talkies" had come in. Each cinema put on two complete programmes every week, Monday to Wednesday, Thursday to Saturday, each programme consisting of "the big picture", usually with well-known Hollywood names, and a supporting

Coedybrain boys being drilled in the 1930s – the class of Mr Howell J Thomas, who lived with his actress wife in Rhiwbina.

Courtesy of Mrs Rachel Thomas

picture of a less prestigious kind; to ensure value for money there was always "The News" (Pathe or Gaumont) and "trailers" for the forthcoming attractions. Typical of the fare on offer were films such as "Charlie Chan", "The Singing Fool", "Tom Sawyer", "King Kong", "Hell Bent for Frisco", "East of Borneo", "Gay Buckaroo", "Expensive Women", "Women from Monte Carlo" and "Murder at Midnight". The "Pictures" were the equivalent of today's television; children would often go two or three evenings a week – fourpence for a seat in the "chicken-run" and change out of a "tanner" to buy an ice-cream or sweets! As early as 1927 the County Council was considering whether to request the District Councils, who exercised juristriction under the Cinematograph Act, to make the issue of licences conditional on the licensees prohibiting the admission of children of elementary school age (5–14 years) into cinemas during school hours; and the School Medical Officer was asked to give his opinion as to what degree children of school age might suffer harm to their physical condition by too frequent attendance at cinemas.

Scholars and smokers In March 1936 Mr Aneurin Davies, aged 25 years, transferred to Coedybrain Boys from Deri Mixed. He had gained his degree and teaching qualification at Aberystwyth before teaching for a year in Dagenham, then returning to his home in Abertridwr. He left Coedybrain in June 1939 for a post in the new Whitchurch Mixed Senior School.

The logbook entries for 1936 include two items of particular interest :-

11 June 1936 Scholarship results – Noel James Fowler was awarded first place in the Caerphilly List.

It was a matter of great pride for any school to have produced the boy or girl who topped the list of those who in March had sat the examination which afforded entrance to the Caerphilly Boys or Girls Secondary School. Noel was the oldest of three brothers, all of whom in turn "passed the scholarship". Noel eventually qualified as an architect and practised in Caerphilly until his retirement; he now lives in Canada.

The other entry seems, for the period, a little surprising :-

1 September 1936 County regulations prohibit smoking but as most members of staff are in to dinner, the room set aside as dining room is used for smoking from 12.05 to 1.20 and the smoking is confined to this room and should not be indulged in on playgrounds, hall or corridors.

Since the danger of passive smoking, as it would have affected the staff or even the children, was not an issue then, perhaps the regulation was intended to protect pupils from modelling themselves on the teachers in this respect; although with the smoking habit so widespread among the adult population and glamorously portrayed in the children's regular diet of Hollywood films, it was unlikely to have any effect. It is interesting to note that as long ago as

January 1905 the anonymous correspondent from Llanbradach whose caustic comments appeared regularly in the Caerphilly Journal had this to say on the subject:

"Is it a fact that smoking among juveniles is still prevalent? Were not a number of little boys seen puffing at cigarettes on Saturday night?
Do they consider themselves of importance with a fag end between their lips?
Why will not the parents look after their children and stop them from being drawn into this pernicious habit?
Is not smoking detrimental to their health and also the means of stunting their growth?"

1938 saw the appointment of two replacement staff. Mr Glynne Walters' place was taken in April by Mr William Walter Augustus Williams, an experienced teacher, a few months short of his 44th birthday. He had trained at Carmarthen in 1914–16 before doing his War Service until February 1919. He then taught at Brithdir Boys and Bargoed North Boys before coming to Coedybrain. He always deputised for Mr Daniels during any of the headteacher's absences and was acting headteacher for a year after Mr Daniel's death.

The other replacement, in July, was for Mr Archibald Williams, the Manual Instructor. The new arrival, taking up his first appointment, was Mr Dillwyn Maddocks, whose career was interrupted by nearly six years wartime service in the R.A.F., returning to his post in October 1946.

Vandals Despite the difficult social conditions of the 1930s the school suffered little from vandalism and theft:-

25 January 1932	Cleaner reports breaking and entering into school premises. Police informed.
1 February 1932	Working lads were again on the premises over the weekend. The cleaner reports that the WCs were made filthy and objectionable words were written on the doorways.
31 October 1936	On this day – a Saturday – a boy in Standard III broke in and stole a quantity of material. He was accompanied by another boy. Police and office told.
18 October 1937	During the weekend an unusual incident took place in WC. The doors were clean on Friday but filth appeared by 9.30am Tuesday. A very definite watch must now be kept.

There were two more incidents of the WCs being abused during 1938.

The prospect of vandalism on an international scale began to enter people's minds during 1938. In September, the month of the Munich Agreement which was meant to satisfy Hitler's demands on Czechoslovakia, the government began preparations for war. Primitive air raid precautions were made in London parks; anti-aircraft guns were positioned; warning sirens were tried over the wireless. Thirty eight million gas masks were distributed to regional centres. An emergency scheme was drawn up for evacuating schoolchildren from London. In October the local A.R.P. Organiser met the committee of Llanbradach Workmen's Institute and Hall to seek permission to present a slide show and talk.

Coedybrain boys in the Baths, August 1939

Back row :   Howard Spragg, Jimmy Gready, Bertie Owen, Tommy Hearn, Ken Slocombe.
Middle row : Ivor Spriggs, Neil Rees, Gary Linder, Fred Gale, Trevor Waite.
Front row : Alfie Thorne, Gareth Hughes, "Kilty" Grainger, Ken Perry, Walter Grainger, Glyn Jones.

Courtesy of Gary Linder

The day war broke out   Nearly a year passed before Germany invaded Poland and the British ultimatum for Hitler to withdraw his armies expired at 11am on Sunday 3 September 1939. The following day Glamorgan schoolchildren should have returned from their summer holidays for the beginning of the new school year, but :

11 September 1939   Reopened – there was one week's closure due to the war emergency.
A number of boys have left for the hop-field.

Although in most ways school and village life carried on as usual there were some immediate changes which affected everyone. Gas masks were issued to all civilians. The public information leaflet described the gas mask as consisting of "a metal container filled with material which absorbs the gas, and a rubber face piece with a non-inflammable transparent window .... it will give you adequate protection against breathing any of the known war gases". The leaflet continued, "It is important to know how to put on your mask quickly and properly. You might need to do this in a hurry. To put it on, hold the mask by each of the side straps with the thumbs underneath and the inside of the window facing you. Then lift the mask to your face, push your chin forwards into it and draw the straps over the top of your head as far as they will go. To remove the mask, insert the thumb under the buckle at the back of your head and then pull it forward over the top of your head so that the mask is lowered downwards from the face". Children as well as adults were issued with a gas mask each which they were advised to store and carry around with them in the special cardboard box supplied. The public were also advised, "If poison gas has been used you will be warned by means of hand rattles. Keep off the streets until the poison gas has been cleared away. Hand bells will be rung when there is no longer any danger". In the event, fortunately, the masks were never needed.

The other civil defence precaution which came into immediate effect was "The Black-out". This meant that all windows, sky lights, glazed doors or other openings which would show light had to be screened with dark blinds or blankets, or brown paper pasted on the glass or mounted on battens. All street lighting was put out. Motor cars were forbidden to use their headlights, but after deaths on the roads increased 100% in September masked headlights were then authorised. The black-out lasted until the defeat of Germany.

Mr David Daniel, the headteacher, attended the funeral of Alderman William Bowen, of Garden Avenue, on 23 January 1940. The next day he was absent from school, due to sickness; on 7 February he had a slight seizure and was admitted to Cardiff Royal Infirmary; ten days later he died.

With Mr W W A Williams as acting headteacher, school life continued much as before. The Easter holidays passed without incident at the end of March. The logbook notes that the average number of children on the register during the last twelve months was 208 (the school had been designed to accommodate 364) and the average attendance had been, in fact, 180. This huge "under-occupation" was destined to last only a little longer.

On 10 May 1940 the school broke up for the Whitsun holidays; on the same day, without warning, the German armies invaded Holland and Belgium. On 14 May the schools reopened by order of the Board of Education, and the next logbook entry reads:

16 May 1940   At 2.30pm the three departments (Boys, Girls and Infants) had an "Air Raid Practice" when all the children ran home (if within 5 minutes distance) or to accommodation addresses found for them. All the boys got to their places well within four minutes.

Evacuees On 27 May the evacuation from Dunkirk began and was completed by 3 June. The fear of enemy bombing and invasion of the south coast of England caused authorities to carry out the immediate evacuation of children from the area. On 5 June all the Llanbradach schools received a large intake of children. Whole schools, children and their teachers, were transferred to Caerphilly and the surrounding district, the children billeted with families and shared among schools. Coedybrain Boys received 57 evacuees from the George Spurgeon School, Folkestone and one from All Saints, Folkestone.

10 June 1940   13 evacuees have been absorbed into our classes. The 45 left have been divided into two separate classes under the direction of their own teachers, Mr Chislett and Mr Duffy.

Mr Duffy was instructed to attend at Cardiff on 23 July for a medical exam under the Military Service Act and he left Coedybrain on 30 August for R.A.F. Uxbridge. Mr Chislett also reported for service with the R.A.F. at Blackpool at the end of November and was immediately replaced by another Folkestone teacher, Mr Diplock, who was transferred from Taffs Well school; Mr Diplock remained at Coedybrain Boys until he reached retirement age in April 1943 after a teaching career which had lasted 42 years. Mr Duffy's place was not filled until five months after his departure when Mrs Parsons, another Folkestone teacher, transferred from Cwmaber Infants in February 1941. By this time the number of evacuee children had fallen to 46, all of whom were now shared between their own two teachers. By the time Mrs Parsons was recalled to Folkestone in October 1942 most of the first wave of evacuees had already returned to their home district or to other destinations in London, Kent and Surrey. A mere handful stayed through 1943 and 1944. Sadly, one boy, Cyril Woods aged nine years, did not return home to his parents, dying of meningitis only six months after coming to the village; the headteacher noted that 37 boys attended his funeral, all of them belonging to the Boys Brigade.

On the alert The first air-raid warning to affect the village schools came on Monday 15 July 1940; only half an hour elapsed before the All Clear was sounded, but in that time the children were dispersed to their homes or to the homes of other children and were back in their classrooms within 35 minutes. This was the first of many such interruptions over the following twelve months; by the end of December 1940 the school had been evacuated on 36 occasions, often twice during the same day. The sirens sounded 14 more times during school hours in 1941, the last occasion being in mid–July. No bombs fell on the village and few aeroplanes were seen overhead, but the excitement and the apprehension caused by the air-raid warnings never entirely evaporated, and even now the familiar siren sounds are very evocative for those who heard them during the war years. In Llanbradach it was the pit hooter which gave out the warning and all clear signals. Of course, for anyone who lived near Cardiff the air-raids, which often came in the hours of darkness, were a more frightening and dangerous affair :–

29 August 1940   Mr H V Williams absent – shock following an air–raid near his home in Taffs Well.

The Battle of Britain, during which the Luftwaffe tried to destroy the RAF fighter bases in Kent, lasted from mid–July to mid–September, and was intended to prepare the way for a German invasion. When this plan was foiled the Luftwaffe concentrated its bombs on London ("The Blitz"), attacking the capital every night from 7 September to 2 November causing the deaths of nearly 14,000 people by the end of the year. Children were evacuated from London; Coedybrain Boys received its small quota of eight from parts of south–east London (Camberwell, Brockley, Nunhead). Of these four had returned home within three months and another two within a year. Eleven year old Patrick Gall was joined by his younger brother, Alan, in January 1941 and they lived with a family at 40 Central Street, Pwllypant, until July 1942.

I wonder what the Folkestone and London boys made of their new temporary homes in a South Wales mining community? However kindly they were welcomed by their host families, they must have been homesick for their own families and the familiar sights and sounds of the big city or the seaside town; they must have longed sometimes, surrounded by the speech patterns and Welsh lilt of Llanbradach people, for the language of their own kind. Probably school life, where most of the boys were taught in evacuees classes with their own teachers, played an important part in helping them to adjust to the new environment:–

28 February 1941   St David's Day Celebrations. Before play special lessons were given in the class rooms. After play the boys assembled in the hall and choruses and solos were sung. This proved a praiseworthy event as the Folkestone Evacuees took an active part and sang several Welsh Airs. Alert sounded at 10.20. boys quickly sent home. The "All Clear" went at 10.50. St David's Day celebrations continued at 11 o'clock.

On 3 March 1941 Mr W W A Williams, acting headteacher, handed his duties over to the newly appointed head, Mr Thomas Howell Jones. Then aged 42 years, Mr Jones held the post until his retirement in July 1964. He had previously taught at schools in Rhymney Bridge, Deri and Abertridwr.

In January, March and April 1941, Cardiff suffered from three especially heavy air–raids in which 248 men, women and children were killed and many hundreds more were wounded and made homeless. During these months a steady trickle of evacuees arrived from London and Bristol but mainly from Cardiff, and then in June 1941 the trickle became a flood when 38 children came in from Cardiff, most of them from Kitchener Road School in the Canton area. About half of the Cardiff children returned home before the start of the summer holidays, and all bar one had done so by the following Easter. To help cope with the extra numbers and to make up for the earlier departure of Miss Black and

Mr Rees, a new teacher was appointed to the staff before the end of the month. This was Miss Sarah G Phillips, aged 22 years, whose first teaching post had been at a boys school in Sheffield, although she trained at Barry Training College and was from Abertridwr. She remained at Coedybrain Boys for almost three years, leaving to get married and live in Hull. She returned, as Mrs Davies, in June 1945 and taught the boys for another two years before transferring to Coedybrain Girls in July 1947. She was granted six months maternity leave in October 1949 but never returned.

Unclean boys and slovenly work   In July 1941 the school was inspected by Mr David Jenkins, HMI. The headteacher reported that his comments concentrated particularly on the following points:-

1. Cleanliness of Boys. More attention to the physical well-being of boys (games and PT).
2. Encouragement of swimming as an inducement to Cleanliness.
3. Insistence daily that whatever is done in exercise books should be done neatly and well arranged – no slipshod, slovenly work should be tolerated.
4. Punctuality must be adhered to, as a good habit for boys in after-life. Referred to stragglers arriving at 1.40 instead of 1.30. Thought the emergency 1 hour for lunch was insufficient, proposed at least 1¼ hours.
5. Referred to large number of Retarded Children scattered throughout classes, as a result of merging Dull and Backward Class disbanded through transfer of Miss Black.

Miss Black, who joined the staff in 1922, had been selected from 1928 to specialise in teaching children with special needs, although in those days they were grouped in what was variously known as the Mentally Deficiency, Mental Progress or Special Difficulty Class.

During September another seven Cardiff evacuees came in, accompanied by Mr Moses Samuel, a teacher from the Herbert Thompson school, who was recalled to Cardiff in June 1942, although three of this latest batch stayed at Coedybrain Boys for three or four years; one boy stayed on until he reached school leaving age, another left when he contracted T.B., and the third boy, Leonard Humphries, passed the scholarship exam in 1945 but did not enter Caerphilly Boys Secondary School – perhaps he returned to Cardiff to pursue his secondary education.

On the look-out

7 November 1941	Today Sgt. Jones called and inquired whether Fire Watching of School Premises had commenced. I showed him sleeping bunks, torches, blankets, tin helmets – and that all was in readiness. I had submitted list of men

teachers available and had informed Mr T F Owen (Clerk, Caerphilly Urban District Council) I required 30 men to complete my Rota (5 each night).

Mr G O Thomas, Mr H V Williams and Mr H J Thomas are exempted owing to Warden's Duties at Rhiwbina, Whitchurch and Taffs Well.

Copy of letter I had addressed to Clerk, CUDC, explained position, he saw that blame of not commencing was due to the delay by Council in sending lists of 30 Compulsory Residents from the place ..... As Officer in Charge of Fire Watching, I was awaiting outside helpers to supplement staff.

14 November 1941 County Councillor Westhead (Chief of Fire Watching Service in the village) called and stated that Fire Watching of schools was to commence from 17 November and that I as O/C could make my arrangements.

As the Civil Defence information leaflet stated "It is probable that in an air attack on this country an enemy would make use of fire bombs. The object would be not only to destroy property but also to create panic ..... The ordinary fire bomb is not in the least like a high explosive bomb. It may weigh as little as two pounds or so. It may not explode at all, but will blaze up and may scatter burning material in all directions .... It will go through any ordinary house roof if dropped from sufficient height, but a small bomb will probably come to rest on the first boarded floor below the roof. Fires will thereafter mostly break out in roof spaces and attics". the public were advised to keep ready several buckets of water or sand and, if possible, a stirrup pump; they were urged to act quickly if an incendiary bomb (as they were commonly known) landed on their property as "All large fires start as small ones".

The Coedybrain Schools were guarded at night for two years without, as far as I know, any incendiary bombs falling on the buildings.

A variety of visitors On 17 November 1941 Mrs Catherine Burdon, a London County Council teacher, joined the staff and was put in charge of a class of 20 evacuees, most of whom were children from London who had arrived in Llanbradach at various times from October 1940 onwards. Mrs Burdon remained at Coedybrain Boys until early 1944.

The logbook records events which brightened the children's lives at this time :-

11 December 1941 The King and Queen went through the village this morning by car en route for Treforest Estate. Schools were marshalled and lined up in streets to witness the event.

17 December 1941 No school today. Juniors had a cinema show in the Workmen's Hall in afternoon and Seniors in morning – Christmas Treat.

 C. Cllr. Westhead is to be thanked for the excellent

arrangements made to provide boys with this show – for all school departments in the village.

Cllr. Bill Westhead had earlier been treasurer to the Workmen's Hall and Institute, then was employed during the 1930s as operator (or projectionist) before being made operator–manager in February 1940.

Llanbradach's Home Guard Unit in the Coedybrain Boys playground. From the top lefthand corner : Ron Sargent, Tom Davies, Idris Davies, Fred Walden, Bill Kenyon, Jim Hoare, Ron Bendry, Arnold Williams, John Wiltshire, Bill Jones, Ivor Murphy, ? Jones, Geo Jones, Bernard Lee, ? Gater, Tom Lane, Tom Vernalls, ? Talbot, ? Davies, Victor Moore, Bill James, Arthur Keirle, Tommy Jay, Tom Conniff, O Ford, ?, Evan Jones, Alf Hawthorne, Trevor James, Geo Chinn (Snr.),? Taylor, Moses Dowling, Glyn Williams, Rowley Isaacs, Geo Chinn (Jnr.), Trevor Dole, Ted Keynon, Bernard Lee, Ivor Gristock, Cliff James, ?, Dennis Mortimer, Arthur Seabourne, Maldwyn Keirle, Danny Seabourne, Philip Gater, Bill Evans, Wilfie Davies, Charlie Odey, John Gater, Harry Wards, ? Brimble, Ron Barnard, Cliff James, Tom Dobbins, Tom Smith, Frank Brimble, Ted Turner, Alfie Flowers, Treherne Bramble, Emlyn Samuel, Frank Stone, ?, Jack Roach, Bill Perry, Bill Sargeant, Llew Evans, Herbert Williams, Jack Hughes, Bob Davies, Glyn Williams, Arthur May, Harold Davies, Noel Butler, Carson Gibbs, David Williams, Noel Thomas, Reg Davies, Fred Gristock.

Courtesy of late Vic Stone

5 February 1942	An ex-professional actor entertained the boys for a short period with extracts from Pied Piper, Peter Pan, David Copperfield and Shakespeare's plays. The boys thoroughly enjoyed his dramatic representations, as all were of an educative nature.

The Coedybrain Girls logbook identifies the actor as "Mr Ulick Burke of London".

Surprisingly, the headteacher, Mr Tom Jones, makes no reference in the logbook to the arrival of yet another influx of evacuees on 10 December 1941. The admission register shows that on this day a total of thirteen boys from several Birmingham schools were admitted to Coedybrain Boys. A year later all but two had left Llanbradach.

1942 The logbook gives only a fragmentary picture of school life during 1942, the year when Hitler turned his attention towards the Soviet Union and the Japanese sank most of the American fleet at Pearl Harbour. The older boys were shown a film advertising Warship Week in January, and the "Hygiene and Temperance Lecturer" gave lessons the whole of one day; Mrs Burdon, the LCC teacher, was absent for two months owing to her husband's severe illness; Mr Jones informed his staff that "no scrap paper whatsoever was to be taken home by pupils or sent down to Coal House to be placed in bins" as it was a serious offence in wartime; classes were reorganised in June as the number of Folkestone evacuees diminished; Mr Jones assembled everyone in the playground and gave a short address on Safety First, with posters to drive home the lesson; many boys went hop-picking in September, and in the same month Mr Jones gave permission for the classes to go out collecting blackberries to be sent for making jam at the Council Offices, Caerphilly, under the direction of Mr T F Owen, Executive Food Officer; and before breaking up for the Christmas holiday, the headteacher assembled the children and addressed them re their term's work, leavers, Top Boys etc.

1943 The year in which British and American forces recaptured North Africa and invaded Italy is only patchily recorded in the Coedybrain logbook.

19 February 1943	Air Raid Warning at 3.15. All Clear at 3.40. There were no incidents.

(There had been no alerts recorded since March 1941, and this is the last one to be entered in the logbook, but there were air raid warnings outside school hours, as the following entry shows) :-

18 May 1943	All the staff present. Most reside in Cardiff area. There was a heavy air raid on Cardiff last evening, and most of the children must have had a troubled night. Yet they attended remarkably well on this sunny morning.

Mr Jones listed all the teachers currently on the staff in the same month:

Standard 7	Mr Wm. W A Williams	Senior Assistant
Standard 6	Mr Frank T Phillips	
Standard 5	Mr G O Thomas	
Standard 4	Mr Howell J Thomas	
Standard 3	Mr Harold V Williams	
Standard 2	Mrs C Burdon	
Standard 1	Miss S G Phillips	

30 July 1943 School broke up for Summer Holidays.
I assembled boys in Hall and talked of Conduct and Safety First during the holidays. Also had Scholarship, Technical Leavers and Top Boys of every Standard assembled on the platform. They were heartily cheered by boys.

1 September 1943 Reassembled after holidays.
Number of boys absent – gone hop–picking and fruit–picking with their parents.

9 September 1943 It is worthy to record that yesterday at 5 o'clock on BBC it was announced the Italians signed an armistice (unconditional surrender). There was a noted cheerfulness among children and staff.

30 September 1943 The Director of Education, County Architect and Clerk of Works called regarding proposed plan to extend school feeding facilities by building annexe to main hall for kitchen.
I had to leave at 3.35pm to attend funeral of late scholar John Mullane, who lost his life by being killed by a lorry at hop–fields (London Unofficial Evacuee). The funeral took place at Penyrheol Cemetery and 6 senior boys acted as bearers.

The admission register shows that John was two months short of his ninth birthday. He had enrolled at Coedybrain Boys on 29 March 1943 having previously been a pupil at St Joseph's Roman Catholic School, Battersea. His local address is given as 25 Central Street, Pwllypant.

6 December 1943 Fire watching duties ceased at this school on Saturday night December 4th by official instructions.

1944 In April when Miss Sarah Phillips left for marriage and Hull, she was replaced by Mrs Nellie Williams, aged 41 years, who trained at Swansea in 1921–23 but had given up teaching on getting married in 1926.
 The Allies invaded France on 6 June. On 12 June the Germans began bombarding London with flying bombs ("Doodle-bugs" or Buzz-bombs"). During

June and July the school received another influx of London evacuees from Islington in the north and Wallington in the south. There were 50 in number, but by the end of the year the great majority of them had returned home, only seven remaining with their host families in Llanbradach and Pwllypant until the following May or July. In September another ten boys arrived from London and Maidstone, and nine who had been billeted in the district since July came up from the Infants. Most of them returned to their own homes within the next six months. During their stay the London boys had an LCC teacher, Mr Wilson, on the school staff, Mrs Burdon having left by then. The headteacher noted in December that there were still 36 evacuees in the school, all from London, as the last two Folkestone evacuees had just gone home.

The end is in sight   At the start of the new term in January 1945 Mrs Madge Clement joined the staff, replacing Mr Glanffrwd Thomas who, after 16 years, had transferred to Taffs Well. Mrs Clement had last taught at Aberbargoed Girls in 1940. She left Coedybrain Boys and the teaching profession in September 1946 to live in St Ives, Cornwall.

A very heavy fall of snow towards the end of January completely disrupted school life for more than a week :-

25 January 1945   Very few children turned up, and hardly a single child in other departments. No child could possibly reach the lavatory over the playground.

County Councillor Westhead, one of the school governors, confirmed the headteacher's action in closing the school for the day. However, the next day County Hall instructed Mr Jones to keep open despite the small attendance, 46 out of 238 pupils. Conditions had not improved after the weekend and Mr Jones took it on himself to close the school for the next three days:

29, 30, 31   School conditions in my opinion were a danger to the few
January 1945   who turned up.

The heating system had broken down, there was no water supply in the lavatories, and the roof was leaking into the corridor and two of the classrooms. School reopened on Thursday and Friday but less than half the pupils attended. Things did not return to something like normality until after the second weekend.

The war in Europe was now approaching its end. In March the Allied armies crossed the Rhine, in •April the German forces in Italy capitulated. The Germans surrendered unconditionally on all fronts in the early hours of 7 May.

7 May 1945   I visited Secretary of local Cheer and Goodwill Fund to have a list of Coedybrain Boys who had lost their lives in World War in preparation for Special School Religious Service.

	The very welcome news came this afternoon at 3 o'clock that the German Supreme Commanders had broadcasted of their complete unconditional surrender – this I informed the children and the likelihood of òfficial announcement by Prime Minister Winston Churchill later in the day – news was greeted with loud cheers.
10 May 1945	At 6 o'clock May 7th it was officially announced there was to be 2 full complete days' holiday. Thus the school was closed Tuesday and Wednesday owing to the cessation of Hostilities in the European War.
	There was great rejoicing, and children had a wonderful time, street tea parties, bon fires, dancing in the streets – relayed by amplifier – processions through the village. Many children failed to turn up this morning, probably due to late hours last evening dancing and merrymaking in streets.
	I record here, for future reference, the great joy and rejoicing that the European War is over, the complete capitulation and unconditional surrender of all German Forces, and the Thanksgiving and Prayer Services held in every village during the 2 days holiday granted.
18 May 1945	Closing for Whitsun Holidays.
	The last Evacuation Teacher (LCC) Mr C P Wilson leaves today for his return to London Authority. He gave a few words to all the boys – which were much appreciated. It is worth recording here that today practically all the evacuees (now only London boys) return to their homes this week in London.
	There will be a few boys remaining here, through no cause of their own – bombed homes, or inability to trace parents.

No homecoming for some   Although Llanbradach, along with the rest of the country, shared in the wartime restrictions – the blackout, food and clothes rationing, direction of labour – it suffered no damage or deaths through enemy bombing (nationally, 60,000 civilians were killed by bombs, many thousands more were injured and made homeless). However, there are 31 names on the war memorial. The headteacher did not record the list of Coedybrain boys he obtained but from the admission register it is possible to identify several whose names are inscribed on the war memorial: Edwin Buck (aged 30 years in 1939) of 37 Garden Street or Edward Buck (17 years) of 11 School Street, Fred Busby (19 years) of 3 New Street, Pwllypant, Trevor Crowe (26 years) of 39 School Street, James Lannon (34 years) of 18 Thomas Street, Gwilym Mathews (18 years) of 10 Mountain View, Pwllypant, Glyn Morris (36 years) of 17 Garden Avenue, Ronald Rudge (17 years) of 94 School Street, Henry John Rowberry (25 years) of 18 High Street, Howard Skym (24 years) of 64 Garden Street, Francis

Ceremony at the cenotaph to mark the unveiling of WW2 names.

Vernalls (24 years) of 6 Oak Terrace and Horace Webb (25 years) of 12 Coedybrain Road. Young men of military service age who were eligible to claim exemption and go into the reserved occupation of coal mining appear not to have done so. The directors of the Cardiff Collieries Company, owners of the Llanbradach colliery, complained regularly at their Annual General Meetings during the war years that the company was unable to recruit sufficient skilled workers to boost production to its potential level, despite the urgent national need for coal. In fact, production at Llanbradach fell year on year between 1939 and 1945 from 444,806 tons to 286,705 tons. During these years the range of fathers' occupations shown in the admission register has somewhat widened compared with the 1914–18 period; as well as the multifarious colliery job titles, the tradesmen and the time–served men, there are men working in factories and foundry, docks and aluminium works, garage and munitions.

Coedybrain Boys, Standard 3, 1948

Back row : Mr B M Moore, Cliff Harman, Alan Conniff, ?, John Meade,
Doug Powell, Christopher Bell.
Centre row : David Bevan, Byron Date, Keith Edwards, Evan Phillips, Adrian Powell,
Granville Wise, Michael Evans, Perry Stadden, Keith Harvey, ? Simons,
? Bryant, Robert Greenwood, Keith Brimble, Keith Thomas, Joseph Kidley.
Front row : Keith Fox, Hedley Kemp, Tony Willis, Courtney James, John O'Leary,
Gareth Cassam, Bertie Stone, Keith Spencer.

Courtesy of Cliff Harman

118

Nearly full circle   The Labour Party was swept into power in the July 1945 General Election, which was followed by the gradual implementation of the Education Act 1944. This raised the school leaving age to 15 in 1947 and slowly opened up a tripartite form of secondary education – grammar, technical and modern – to all children. However, as late as the end of 1957 the Coedybrain Boys remained in the village school until the age of 14 years, only then transferring to the Twyn boys Secondary Modern in Caerphilly. It was not until January 1958 that boys aged 11½ years or more were transferred out, allowing Coedybrain to be properly reorganised as a Junior Boys School. When Miss Lydia Williams, headteacher of the already reorganised Junior School for girls, retired in December 1959, the two schools amalgamated on 4 January 1960 as Coedybrain Junior Mixed School under the headship of Mr Tom Jones.

Thus the story of the Coedybrain Schools came (almost) full circle, and the children, boys and girls, at least the younger ones, were once again to share classrooms, as they had done until 1913.

Chapter Six

COEDYBRAIN INFANTS 1900 – 1956

After opening its doors on 10 September 1900 the Infants Department of the Coedybrain Schools suffered almost the same degree of overcrowding as the Mixed Department. Built to accommodate 130 children, by the end of September a total of 149 had been registered. To cope with an average attendance of 85 per cent, about 123 children, the head teacher, Miss Minnie Jones, had two assistant teachers, Mrs Annie Jarvis and Miss Elizabeth Evans, and a first year pupil teacher, Annie Powell, 16 years of age. In June 1902, with the same teachers supplemented only by a 14 year old probationer, the number of children on the books had risen to 188 and an average weekly attendance of 163. The H.M.I. visited the school in September and reported:

"The aims are very good and the condition of the school is generally satisfactory, although the rooms are decidedly overcrowded".

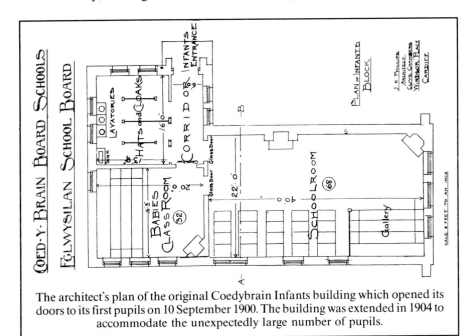

The architect's plan of the original Coedybrain Infants building which opened its doors to its first pupils on 10 September 1900. The building was extended in 1904 to accommodate the unexpectedly large number of pupils.

Courtesy of Mrs Aurelia Jones

The design of the school can be seen in the adjoining illustration. It consisted of a large room called the Schoolroom and a smaller one for the Babies (the under five year olds). Each room had a gallery, an ascending series of platforms on which the children sat at their desks, allowing the teachers and pupils a better view of one another. Only three lavatories were provided for pupils and teachers and there was no staffroom. The building was heated by three open fires and lit by gas.

The Eglwysilan School Board which had built the Coedybrain Schools went out of existence at the end of September 1903, handing its responsibilities over to Glamorgan County Council. One of the Board's last decisions was to accept a tender of £3900 from Hamilton and Millard, the Caerphilly builders, to extend the schools; one of Glamorgan Education Committee's first decisions was to confirm acceptance of the tender. J H Phillips, the Eglwysilan School Board architect who had designed the original schools, was also responsible for the new work. (He died at his home, "Gwyfa", St Martin's Road, Caerphilly in 1921). The additions made to the Infants School during the summer of 1904 resulted in the schoolroom being extended, another two classrooms were built on its south side, and a small room provided near the entrance for the head teacher. It was probably at this same time that the internal lavatories were replaced by handbasins in the cloakroom and the row of outside lavatories was built in the playground. The building was now officially designated to accommodate 252 children. There were times towards the end of the decade when the number of pupils on the books exceeded 300 but the actual attendance figures did not exceed the accommodation, and up until the end of WW2, even with the evacuee children, the school never had more than 235 on the books and attendance did not rise above 208; although when the National School was closed down suddenly in April 1952 the 53 Infants transferred to Coedybrain created an over-crowded situation which necessitated one class being accommodated temporarily in the Girls Department.

The main room, as the Schoolroom was later called, continued to hold two large classes (the HMI commented in 1910 that the classes greatly interfered with each other) until it was partitioned in August 1921.

In the summer of 1936 the outside lavatories were demolished and rebuilt. In the winter of 1937 the open fires were replaced by coal-fired central heating. It was not until February 1957 that the school was provided with electric lighting and an indoor lavatory for the staff.

Excellent reports   HMI Mr W Edwards inspected the school in July 1910 and reported:

"The school fully maintains its reputation for the rigorous and intelligent manner in which the lessons are conducted. Sound methods of instruction are employed as regards the rudiments of reading, writing and number, and much attention is given to the development of the powers of observation and self-expression".

He carried out another inspection in November 1912:

"The head teacher is an enthusiastic and progressive educationalist and is assisted by a staff of devoted and capable teachers. The lessons are carefully prepared and illustrated and are of a stimulating character, while the scholars are thoroughly responsive and interested in their lessons. The Mistress bestows great pains on the training of her pupil teachers and her criticisms are very helpful and practical.

The elements of reading, writing and number are systematically and successfully taught, while nature study and hand and eye training are skilfully developed.

The recitations and stories are dramatised and special attention is given to the training of the children in oral expression. The singing and games are conspicuous features and are fully enjoyed by the children".

Teaching staff of Coedybrain Infants, December 1928

Standing : Miss Dulcinea Hughes, Miss Elsie Ridge, Miss Harriet Powell.
Sitting :   Mrs Annie Jarvis, Miss Minnie Jones (headteacher), Miss Olwen Thomas, Miss Annie Reynolds.

This photograph probably marked the retirement of the headteacher after 28 years in post; Mrs Annie Jarvis, who also taught at Coedybrain had retired in December 1927.

Courtesy of late Miss Elsie Ridge

In September 1922 another HMI, Mr H Price, reported as follows:

There is an excellent tone in this school. The Head Mistress and her loyal staff do all they can to promote an atmosphere of cheerfulness as well as work and play in the school, and the rooms are rendered attractive and bright by means of pictures and window plants. Every endeavour is also made to encourage the natural freshness and activities of the children; and by means of a well selected scheme of "occupations" initiative, self-expression and self-reliance are cultivated. The series of special sense-training exercises form a very good feature of the work. The head teacher has kept herself abreast of educational developments by reading and by attending courses of lectures bearing on Infant School work. She is thus enabled to give excellent guidance to her teachers and there is every indication that she has succeeded in inspiring them with her own high ideals.

The reading is fluent and expressive in the First class and the little ones get their first conception of number in a very interesting and intelligible manner. Script writing is exceedingly well done in the First and Second classes.

Drawing is a strong subject; and the children take great interest in illustrating their stories by means of the crayon.

The Songs are carefully selected and are combined in many instances with dramatic action. The children are trained to sing sweetly and softly, and pianoforte accompaniment is very helpful. The little ones seem to catch the spirit of the words, which are also clearly enunciated.

The large main room has been divided recently by means of a wood and glass partition which greatly facilitates the work of organisation.

Miss Minnie Jones, the first head teacher of Coedybrain Infants, remained in post from the opening in 1900 until she reached retirement age at the end of 1928. (She applied unsuccessfully for the headship of Twyn Infants in 1914 and of Senghenydd Infants in 1919). She was appointed on an annual salary of £50, although this was supplemented (and could be almost doubled) by receipt of half of the annual grant made by the Board of Education. This grant was based partly on the result of the HMI inspection and partly on the average attendance figure for the year – this accounts for the frequent logbook references to attendance, and also for the stories told by former pupils of how children were encouraged to attend even when not feeling well. Minnie Jones taught several generations of village children and kept the school logbook for 28 years yet it is only in the HMI reports that one has glimpses of her personality and dedication to her work. After retirement she lived at Underwood, Caerphilly.

Mrs Annie Jarvis, one of the original staff, was 33 years old at the time of appointment. She appears to have made one attempt to leave Coedybrain Infants when, in 1901, she applied to work in one of the South African refugee camps during the Boer War. Nothing came of this and she continued at Coedybrain, in charge of "the Babies", until she finally left in December 1927 following her 60th birthday. In her younger years she was one of several Coedybrain teachers who were members of the Llanbradach Ladies Choir at the time of their success in the Rhyl and Caernarfon National Eisteddfodau.

Coedybrain Infants, Class 1a, 1930

Courtesy of late Mrs G Coppage

The youngest and lowliest member of staff in the early days was Miss Harriett Powell. She joined the staff on 1 April 1901 as a probationer or monitor one month before her thirteenth birthday. A probationer was a young person who aspired to become a teacher by a route other than that of higher education. A qualified and certificated teacher had usually, by means of passing the County entrance examination and being awarded a scholarship, gone to a County School (such as the ones for girls at Hengoed and Pontypridd) for four or five years, then to a Teachers Training College for a further two years. The route which Harriett Powell took involved helping in the school while continuing her studies; as a probationer or monitor she was paid thirteen shillings a month. On 1 April 1904, nearly sixteen years old, she became a pupil teacher on a monthly salary of £1–13s–4d. During her apprenticeship, which terminated in December 1906, she learned the practical skills of teaching under the guidance and supervision of the head teacher, and studied to take the Preliminary Examination for the Elementary School Teachers Certificate. She failed Part I in December 1906 but was allowed to extend her apprenticeship. She passed Part I in December 1907 and Part II six months later. Harriett was then classed as an Uncertificated

Teacher which gave her a salary of about £35 - £40 pa. She spent the next year on the staff of Abertridwr Mixed before returning to Coedybrain Infants in October 1909. Although there are few references to her thereafter (usually a day's absence to attend family funerals) she taught at Coedybrain Infants until her retirement in May 1947, by which time she had served a total of 45 years there as a probationer, pupil teacher and teacher. She was one of the Powell family who kept the Pwllypant Post Office for many years.

Miss Sarah Major, previously teaching at Tondu National School, came to Coedybrain in January 1903. Before leaving in September 1911 she is mentioned once in the logbook:

24 March 1908   Miss S A Major absent this morning in order to attend Caerphilly Police Court to answer a charge which has been brought against her by a parent for punishment inflicted upon a scholar, John Goldsworthy. Mrs Watkins who teaches in the same room has been subpoenaed and is also absent.
Afternoon. Both returned. The case was dismissed as there was no evidence.

Miss Olwen Thomas joined the staff as a trained and certificated teacher in August 1919 straight from her two years course at Bangor Normal. She was 27 years old. Her family home being in Blaenau Festiniog she was usually given permission at the start of the Easter holidays to travel home by train on the Thursday, the last day of term, as there was a limited service on Good Friday. In September 1929 she was given three days leave of absence to attend for a job interview at Dolgellau but nothing came of it and she continued at Coedybrain. She had to take time off in the autumn of 1938 when her mother was ill and in the spring of 1942 when her mother died. A happier cause for absence occurred in February 1944, just after her 52nd birthday, when she had a week off to get married to Dick Williams who was employed as a winder at Llanbradach colliery. Benefiting from the wartime relaxation and the post-war abolition of the regulation concerning the employment of married women teachers Mrs Williams remained in post at Coedybrain Infants until her sudden death in February 1957. She was in her 65th year and due for retirement.

Miss Annie Reynolds started at Coedybrain Infants in August 1924. Before she left to get married in April 1935 there is one reference to her in the logbook:

3 December 1929   Miss Reynolds absent today and until the house is fumigated. Her sister has been taken to hospital suffering from Diphtheria.
(She returned to school on 5 December).

Miss Elsie Ridge, the elder of two sisters who taught at the school, came there, aged 20, in March 1927. Miss Doris Ridge joined her on the staff in November 1932, also aged 20 years. On account of their differing statures they were known to generations of children as Big Miss Ridge and Little Miss Ridge. They had moved with their parents from Birkenhead in December 1913 to 58 School Street, and in March 1916 to Caerphilly, in time to receive their secondary education at Pontypridd County Girls School. Doris taught at Coedybrain until, on her marriage in 1948, she left in September 1949 to start her family. Elsie never married and remained on the staff until her retirement in July 1972, having been appointed deputy head teacher in 1969. Three months before she retired she had a bad fall in the school hall which caused severe bruising to her head, neck and back, but after X-ray examination at the Caerphilly Miners Hospital she insisted on returning immediately to her duties. Elsie spent her retirement years in Caerphilly and died shortly after her 90th birthday in 1996.

Miss Hannah Evans, of Ynysmudw, taught at the school between 1929 and 1939, leaving to get married.

Miss Eunice Howells was on the staff from April 1935 until March 1941 when she transferred to Coedybrain Girls School.

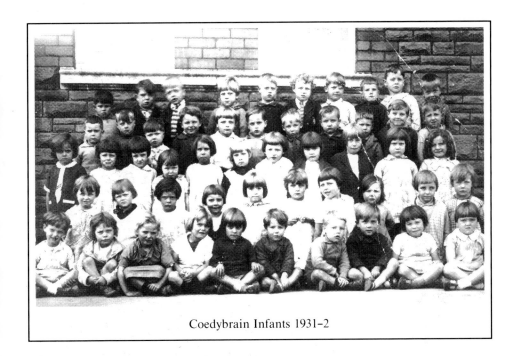

Coedybrain Infants 1931-2

126

Coedybrain Infants teachers, 1947, on the occasion of Miss Harriet Powell's retirement.
Standing : Mrs Ann Coleman, Mrs Elsie Bowsher, Miss Olwen Thomas, Miss Kitty Hughes, Miss Elsie Ridge.
Sitting : Miss Doris Ridge, Miss Harriet Powell, Miss Carbetta Morris

Courtesy of Miss Kitty Hughes

The head teacher who succeeded Minnie Jones in January 1929 was Miss Carbetta Morris who had previously taught at Senghenydd Junior School. She came to live in the village, lodging at 19 Garden Avenue. In the summer of 1942 she married Mr Bill Williams, a teacher in Coedybrain Boys. She was allowed to keep her post, despite the usually stringent peacetime policy requiring women teachers to resign immediately on this event, and she remained head teacher until her retirement in July 1956.

Teachers and villagers on an unknown occasion c. 1946–7
Standing : ?, ?, Cissie Clarke (née Shannon), Clara Dole (née Watts), Louie Roberts, Mrs Colson, Dorothy Logan, Betty Gardner (née Moore), Margaret Carter (née Blackledge), Bill Williams (Coedybrain Boys), ?, Tom Jones (headteacher, Coedybrain Boys), ?, Bill Roach (caretaker), Cllr. George Smith, Winnie Jones (née Preece), Edith Rees, Vi Rowlands (née Bowen), Glenys Britton (née Lewis), Ella Jones, Pat Roach (now Linehan). Sitting : ?, ?, Lilian Morris (née Blackledge), Elsie Ridge (Infants), Doris Ridge (Infants), ?, Kitty Hughes (Infants), Carbetta Morris (headteacher, Infants, married to Bill Williams), Olwen Thomas (Infants, married to Dick Williams), ?, ?, Gillian Gardner, May Moore, Florence Roach.

Courtesy of late Miss Elsie Ridge

Miss Kitty Hughes joined the staff in May 1943. Miss Hughes was born in the village, the only daughter of Cornelius (Ellis) Hughes and Catherine (Kate) Prout. Her father, a Carmarthenshire man, left school at 14 to work in the pits, moving to Llanbradach three years later, in 1906, to join his older brothers, William and Dan, who were already employed in the colliery; ambitious and always eager to learn he qualified as a mining engineer and eventually became manager of No.3 pit at Llanbradach colliery. Kate Prout came to Llanbradach from Brynmawr with her parents in 1896 aged four years; she was a pupil in the National School where she gained a scholarship to Hengoed County School for Girls in 1905; she later taught at various times in the Llanbradach Mixed (as the National became in 1903) and Coedybrain Mixed. Miss Hughes followed her mother as a pupil in the Llanbradach Mixed before proceeding to the Caerphilly Secondary School in 1926 and hence to Swansea Training College in 1932. On completion of her training she taught at a school for mentally handicapped children in Birmingham until 1939, then in the small village school in Penally, Pembrokeshire, before returning to Glamorgan, first of all in Nelson, then in Coedybrain Infants in 1943. She became head teacher in September 1956, the post from which she retired in December 1974. Miss Hughes continues to lead an active life in her beloved native village.

Chapter Seven

COEDYBRAIN GIRLS 1913 – 1950

Women teachers: career or marriage?   When the Mixed School was separated in September 1913 into Boys and Girls Departments, the Girls remained in the original building, the Boys transferring to the new building alongside. The old building, with five classrooms and a cookery room, was designed to accommodate a maximum of 350 pupils; in September 1913 there were 292 girls on the books and an average attendance of 265. The newly appointed headteacher, Miss Ellen Williams, formerly of Blaenllynfi Council School, had five teachers and one pupil teacher to cope with these numbers, and Miss Williams was obliged to take charge of Standard One until Mrs Tydfil Jones was appointed in March 1914 when the class had 58 children on its register.

During the first term two of the teachers appeared in Caerphilly Police Court: Miss Catherine Davies appeared to answer a charge brought by a parent but the case was dismissed: Miss Coe was assaulted on the school premises by a parent, the case being decided in the teacher's favour. It appears that violence in the classroom is not an entirely modern phenomenon, although these cases involved adults rather than children. Neither of these teachers stayed for long at the school.

On the other hand, Mrs Tydfil Jones remained on the staff until her retirement in 1943 and was known to generations of children. She was the Miss Tydfil Davies mentioned in my first book who taught in Coedybrain Mixed under the headship of Tom Moses. She married Thomas Jones and had two sons by him before he died tragically in Llanbradach colliery, aged 25 years, in January 1908. She had given up teaching in May 1905 on marriage, as required by the County, but as a widow she was allowed to resume her teaching career. Having earlier lived at 9 Glen View Terrace, her home in 1914 was Brynderwen, 37 High Street. She was often marked as absent from work, due to illness, in the years up to 1921, the year in which her younger son, Emlyn, left Coedybrain Boys. The death of her mother shortly after she returned to teaching must have made her position as a lone parent even more difficult in those early years. She receives little mention in the school logbook thereafter, apart from attendance at family funerals, until her retirement :-

26 January 1943 Mrs Tydfil Jones is retiring on pension today after serving 30 years as a member of the staff of this school. She was presented with a cheque from the scholars. Tea was subsequently partaken of in CDS (Cookery and Domestic Science) Centre when Mrs E Bowen–Davies, Cardiff, and Miss Lydia F Williams on behalf of past and present

members of the staff presented her with a cheque. C.Cllr. Westhead and Reverend Bernant Rees also expressed their good wishes for a long and happy retirement. Mrs Jones and her father, Mr D Davies, a nonagenarian, suitably responded. Several old members of the staff attended the presentation.

David Davies, her father, had been the colliery lampman before his own retirement. Unfortunately, Mrs Jones' retirement was not long as she died in July 1947 aged 69 years.

Two other long serving teachers should be mentioned: Mrs Kate Knight, whose home was School House, Caerphilly, had been appointed to Coedybrain Mixed in January 1906, a certificated teacher who had not been in employment for some time. She must, by then, at the age of 40 years, have been a widow as the County Council regulations would otherwise have barred her from their employ. She transferred onto the Coedybrain Girls staff where she remained until she went to one of the Caerphilly Schools in January 1917.

Miss Mary Grimes had been a pupil teacher at the Caerphilly National School before being appointed to Llanbradach Mixed in May 1903. She transferred to Coedybrain Mixed in December 1906 aged 21 years, and then to Coedybrain Girls. She remained here until January 1918 when she went to the Twyn School, Caerphilly.

Coedybrain Girls Council School, Standard IV c. 1914

Courtesy of Ellis Stanbury

The first headteacher, Miss Ellen Williams, was obliged to give up her post after only five years when she married, but her successor, Miss Elizabeth M Roberts, who had been teaching at the Twyn School, arrived at Coedybrain in October 1918 and remained in post until she reached retirement age in August 1950. Until after WW2, when the discriminatory policy against married women was abandoned, the teaching profession relied heavily on those women who, whether by choice or otherwise, remained single. In Coedybrain Girls alone, between 1918 and 1945, twenty one members of staff were forced to give up their teaching careers when they opted for the married state. One can only reflect on the personal frustration and disappointment caused by this policy, the waste of talent and maturity, and the disruption to the children's education.

Keeping the Welsh language alive   Miss Roberts was a native of North Wales and always returned to her family home during the school holidays, although on her retirement she continued to live in St Martin's Road, Caerphilly. Despite the anglicised nature of the community in which she spent her working life, she was very keen to promote the Welsh language and culture among her pupils. St David's Day was an important date in the school calendar from the beginning, with lessons on Patriotism and Welsh heroes, Welsh airs and folk songs. Miss Roberts gradually developed the celebrations during the 1920s. In 1921 two hundred parents attended a concert in the school hall; the Rev. J N Jones of Caerphilly spoke about Sir O M Edwards and a portrait of the great man was unveiled by Mrs Joseph Morgan (she was the daughter of the poet Taliesin O Eifion, lived in St Martin's Road, Caerphilly and was otherwise known by her bardic name of Mair Taliesin). The following year another bard, ap Glaslyn, gave an address on St David and the importance of Welsh parents teaching their children to speak Welsh. (Ap Glaslyn was the bardic name of the Rev. John Owen, minister of Moriah, the Calvinistic Methodist church in Llanbradach, who was in great demand as an adjudicator and conductor of eisteddfodau, and in his younger years was a well known baritone and one time member of the Carl Rosa opera company. He died in 1934 at his home in 8 James Street). In 1924 the celebrations took place in the Workmen's Hall, attended by more than 600 people; there were selections on the harp, folk songs, dances and the ceremony of the Chairing of the Bard took place. The same venue was used in 1925 when Annie Lannon of 19 Thomas Street was chaired for her poem "The Harp", the ceremony performed by ap Glaslyn. In 1927 the chair was won by Kathleen Dando of 25 Thomas Street, the second prize going to Mary Ingram of 33 Garden Street; the Rev D Tafwys Jones of Caerphilly spoke to the large audience on the importance of keeping the Welsh language alive. In 1928 a poem on "The Sea" won the prize for Letitia Piper of 3 Monmouth View, the competition being judged by Elfryn (Mr Edmund Evans, the Coedybrain teacher). In 1929 the usual St David's Day celebrations were followed by a Welsh Week when all the reading and writing were to be in Welsh and "as far as possible all lessons will be in the vernacular".

The Workman's Hall was used as a venue for the last time in 1930, after which the celebrations became a more modest affair in the school hall once more and on several occasions were not even mentioned in the headteacher's logbook, although in 1936 there was another Welsh Week.

1 March 1938   St David's Day Concert – Welsh songs, recitations, dances and historical plays.
The Chairman, Mair Taliesin, urged the girls to keep the Welsh language alive and to foster Welsh culture.

Llanbradach Operatic Society, 1928. The cast for a production of "Blodwen", the opera composed by Merthyr-born Dr. Joseph Parry.

Top row :   Levi Williams, Dai Morgan, Lloydie Jones, ?, Hugh Griffiths, "Mousey" Davies, ?, Richard Ll Jones, ?, ?, Dicky Dole.

Second row : William Davies, Myra Williams (née Jarman), Cassie Davies (née Williams), Lydia Williams (Coedybrain teacher), Hannah Bowen, Miss Pritchard, Mrs Glaslyn Davies (daughter of "Glaslyn", Rev. John Owen), ?, Caradoc Skym, ? Thomas, Morgan Jones, ?, Arthur Jones.

Third row :   Reuben Evans, Dai Carlick, Mrs Tom James, Mrs Fred Carter, Mrs Phil Price, Mrs Bevan, Mrs G L Evans, Ionwy Davies (née Parry), Mabel Barnard (née Selby), Phyllis Rees (Coedybrain teacher) Ceinwen Nicholas, Vi Bowen (later, Mrs Bert Rowlands), Priscilla Williams (née Davies), Gladys Hughes (née Parry), ? Thomas, ? Preece, Bill Hughes.

Front row :   Llew Lewis, three soloists from outside the village, Ethel Crates, Dave Harry (from Llanelly), Dan Hughes (made a bard in 1930, "Alaw Gwendraeth"), "Blodwen" (not known), Mrs Owen, Laura Davies (née Williams), Gertrude Prout (pianist), Maenwen Parry (now Glendinning), Elenid Owen.

Courtesy of Miss Kitty Hughes (photo)
Mrs Marion Viney (names)

133

1 March 1939	Gwyl Dewi celebrated this morning by a concert in the Central Hall. Cllr. Roach, Chairman of Caerphilly Council (and an old pupil of this school when it was a Mixed Department) attended wearing his badge and chain of office. He addressed the girls about ideals of Wales and the traditions of this locality.
1 March 1940	Gwyl Dewi celebrated ..... Rev Bernant Rees addressed the girls about Welsh ideals as personified in St David.
28 February 1941	St David's Day celebrations. Concert in the Central Hall. Mair Taliesin attended and distributed pennies to all the girls. Air Raid Warning 10.15 – All Clear 10.45.
27 February 1942	St David's Day. Conducted entirely in Welsh. Attended by Rev. Morgan Watcyn M Price, Caerphilly, and Mair Taliesin in Glamorgan Welsh Costume. (This is Mrs Joseph Morgan's last recorded visit to Coedybrain Girls. She died in May 1942).
26 February 1943	The celebration of our Patron Saint takes place this morning. Ceremony of Chairing the Bard – Mr E Evans (Elfryn) a member of the Gorsedd acted as adjudicator and Archdruid. Mary Greenaway (8 Garden Street) won the prize and was duly chaired. An address was given by Rev Rees Hughes, Congregational minister, on "The Culture of Wales".
1 March 1944	St David's Day concert.
2 March 1944	Repeat of yesterday's concert for parents. C C Westhead addressed the parents about the importance of regular attendance at school and also of fostering the Welsh language. Mr Wheeler, headmaster of Folkestone School, attended and thanked the parents for what they did for the Folkestone Evacuees in Llanbradach.
1 March 1945	St David's Day. Rev. Idris Jenkins, Caerphilly, talked about Dewi Saint and the local celebrity Dr Morgan John Rhys.
2 March 1945	Parents Day. 150/200 came for repeat performance of yesterday's programme. Mrs Sargent, School Manager, present.

As the exhortations to foster the language show, it was an uphill task to encourage the use of Welsh among the children of English-speaking parents or even to preserve its use by the minority of children with one or more Welsh-speaking parents. In July 1926 Miss Roberts had written to the Caerphilly Group Managers pointing out that only one of her staff, apart from herself, was competent to take Welsh conversation. When the Urdd National Eisteddfod came to Caerphilly in 1933 two Coedybrain girls won prizes but in non-linguistic categories : Edith Olwen Bevan (10 Glen View) took first prize in the cookery competition and Dilys Jones (7 Pencerrig Street) gained a second prize with her fruit cake.

Cookery centre   An improved Cookery Centre was opened in the school in May 1918 and girls from Standards V, VI and VII attended courses in Housewifery and Cooking on Wednesdays, Thursdays and Fridays, the Llanbradach Mixed girls attending on the other days. The CDS mistress from November 1924 until her marriage in October 1934 was Miss Olwen Isaacs. There were several short-term replacements until Miss Olga Griffiths took up her duties in December 1937. Although Miss Griffiths married in April 1944 (to Mr Reuben Baillieux) she remained in post until the end of May, when she and her husband, also a teacher, moved to Bristol. The couple returned to Caerphilly when Mr Baillieux began teaching at the Boys Secondary School, and in March 1947 Mrs Baillieux returned to Coedybrain Girls, benefiting from the change of policy regarding the employment of women teachers. When she transferred to Caerphilly Secondary Modern (Girls) in September 1951 the Coedybrain Cookery Centre closed down.

Teachers   Fortunately for the pupils and the headteacher there was one member of staff who provided a measure of stability and continuity for four decades. Miss Lydia Williams was brought up in the village, receiving her elementary schooling in Coedybrain Infants and Mixed before going on to Hengoed County School in 1912. She went as a student teacher to Coedybrain Girls in July 1917, then transferred to the Boys School in October 1918 on an annual salary of £65. She returned to the Girls School in April 1919 and in September was admitted to Swansea Training College for her two years of teacher training. On completion of the course she returned in July 1921 as a trained and certificated teacher to Coedybrain where she remained until her retirement (by then headteacher) in 1959. Miss Williams' father was Griff Williams, a winder at Llanbradach colliery, whose home was at 2 Central Terrace (now Park View); he was also secretary of the Workmen's Institute for ten years until his resignation in 1921.

There were several teachers who remained in post rather longer than many others during the 1920s. Eva Lloyd taught at Coedybrain from February 1917 until October 1923 when she became a headteacher at Pengenfford, Breconshire. In September 1937 Miss Roberts recorded in the logbook that Miss Eva Lloyd, now Mrs Swan, passed away during the Midsummer Vacation. Miss E J Bowen, appointed in Octboer 1918, suffered from nervous disability early in 1922 and was off work for a year before resigning on health grounds in 1928; but as Mrs Bowen–Davies, she represented the past members of staff at Mrs Tydfil Jones' retirement in 1943. Miss Maggie E White, a former pupil of Coedybrain Mixed School, obtained a scholarship to Pontypridd County School in 1910. After completing her secondary education she returned briefly to Coedybrain Girls in 1916 to gain some practical experience before going on to Hereford Training College. She joined the staff, as a certificated assistant teacher, in July 1919, but left in January 1923 to get married. Her career was closed to her at the age of 25

135

years. Miss Gertrude Fuell, already mentioned in earlier chapters, was on the staff through most of the decade, finally leaving for a new life in England in 1929. Miss Kate Morgan arrived in June 1921 and left to get married in the summer of 1930. During these nine years she twice applied for headships within the County, at Nantgarw and Seven Sisters. When the headteacher was absent for a fortnight in 1929 due to a family bereavement it was Kate Morgan, who was put in charge of the school, a clear testimony to her ability, and yet, like so many other women of her own and later generations, her career was sacrificed on the altar of marriage. Miss Grace Bennet came from Nelson Mixed to Coedybrain in 1919, leaving for marriage in September 1925. She had been made Senior Assistant during her time on the staff and was left in charge during Miss Roberts' absences, such as the headteacher's attendance at the formal opening of the new Twyn School, Caerphilly in January 1924. Miss Vera E Arnold, from Ystalyfera, was appointed in June 1926. In July she had leave of absence to attend the graduation ceremony at University College, Swansea, where she received her B.A. Degree. In 1930 she applied unsuccessfully for the post of English Mistress at the new Cadoxton Central School, Neath. In March 1934 she left to get married to Bert Gardner, a colliery official, and made her new home in Woodlands, the semi-detached house above the Pit Road. Miss Phyllis J Rees of Trelewis, joined the staff in November 1926. She was in the process of

Coedybrain Girls, Standard V, 1930 Teacher : Miss Phyllis Rees.
Among the pupils are : Nancy Jones, Lilwen Davies, Margaret Denison, Elenid Owen, Renee Richards, Jessie Hayward, Anita Fennell, Betty Moore, Molly Wright, Amy Bassett, Iris Bramhall, Myra Lewis, Olwen Bevan.

Courtesy of Miss Elsie Davies

studying, in her spare time, for her B.A. Degree; she sat the Finals in June 1927 and graduated the next month. In May 1930 she accompanied pupils for a fortnight's stay at the Pendine Holiday Camp. She left Coedybrain to be married in April 1932.

An inspection   The school was inspected in September 1922 by H.M.I. Mr H Price. He reported as follows:-

1. The tone continues excellent and the staff co-operate heartily to keep in touch with old scholars by means of correspondence and occasional visits to the school.
    The 'Prefect' system is adopted : this promotes a sense of responsibility, initiative and self-reliance amongst the senior girls, whilst it helps materially the organisation of the school. The staff conferences are helpful to secure unity of aims and methods, and the teachers spare no efforts to make their lessons interesting.
2. As far as possible a Welsh atmosphere is maintained in the school, and a spirit of patriotism is fostered by means of the History lessons and in other ways.
    Attention is also drawn to "Welsh Worthies" and by means of the excellent material contained in Cartrefi Cymru the children are made acquainted with the scenes of the early days of our great men and women of the past.
    It was noted, however, that there was only one framed picture of eminent Welshmen on the school walls. The broad principles of Citizenship, which secure common consent, are also taught to older girls.
3. Some good lessons were given in Geography on the day of the visit, but the instruction is somewhat hampered by the absence of good geographical wall-maps or wall atlases, covering the year's work in this subject. Their need is especially felt in the classes receiving "Advanced Instruction". The maps drawn by the girls deserve praise. Handwriting and the general neatness of the written work should receive more attention. Although the number of Welsh-speaking children in attendance is very small, the instruction in the Welsh language is given very successfully by a competent teacher. The arithmetic generally is well taught.
4. As soon as financial conditions become easier a fresh supply of framed pictures should be obtained to decorate the walls of the classrooms and central hall.
    There appears to be some laxity in enforcing the attendance to the end of term of those girls who attained their 14th birthday in the middle of term.

In contrast to his comment on Coedybrain Boys, also visited in September

1922, the H.M.I. pays much more attention to the Welsh atmosphere of the Girls School, obviously a reflection of Miss Roberts' influence. However, the headteacher's determination to encourage her pupils' interest in the Welsh language and culture did not deflect her and her staff from achieving a high stardard of performance in the rest of the curriculum, as can be seen in the numbers of girls who passed the Scholarship Examination each year and moved on to Caerphilly Girls Secondary School or one of the older, more prestigious, County Schools at Hengoed and Treforest.

Attendance   The school attendance figures were, as always, a matter of concern to the headteacher and the L.E.A. After the opening of the new cookery centre the school accommodation was reduced from 350 to 300 (in July 1919). Although the number of girls on the register often exceeded 300 the average attendance during the 1920s was usually between 250 and 270. In 1920 a system of awarding merit certificates was introduced. In 1922 one pupil, Olive Watt of 116 School Street, received a wristwatch for five years perfect attendance; a year later she was awarded a gold medal for six years; and finally, for seven years perfect attendance, she was given a gold chain and pendant.

Llanbradach Park, 1940s, showing the paddling pond or "canal"
which ran across the park into the river.

Attendance was affected by a number of factors, some of longer duration than others. In the autumn of 1920 an outbreak of scarlet fever and measles kept between 16 and 30 girls at home; after the Christmas break the situation deteriorated and the school (along with all the other schools in the village) was closed throughout January 1921 on medical advice. During January and February 1922 many pupils suffered as a result of the influenza epidemic, but Miss Roberts noted that a contributing factor to the poor attendance was a "lack of boots". In September 1922 a few very wet days and "boots in very bad condition" brought attendance figures down to 80 per cent, although there were also several girls who had gone to the Kent hopfields with their parents. In July 1923 "measles and excessive heat" reduced attendance. In succeeding years snow and rain had a temporary effect on numbers. In July 1927 a hundred girls went on the Sunday Schools' outing to Barry Island. In April 1929 five girls and eight "contact cases" were absent due to an outbreak of smallpox which necessitated the fumigation of a classroom; other girls were badly affected following vaccination.

Malnutrition and milk   The depressed economic and social conditions of the 1920s worsened during the 1930s, and one of the headteacher's first logbook entries for the new decade sets the tone :

5 February 1930	Boots (21 pairs) given out this afternoon to the girls of the unemployed – received from the Caerphilly and District Distress Fund.
23 May 1930	Miss P J Rees absent next two weeks in order to superintend as teacher at the Pendine Holiday Camp.
5 December 1930	Eleven girls receive milk in school daily this week as they are medically certified malnutrition cases.
30 June 1932	Four girls have been chosen for Pendine School Camp.
4 May 1933	Dr Gladys Evans examined 276 girls for malnutrition. One girl excluded for scabies.
17 May 1933	Thirty three girls now receive milk.
6 October 1933	Attendance greatly affected by Diphtheria and Scarlet Fever – 19 cases.
31 October 1933	Pupil Doris Evans died suddenly this weekend.
18 May 1934	Closing for Easter. Milk to be distributed to all malnutrition cases during the holiday.
13 June 1934	Edwina Willis died suddenly this week.

Doris Evans, whose address in the school admission register in 1927 is given as 1 New Houses, Pwllypant, was 12 years old. Edwina, only 9 years of age, lived at 9 Mountain View, Pwllypant. The register records another two deaths in this decade: Rachel Dowling of Hillside Bungalow, 13 years old, and Rose Reed of 10 Lewis Terrace, also 13 years.

Throughout the 1930s there were regular malnutrition surveys which resulted in the County council supplying free milk to numbers of girls throughout the year, school holidays included. The holiday arrangements were supervised not by the teachers but by local school managers and others, among whom were :

Demolition of Llanbradach Viaduct began in June 1937. The eleven lattice steel girders, each 162 feet in length, were jacked off the supporting pillars, this one coming to rest across the river. Four months of careful dismantling produced about 2,000 tons of scrap metal.

Courtesy of the late V.C. Hardacre

The demolition of the viaduct was completed in 1938 when the ten brick pillars, the highest being 100 feet tall, were blown up. Some of the demolition work was filmed to be shown in cinemas around the country and there was also live commentary on the wireless.

Courtesy of the late V.C. Hardacre

County Councillor William Bowen (and Mrs Bowen), Mr David (Dai) Carlick, Mrs Ionwy Davies, Mrs J Roach of 58 School Street, the Rev. Esias Hopkins (minister of Seion) of 9 Central Terrace, and Miss E Hendy.

Every year a number of girls, from two to thirty, were sent to holiday camps at Pendine, Pembrey or Rhoose, often accompanied by one of the Coedybrain teachers, Miss Amelia Hall.

Teachers present and future During the 1930s nine teachers remained in post for two years or less, the majority leaving due to marriage. There were six teachers who remained for longer periods before getting married or moving elsewhere: Miss Prydwen Williams, whose home was in Ystalyfera, transferred from Tonyrefail Girls School in May 1932. She remained on the staff until her marriage in February 1938 when she became Mrs Whatley and made her home in Grove Street. She returned to teaching in May 1947 and served at various times on the staff of Coedybrain Girls, Llanbradach Mixed, Abertridwr Infants and Coedybrain Infants into the 1960s. In November 1932 Miss Elizabeth (Bessie) Williams, from Resolven, came to Coedybrain Girls. In July 1934 the logbook notes that she had an accident on her way to school and broke her collar bone; the headteacher anticipated a long absence but she returned to her duties within a month. In September 1937 she went to Swansea Training College and is not heard of again. Miss Amelia Hall, from Clydach, arrived in October 1933. It was she who accompanied the Coedybrain girls to nearly all the summer and winter camps. Miss Roberts must have been very sorry to lose her:

4 February 1940   Miss Amelia Hall leaves today after a long service (6 years) to take up duties as County Supply Teacher.

Miss Ida Griffiths, also from Clydach, joined the staff in April 1934, leaving in February 1941 on her marriage to Mr Bill Williams who was a teacher at the Llanbradach Mixed School. Miss Phyllis John, from Brynmenyn, came in September 1934. Miss John, a graduate, applied unsuccessfully for a post as History Mistress in 1937 before transferring to Bargoed Senior School in March 1938. Lilian Humphries, an unqualified probationer, came in September 1937 and left in May 1940 to get married.

A few years earlier Miss Roberts had noted, with a degree of satisfaction, I am sure :

6 April 1936   Misses Gwyneth Richards and Iris Wright (two ex-pupils), who are to go to Barry Training College in October, are here for observation work this week.
15 July 1937   Misses G Richards and I Wright, students from Barry Training College, are here for three weeks school practice – both are old pupils of this school.

Gwyneth and Iris had come up together from Coedybrain Infants in April 1925 and had both passed on to the Caerphilly Secondary School for Girls in

1930. Gwyneth lived at 26 Thomas Street and Iris at 15 Rees Terrace. Iris, better known in the village as Mrs Molly Tudor, taught in Norfolk, Newport and Trelewis before joining the staff of her old Infants School in the 1960s, where she remained until retirement.

A good year   After a fifteen year interval the school was again inspected in November 1937. H.M.I. Mr A G Prys-Jones reported:

Premises – This is a fairly modern building comprising seven classrooms which are situated on three sides of the central hall. One of these classrooms has been adapted for use as a Domestic Science room. One class is accommodated in the central hall. The central heating which was installed about a year ago (January 1937, in fact) is in effective working order. The interior has been recently redecorated. The playground is level and spacious. It is suggested that the possibility of renting one of the fields in the neighbourhood of the school for purposes of games should be explored.

Staff. The headteacher appointed about 19 years ago has rendered devoted and valuable service to the school. She is conscientious in the discharge of her duties and exercises a wholesome and refining influence upon the girls placed under her care. She is assisted by an energetic staff, nearly all the members of which have had but short experience of teaching.

Standard of Work. The standard attained in music is not as high as might be expected; this is chiefly due to the fact that, at present, there is no-one on the staff who is really competent to teach it. It is hoped that this deficiency will be made good when the next vacancy occurs. Greater attention should also be given to methodical and progressive instruction in art.

In other subjects, in spite of the frequent changes which have taken place in the staff during recent years, good progress is being made.

Schedules of work have been thoughtfully drawn up, and terminal tests are carefully carried out. In the two upper groups (Forms 1A and 1B), though spelling is weak in a number of cases, the work in written composition reaches a commendably high standard. Much originality is shown in teaching mathematics, geography and history. In the lower of these two groups every effort should be made to ensure neater and more careful writing. In the middle and lower schools (Standards I to V), although a few girls in each class are backward, sound training is given in the basic subjects. Reading, on the whole, is fluent; but even the best pupils, in their eagerness to read quickly, fall into minor errors. Much care is taken to teach good penmanship.

The general demeanour of the girls reflects credit upon the Headteacher and Staff who make praiseworthy efforts to train their pupils in habits of helpfulness and self-reliance. Slow and backward pupils receive every encouragement and sympathy. In general, the girls respond freely and naturally to oral questions.

World War Two   The first effect on Coedybrain Girls of the declaration of war on Germany was the arrival, in September 1939, of fourteen children who were sent away from London, Reading, Dagenham and Coventry by anxious parents to the safety of relatives in Llanbradach; once the first alarm was over they returned quickly to their home areas. It was not until early June 1940 that the school, along with all the others in the village, received its first batch of official evacuees: 33 children from Mundella Girls School, Folkestone, accompanied by one of their own teachers, Miss Brown. However, the headteacher, after testing the evacuees, decided to absorb them into the local children's classes as there was plenty of room to do so.

Coedybrain Girls, Standard IV, 1939

Back : Vera Thomas, Norma Dole, Jean Butler, Eileen Bouse, Elsie Davies, Mona Langdon, Edna Jones, Margaret Mapps, Joyce Davies, Betty Haskins.
Centre : June Strong, Gwen Carter, Muriel Hawthorne, ? Gardiner, Elsie Briffert, ?, Doreen Hughes, Edna Powell, Betty Ricks, Joyce Sergeant.
Front : Dorothy Spencer, Muriel Smart, Beryl Simons, Violet Gurner, Nancy Evans, Doreen Stride, Lily Evans, Marjorie Fry, Pam Jones, Perys Rees, Violet Proctor.

Miss Roberts' logbook, contrary to the entries in the Boys and the Infants logbooks, dates the first daytime Air Raid Warning on 3 July 1940, nearly a fortnight earlier – this was probably because the Alert and the All Clear occurred within the normal dinner hour and so the school did not have to be evacuated. The next Air Raid Warning came on 15 July, when the children were sent home for three quarters of an hour. The entry concludes :

15 July 1940	According to instructions received school starts an hour later from today in order that the children have more rest as they are disturbed in the nights by continual air raids, bombs have dropped recently in the vicinity (Caerphilly and Bedwas) but no casualties.

There were another 34 daytime alerts before the end of the year, as well as the night time ones. The County Architect visited the school to see which classrooms would be most suitable for safety in an air raid and should have anti-splinter varnish on the windows; an additional precaution was the fixing of wire netting over the windows.

The Cardiff Blitz Between October 1940 and March 1941 a trickle of London evacuees, sixteen in all, joined the Folkestone girls. Most of the Folkestone evacuees had left Llanbradach by the end of 1941, but at least four of them stayed in the village for three, four and nearly five years. The London evacuees had all left by the end of 1942. In June 1941 there was an influx of more than thirty Cardiff girls from the Canton district, most of whom stayed only a few weeks before returning to their own schools in Lansdowne Road, Kitchener Road and Severn Road. The first major raid on Cardiff occurred during the dark hours of 2 January 1941 when 100 aircraft came over the city and dropped 150 high explosive bombs, 14 parachute mines and about 5000 incendiaries, leaving 156 dead and 427 seriously wounded. Lansdowne Road School was hit during the second major raid on 3 March when the Luftwaffe dropped about 60 high explosive bombs and 7000 incendiaries, killing 51 people in the residential areas and injuring 243. On 29 April another heavy raid left 41 dead throughout the city. The last major raid took place on 18 May 1943, 50 aircraft causing another 45 deaths. Between June 1940 and May 1944 the cost to human life and property was considerable:

	Killed	Injured	Premises
Men	151	607	damaged 29,998
Women	147	254	demolished 600
Children	47	75	
	345	936	

German bombs claimed no lives in Llanbradach, but natural causes ("heart trouble" according to the logbook) resulted in the deaths of two Coedybrain girls on successive days in March 1941 : June Edwards of 22 Thomas Street and Connie Butler of 18 De Winton Terrace, aged 10 and 11 years. Their classmates attended the funerals and sang a hymn. In December 1941 eleven girls from Birmingham were admitted to the school, taking the places of those who had by now returned to Folkestone, London and Cardiff. Most of them returned to Birmingham within the space of a year.

1942   From the beginning of the year the girls whom the school medical officer certified to be suffering from malnutrition were given hot dinners in the cookery room. This scheme was already operating in the Gwyndy Senior Girls School, Caerphilly, which the headteacher and the domestic science teacher had visited to observe the arrangements. The provision of milk was extended, too :

2 March 1942   New scheme for milk starts. Means Test for free milk and other girls can pay 1½d per pint.

During 1942 Miss Roberts had the worry of her sick mother in North Wales. She was called home suddenly in January and stayed there for a month, only to be summoned again by telegram in March. In May she lost her old friend, Mair Taliesin.

22 June 1942   Miss Bregeon of the Caerphilly Labour Exchange and Mrs Ellis Hughes, member of the Employment (Juvenile) Committee, interviewed all the leavers.
                        Mr Blatchford, Attendance Officer, paid a special visit to each class today and warned them about the new penalties for non–attendance at school.
25 July 1942   Joan Pugh (69 School Street), a pupil in Standard I, died this week of Diphtheria at the Isolation Hospital.
31 July 1942   Closing for Midsummer Vacation.
                        Dinners will be provided during the holiday for the children who have applied for them. These will be prepared and served in the C.D.S. Centre and a teacher will be in charge of registration.
                        Attendance for dinner during holidays – 26 on books, average attendance 20.4.
9 September 1942   Dr Clarke and nurse visited. Immunised 30 girls against Diphtheria who had not been done at the previous times.
10 September 1942   Standards IV and V and teachers went for a Ramble this afternoon to pick Blackberries for preserving.
30 September 1942   Nurse Radcliffe visited. Examined 213 girls, 17 with unsatisfactory heads.
                        Swimming lessons finish after today.
11 December 1942   Attendance very low this week on account of Influenza Epidemic.

More teachers   Miss Glenys Davies, from Rhymney Bridge, was the first teacher to be appointed after the outbreak of WW2. She arrived in February 1940 and left for South Bargoed Junior Girls in September 1943 without receiving any other mention in the logbook. Miss Bronwen Davies came in February 1940 and left in June 1943 on being appointed Youth Organiser for the Co–operative Union in Manchester. Miss Gwyneth Morgan transferred from Hendre Infants in June 1940. She moved to Nelson Infants in July 1951. Miss Eunice Howells, who had been teaching in Coedybrain Infants since April 1935 transferred to the Girls School in February 1941. She married in July 1945, becoming Mrs Thomas, and left in March 1946. Miss Dilys Evans joined the staff in December 1941, and applied unsuccessfully for the headship when Miss Roberts retired in 1950. As the only graduate on the staff at this time she was able to transfer to the Caerphilly Secondary Modern in July 1953 to teach mathematics. In June 1942 Miss E J Jones, who had accompanied the Birmingham evacuees to South Wales, was transferred to Coedybrain Girls. On marrying in August 1943 she became Mrs Wilding. At some point she ceased to be an evacuee teacher and remained at Coedybrain as a Glamorgan County Council teacher until she was transferred temporarily to Fochriw in May 1947 and then permanently to Tiryberth Infants in July 1947. Miss Muriel Jones was appointed in September 1943. She was transferred in May 1947 to a Whitchurch school in order to be nearer home. Miss Annie M Davies also came to Coedybrain Girls in September 1943 and left in November 1950 to become headteacher of Rudry Village School and, later, of Twyn Infants, Caerphilly.

1943   The logbook entries are fairly sparse :

1 March 1943	Dr Pendse and Nurse visited. Immunised 13 girls against diphtheria.
31 March 1943	Annual Returns – average on register 244.9. Average attendance 206.6 – 84.4 per cent.
3 May 1943	Swimming Instruction starts.
21 June 1943	Reopened after Whitsuntide Holiday. Headteacher absent due to her mother's illness.
24 June 1943	Miss Bregeon and Mrs Watkins, J.P., visited the school to interview the leavers.
1 September 1943	Reopened. Headteacher back after being absent since 21 June owing to her mother's illness and subsequent death.
2 September 1943	Miss Connie Wayt, Maid at the School Canteen, is ill so a new maid has to be appointed temporarily. (Connie, of 9 Wingfield Terrace, then aged 19 years, had been a pupil in the school. Her illness kept her off work for over a year, but in September 1945 she gave up her post in order to take a course at Bristol Domestic Science College. She did not return to Coedybrain Girls). 50 girls have gone hop-picking to Hereford.
4 October 1943	The hop-pickers returned to school today.

1944   The noteworthy entries for this year are also sparse :

16 March 1944	A girl from this school, Maureen Harding, was killed yesterday evening, knocked down by a bus. Special lessons on road safety have been given today. (Maureen, of 21 Richmond Terrace, was eight years old).

5 June 1944	Exhibition at Caerphilly for "Salute the Soldier" week.
14 July 1944	14 evacuees from London admitted this week owing to the pilot-less planes danger.
17 July 1944	12 official London evacuees admitted this morning.

During July, August and September a total of fifty London evacuees came into the school, most of them from Islington and Wallington. All but a handful had returned home before Christmas.

1945 The severe snow blizzard towards the end of January 1945 brought everything to a halt for more than a week. No children turned up on 25 January and only five the next morning.

| 29 January 1945 | All the staff and more children present but the water is frozen outside and thus none obtainable in school. The lavatories are frozen so there is no sanitation here. After consulting County Councillor Westhead, I closed the school and sent the children home. |
| 1 February 1945 | Reopened as the snow has cleared and the pipes have melted. Attendance very poor. |

Miss Roberts' continuing influence on her pupils' interest in Welsh culture is shown by their success in a local eisteddfod :

| 11 March 1945 | Standard V girls won first prize for Country Dancing at Undeb Cymru Fydd Eisteddfod at Caerphilly last Saturday. Form 1B won first prize for Welsh Action Song, "Y Sipsi" (Crwys). The school choir tied with Abertridwr for first prize for song "Clychan Cantrer Gwaelod". |
| 16 April 1945 | Miss Betty Hughes an old pupil is here today and for this week for observation purposes before she enters a Training College. |

(Betty, of 2 Tynygraig Road, passed the scholarship examination in 1938 and went on to the Caerphilly Girls Secondary School. She returned to Coedybrain Girls in July 1946 to do some of her teaching practice while studying at Barry Training College).

8 & 9 May 1945	General holiday by Wireless News at 9pm on 7 May. V.E. Day and VE II celebrations general throughout the village and children congregated together to have teas in the streets where they live.
5 July 1945	Closed for General Election.
30 July 1945	Parents Day. P.C. Thornton visited to give a talk on "Road Safety" but as only two turned up he gave a talk to the senior girls as well as the parents.

147

26 October 1945   Closed at end of day for Mid-Term Holiday and two VJ days.

From September 1946 school dinners were prepared in the new prefabricated kitchen in the Boys School and served in the Boys School Hall. 54 boys and 54 girls were given their first meal in the new surroundings, some of them paying. A cook and two maids had been recruited for the new facility.

In September 1948, Arthur Wint, the Jamaican athlete who won the 400 yards race in the London Olympics of that year, called at the school. He was visiting friends in Llanbradach, the family of Miss Kitty Hughes whose brother, Glyn, had befriended the athlete during their student days in London.

In December 1949 Mr Bill Roach of 35 De Winton Terrace died, having been full time caretaker of the Coedybrain School since January 1937. He was appointed to this position a few months after the sudden death of Mrs Voyzey who had been the school cleaner since January 1909.

Coedybrain Girls teachers, c 1947–50
Standing : Mrs Olive Baillienx (née Griffiths), Miss Sally Phillips,
Miss L M Roberts, (headteacher), Miss Dinah Lloyd, Miss Lydia Williams
Sitting : Miss Annie Davies, Miss Gwyneth Morgan, Miss dilys Evans

Courtesy of Mrs Olive Baillienx

The last days of Coedybrain Girls

28 July 1950   I, E M Roberts, resign my post as Headteacher by
31 August 1950 so am leaving today as I have reached
retirement age.
Closing for Midsummer Vacation.
Miss L F Williams will take up her position as
Headteacher from 4th September 1950.

Two months before Miss Roberts retired H.M.I. Miss D Rees carried out a
three day inspection of the school premises and facilities and her report was
entered into the logbook :

"This school, originally opened in 1900 as a mixed school, is pleasantly
situated away from the main road and adjacent to the Boys and Infants
schools. The premises consist of seven classrooms leading from a central
hall; one room is adapted for Housecraft teaching. There are two cloakrooms
with wash basins, an adequate supply of towels, but no hot water; a small
staff room is used by the headmistress. The lavatories for both children and
staff are in the playground. Every endeavour should be made to keep the
lavatory pans cleaner.
The premises have been redecorated recently and are generally in good
condition. There is no electricity.
There is a good playground but the best use was not made of it, as the five
junior classes used it at the same time. To add to the scope and variety of the
teaching in Physical Education it is essential for each class to have its full
use for the lesson. The senior girls attend the privately owned swimming
baths, a few minutes walk from the school, for instruction in swimming
during the summer term.
The Headmistress who has served in this school for 32 years is assisted by
seven qualified assistants. There were, on the days of inspection, 194 pupils
in attendance; these were divided into seven classes. At the moment, the hall,
which has poor natural lighting, is used by a class. This factor seriously
curtails its use for indoor Physical Education in inclement weather, for
music and other activities. At 14 years of age, the senior girls are transferred
to the Secondary Modern school at Caerphilly. During this session they
were transferred in September and in the next session some of the present
students will only attend at the Secondary Modern for a few months. The
transfer of all the senior children, giving them greater opportunities of
being taught in their own age and ability groups under more specialist
direction, should be considered.
The standard of reading was good, though in each of the junior classes
there were a few girls who were retarded. There is need for simpler books
with a progressive vocabulary for these children as the books in use were
too difficult. The writing books were neat throughout the school, but
insufficient stress was given to exercises which would develop free

149

expression, particularly in the lower school, where the written exercises were almost wholly confined to "penmanship". The written work in Arithmetic showed that progress was being made in each class – Algebra and Geometry formed part of the curriculum in Forms I and II. The value of this is doubtful and the time given to these subjects would be more profitably spent on English and cultural subjects. The equipment for the teaching of Art is poor; the pastel books were far too small to allow scope for free expression. A greater variety of work in Art, including use of powder paints and other media, with larger sheets of paper, should be introduced. The teachers, except one, take their own classes in Welsh. The syllabuses in Geography and History need to be reconsidered, as some difficult subjects are taught at too immature an age. The weather chart seen in Std II was interesting. Some of the materials used in Needlework were very uninteresting and not conducive to enjoyment in the production of good work. A better grading of the work was necessary to produce a more satisfactory standard of work. There were two sewing machines but all the seniors could not be taught to use them as the two classes were taught needlework at the same time.

The variety of work done in Housecraft was pleasing, but the conditions of work were not ideal.

A midday meal is cooked in the kitchen adjoining the hall in the Boys School. The lunch was served to both boys and girls at the same time, the staff having their lunch with the children. About 108 girls have their midday meal in school. The children helped to serve lunch at the tables. This training is very valuable; it was pleasing to see the methodical way in which the children accepted their responsibilities; they performed their tasks well. Perhaps the time has now come for the children to be entirely responsible for their own tables and for the staff to dine at a separate table.

A new piano has recently been allocated to this school to replace a piano which was bought through the efforts of the staff. There are no amenities in the form of visual aids, gramophone or wireless set.

The school opens each day with a short service, which is conducted in Welsh on one day in each week.

The teaching is conscientious, but with greater scope to develop their individual best, the variety of the work could be increased."

This HMI is much more critical than her male colleague of 1937 both of the organisation of the curriculum and aspects of the teaching as well as of the lack of material facilities provided by the LEA. And there is, almost pointedly, no praise for Miss Roberts as she comes to the end of her more than three decades in the post of headteacher.

The LEA responded with some alacrity to the suggestion that the older girls would benefit from a longer period of secondary schooling (as envisaged by the 1944 Education Act); from September 1951 all girls over the age of 11 years 6 months were transferred to the Secondary Modern School (Gwyndy Girls) in Caerphilly, and Coedybrain Girls was re-designated a Junior School.

Probably, the shortage of money in these post-war years caused a slower response to the other deficiencies which the HMI had pointed out: although new gas lamps were fitted throughout the school in February 1952 another year elapsed before electricity was installed and an indoor staff lavatory provided, and it was April 1955 when the school received its first radio set with loudspeakers for use in the hall and classrooms.

Miss Lydia Williams, who was a pupil in the Coedybrain Schools until 1912 and had been a member of staff for 31 years since her first appointment in 1917, succeeded to the post of headteacher in September 1950. When she retired at the end of 1959 the Boys and Girls Schools amalgamated as Coedybrain Junior Mixed School under the headship of Mr Tom Jones.

Chapter Eight

I WAS THERE, TOO

I wish to record my debt to the following villagers (some now deceased) who very kindly shared their memories of life in Llanbradach in the early years of this century, and especially Miss Kitty Hughes for allowing me to print a shortened version of her written account.

The official records and documents on which this book is based are an essential source for a factual account of the village history, but these personal memories offer a tiny glimpse of the enormous human richness of the generations who have lived all or part of their lives in this insignificant former pit village.

Mrs Mary Murphy was born in 1892 in Dowlais, although her father, at the time, was helping to sink the Llanbradach pits. The family moved to Llanbradach in 1895. Her stepmother died, her father and siblings moved to Cardiff but she remained with an uncle who lodged with a family in Stanley Row, then known as Hellfire Row or Bottle Alley! She looked after the children in this family and missed much of her schooling. When 12 years old she worked as a cleaner in the Coedybrain Schools before and after school hours. When she married in 1912 her husband's pit wage was £2-10-0 per fortnight; he enlisted in the Army during WWI and died a few days after returning home on leave from the Dardanelles.

Mrs Murphy remembered shopping in the Mile End Stores in High Street ... biscuits sold loose, butter cut and weighed (6½d a pound), rice, raisins and pepper all sold loose, bacon sliced on the machine, rock salt cut into bars big enough to last weeks, stone jars containing from one to seven pounds of jam. In the home she remembered mattresses made of flock or straw; bedroom floors were bare boards partially covered by rag mats which people made for themselves; downstairs there were flagstones in the kitchen and mats made of rag, straw or coconut hair; the flagstones were scrubbed and strewn with sand. As a mother of four children she supplemented her income by taking in other people's washing, charging two shillings for a dozen articles, supplying the soap, soda (to soften the water), blue (to whiten the clothes), and starch; she used a wooden "dolly" to push down and squeeze blankets in the dolly tub. In later years she was a fast and efficient paper-hanger.

Charlie Chrismas, born 1897, lived in the Joinery (Richmond Terrace) when his family came to Llanbradach in 1900. His father was from Eastbourne, his mother from Gwent. He was conscious as a child of being "English". He remembered a tramway taking stone from the quarry near the railway station, going under the main road at the end of Stanley Terrace to a bridge over the river, near the viaduct, and joining the Brecon and Merthyr railway. He was a pupil at Coedybrain Mixed ... Tom Moses, the headteacher, could be sarcastic – Charlie's brother painted a dog-rose which was framed and hung in the school, whereas Charlie's wish to paint a sycamore leaf was derided. Charlie had the "Studying bug" and believed he could have gone to university, but he left school at 14 and took his first job in Evans' bakehouse in High Street, helping to deliver the bread by horse and cart ... he remembers stopping at the Pontygwindy Inn, Charlie had a ginger beer, his boss had a pint. Too small in build to work in the pit he started at the coke ovens in 1912 as a payclerk; in the office on top of the lamp-room ... the large offices in Pit Road were built in 1919. Charlie spent all his working life in the colliery administration, ending up as secretary to the manager, Mr George Budge.

Mrs Gladys Coppage (née Moore), born in Abercarn in 1898 the year her family came to Llanbradach. Her mother, after being widowed by the 1901 explosion, worked as a cleaner at the National School and had thirteen fireplaces to attend to; she also cleaned the Wesleyan Chapel and took in washing to supplement her colliery widow's pension of £2 per month. Mrs Coppage passed to go to Hengoed County School but was unable to take her place as her mother could not afford the cost of train fares and books. She remembered the old tin chapel being pulled down before the present Wesleyan Chapel was built. She met her husband, Les Coppage, the butcher's son, while she worked in John Barry's grocery a few doors down in De Winton Terrace. Her father-in-law, Fred Coppage, also from Abercarn, began his business in Llanbradach in the mid-1890s by carrying mutton and lamb on his shoulders over the mountain, eventually opening the shop at 5 De Winton Terrace and his own slaughterhouse behind School Street .... he later lived in Garth Owen, then Glan Rhymney Farm, before retiring to Malvern.

Mrs Gladys Cordey, formerly Hughes (née Parry), born 1902, was one of eight children whose parents, originally from Treherbert, moved to Llanbradach in 1907. Her father was a timberman in the colliery and in his spare time acted as an agent for the National Insurance Scheme. The children had to do their allotted jobs before leaving home in the morning – polish steel fender and fireguard, blacklead the grate, scrub the passage and front – and were often late for school. During the rationing of food in the 1914–18 war Gladys and her sisters walked to Caerphilly to get half a pound of margarine each from the Maypole for their mother. Family and village life was very bound up in chapel activities most evenings, and there was a weekly visit to the pictures in the Workmen's Hall, admission one penny. Possessed of a contralto voice she sang in concerts and eisteddfodau, and later had lessons with Edward Davies, of Cardiff, formerly a member of the Carl Rosa Opera Company. On leaving school she worked for Marments as a seamstress. Mrs Cordey's younger sister, Llinos, died of pneumonia ... she recalled the medical specialist coming to the house, in Garden

Street, to operate on Llinos in a room which had to be emptied of everything.

Miss Kitty Hughes, born 1914, has recorded the following account:-
My earliest memories are connected with the old National School at Wingfield. I lived at 2, Graddfa Road, in a Colliery owned house since my father, Cornelius Hughes, was Manager of No. 3 Pit.

When my memory begins, I recall walking to school from Graddfa to Tarran–y–Mwrthwl with Annie and her two brothers from Bryn Owen Farm high on the mountain, Kenneth and Claude Evans from Llanbradach Isha Farm, colliery owned; Tom Watkins and myself; Teilo Davies coming from a small holding as it was then, opposite the present entry to B&Q.

We walked to school in all weathers, and there was no bungalow village. We saw the hard work at Tarran–y–Mwrthwl Farm, golden cornfields and all the farm processes through the seasons. Hay-making in the old style, raking, after cutting and drying, with the wooden tooth-like rakes, pitchforks to load the hay on the horse–drawn waggon (gambo), and what a thrill to ride on the gambo at the end of the day. Finally you would see a well-stocked barn. At Graddfa Farm and Ty Isha we saw sheep–shearing, often helping to roll fleeces.

Walking down the lane to school we always wanted to be early before the school bell sounded. Waiting at the end of a long corridor would be the Head-master, Mr T P Davies, wearing a bowler hat, long coat and with a cane flicking behind his back. Woe betide anyone late for school – punishment was a crack of the cane, but exemption if you had a note from a parent. He was a keen disciplinarian – he had to be in those days, since classes were so large, on one occasion as many as 70 in one class.

He had an excellent staff, some commuting from Cardiff. He would brook no interference in his methods of teaching, much work was enhanced by rote, one never forgot tables etc. No one could defy him, and if parents came to ask about punishments he could always defend himself and supply a reason for it. My mother who went back to teach in 1914 recalled an occasion when he failed. Apparently a donkey got into the school corridor – lay on the wooden floor and moved from side to side making a great deal of noise and generally making himself a nuisance. Even T P Davies could not move him, much to the delight of staff and pupils.

The Vicar at the time was the Rev. Edwin Edwards, who went to the school every morning to assist in the teaching of Religious Education.

I remember vividly the teaching of recitation and singing which was always put to good use on St David's Day. The annual school concert always enacted the life of St David. For some years I carried my mother's goat-skin rug to wrap around the character of Caradog, a boy representing St David's father.

Memories, too, are of shops – Mr Fordham at Wingfield and Miss Bartlett at the other end, at the foot of the hill. Gob-stoppers, for 1 penny, that would effectively stop all speech, and sherbet of many colours put into one's mouth with wetted index finger, and sweet bags in triangular shapes. Much liked too were long pieces of Spanish liquorice. Sherbet coloured the index finger, whether red or yellow, and 'Spanish' made vivid brown marks.

There were no school buses or school dinners. We took sandwiches each day and at lunch-time Mr T P Davies would boil a large black kettle of water on the open fire, surrounded with high guards, and would personally pour the boiling water into our cups of sugar and cocoa. We were a mixed school and friends we made then remain the same today.

The Coedybrain Schools built in 1900 had the advantage of a Domestic Science kitchen in the Girls' School and a Woodwork Centre in the Boys' School. The girls from the National School had to walk in crocodile formation to the new school with a 'monitor' in front carrying the register. I never remember any misconduct going or returning.

No 'Flash' or 'Mr Sheen' for us, scrubbing on hands and knees, scrubbing on wash-days on a scrubbing board, not kind to fingers, and 'Monkey-Brand', like a stone that had to be scraped with a knife, to clean the porcelain sink. Many aspects of home-management were taught.

Boys had to attend on other days for their woodwork instruction. They were always taught football or rugby. Later, when the miners gave the park, beautifully landscaped, we could all progress to tennis and golf.

Bank holidays were great times – the whole village turned out on the Wingfield field where all sorts of things went on. I actually danced around a Maypole after months of training in the All Saints' Rooms – we gave a performance on the field after having learned the intricacies of plaiting etc. with coloured ribbons. We would hear the Colliery Band, visit flower and vegetable stalls – all at their best from local allotments. Prizes were given and all sorts of side shows, races for the children.

In my childhood and teens the Colliery was the life-line of the village. It gave employment and a real 'family' feeling was part of our village life. It was always referred to as 'our pit' and 'our village'. There was courtesy, and respect, essential for men working in such conditions, and this overflowed into their home life. Children were well mannered, helpful, and had a firm knowledge of right and wrong. As the village grew, men came with their families to work in the pit and live here. Miners' holidays gave a chance for the pit-ponies to enjoy open-air life for two weeks. It was a delight to see them on the Wingfield field where the bungalows are now. There were quite a few entries to the Secondary School at Caerphilly, and those who chose the pit had family to protect and guide them in their early days, many a father and son worked together in the underground headings.

Never underestimate miners, there were many fine minds, and self education gave them the ability to speak in public debate and aroused motivation for something better for their children and grand-children. Miners have a long tradition for making things available. They contributed most generously for a Workmen's Hall to contain a Library, and a Park for recreation.

There was an expansion of evening classes at the school, many young miners attending to gain knowledge to add to their underground experience and become members of the "staff".

The only 'bad' time I remember was when the miners went on strike, and

155

since there was no money available soup-kitchens were set up in the schools for miners' children to have at least one good hot meal a day. I never saw children without shoes or clothes because contributions came from many sources and clothing was passed around.

The committee of the Workmen's Hall were always generous and gave film-shows for children on Saturday mornings. I recall seeing in serial form 'Dr Fu Manchu', horrifying in places, looking through fingers, and then enjoying 'Tarzan'.

On New Year's Day, every child attending would be given a brand new penny. Many housewives, too, gave gifts of fruit to children who called to wish them a Happy New Year. My mother gave an apple or orange and a 'threepenny bit' as it was called then. These were happy days of childhood.

Later, I remember my father working in liaison for the Colliery with the International Students' Club in Cardiff, and with foreign embassies. Our Colliery was the nearest in direct line from Cardiff. He escorted many people underground, the most eminent being King Freddy of Buganda. He was later deposed, and lived out his life in London. In 1993 his son, Reggy, was recalled and crowned King.

'Our Colliery' was self contained. It had its own Granary, First Aid Post, Ambulance, Lamp Room, Smithy, Wagon-making and repair shop, Laboratory, Washery etc. At the Colliery Farm, next to the school, there were the vets to supervise and care for the ponies. There were coke ovens that spat out red hot coke and, at night, lit up the area, the warmth and heat crossing the railway tracks and colliery yard to warm even Graddfa Road. The engine rooms were spotless and the gigantic machinery so well kept. Here too, were cages of canaries ready to be used for testing for gas. My constant memory, even today, is the sound of miners' boots walking up the Pit Road to go on night shift and a 'smell' of coal.

I remember, too, outstanding shops in the High Street – taking my Grandmother's Christmas cakes to be baked professionally by a village baker, Mr Harry Hutchings. 'Mari Fach' – a Mrs Davies from Grove Street – owned the bakery. She was very small in stature, hence her nickname. In getting bread fresh from the ovens it was a sore temptation to want to eat the lovely crust on the top of the bread.

There was also a Pawnbroker, a Mr Gordon, whose shop was where the paper shop is today. The Llanbradach Hotel was on the opposite corner, and on the road between them the Salvation Army would form a ring every Saturday night and hold an open-air religious service with tambourine accompaniment. My mother, for many years, was asked to preside and present their school prizes, a duty I continued until their closure.

Those, too, were the days of Cockle-Women from Penclawdd, dressed in long, black skirts, white blouses and shawls, with immaculate white aprons, balancing tubs of cockles on their heads, with snow-white coverings, selling from door to door. I recall, too, an oil-van going around selling oil for lamps and cookers, ringing a loud school bell to let everyone know.

Pop-carts, too, went around, 'Dandelion and Burdock' being a great favourite, ice-cream carts and trolleys, and in those early days you took a basin or fruit dish to hold your ice-cream – later came wafers and cones.

The Breton onion sellers were around door to door selling their wares, boats docking in Cardiff, and bicycles with strings of onions on them; always a winter storage hanging in the kitchen or shed with a subtle flavour, and salesmanship with such good humour.

Each church and chapel had individual societies:– Wesleyan – Operettas; Welsh Baptist – Operettas, Drama, Choirs; Moriah – Temperance Society; Bethel – Choirs, Drama; Church – Scouts, Dances in All Saints' Hall, with a local band under the leadership of Mr Tom Pratley; English Baptist – Boys' Brigade. Church choirs would do the rounds at Christmas time with Christmas carols.

For the second world war, this village had a record unsurpassed. A 'Comfort Fund' for serving men and women was set up and the Committee worked tirelessly for funds.

We had, during the war years, Army Cadets, Women's Junior Air Corps, Boys' Brigade, all active in many ways and a flourishing County Youth Club held in the Coedybrain School run by Mr T H Jones, Headmaster. I joined him as an assistant and, when he resigned, I took over with Mr B T J Roderick as assistant. Those were good years for teenagers. The club helped their leisure time and set a pattern for work and social behaviour. I was able to write and produce many pantomimes, our club winning first prize for the County Youth Eisteddfod. It ran for ten years.

I am proud to have been born and raised in this former 'Mining Village' in an age when there was coutesy, respect and good manners among us all.

Mrs Mona Clinch (née Gill), born 1915. Her father, Police Sergeant Gill, was stationed in Llanbradach when his 17 year old daughter began teaching at Llanbradach Infants where she remained until her marriage in 1945. As an uncertificated teacher she started on a salary of £3 per month. During the latter part of her time on the staff she was in charge of the Babies (3 and 4 year olds) .... they were made to sit in regimented rows like the older pupils until she persuaded the headteacher to allow the desks to be put together so that the children could face one another and talk together ... she also got some beds for them to nap on. She went swimming sometimes in the Baths at 7am .... the headteacher, Mr G L Evans, asked her to take a class of girls there on a Tuesday afternoon .... "Don't drown them", he said. After her father moved to Caerphilly on retirement, Miss Gill travelled to Llanbradach on the bus, but on one accasion she missed the bus and hitched a lift from Ivor Evans, the undertaker, in his hearse, and another time she arrived for work on the Corona pop lorry! When a colleague was ill she took charge of his class of older children .... Mr Evans told her, "Don't bother teaching them, just look after them" .... she promised the boys they could play football if they cleaned the classroom floor and got flowers for the windowsill – and they did! Children ran to neighbouring houses during air raid alerts .... Miss Gill used to go to Mrs Vi Viney in the Crescent and have a smoke there .... the evacuee children brought scabies with them, she and some of the local children got it and had to go to a clinic in Castle Street, Caerphilly, for treatment. Dr. Clarke, the village GP, had a four year old son who attended Llanbradach Infants for a while .... one day he was taken to the lavatories by another boy, when he came back he told Miss Gill he had been "pissing for the highest!"

Mrs Kathleen Russell (née Dawes, and known to all as "Busy Dawes"), born 1918. Her parents married in All Saints Church in 1913 and had twelve children. "Busy" was a pupil at Llanbradach Mixed but often had to stay home to help her mother. She remembers that Colonel Lindsay sometimes came for the scripture lessons, he helped to push the wooden partition which divided the main classroom, he was "a darlin' man". The children lined up along the school wall, overlooking Plasturtwyn farmyard, to watch "Stiffy" Lane kill the pit ponies which were no longer useful underground .... T P Davies came along and caned the children from behind. After finishing her schooling "Busy" went into service with the family of the headmaster of a public school, Canford Castle, in Dorset .... when her mother died suddenly in April 1935, one month before her 40th birthday, she had to return home to look after her own family – the five weeks old baby, three children not yet in school, four in school, three brothers and her father all working in the colliery – which she did until she left home on getting married. During this time she also played for three seasons in the village women's football team.

Ken Plint, born 1921 in Cardiff. His father already worked in Llanbradach colliery as a repairer. The family moved to Caerphilly in 1927 and, finally, to 4 Station road, Llanbradach, in 1931. Even before he lived in the village Ken used to walk there to play in the recently opened park – Caerphilly had nothing to rival it. He remembers walking over the disused viaduct to pick crab apples on the Monmouthshire side, playing on the railway sidings behind the Cinema, damming the mountain stream to make a pool, picking wimberries. He remembers the viaduct being demolished in 1937–8, hydraulic jacks were used to raise and tip over the heavy girders. He went to Caerphilly Boys Secondary School in 1933 .... couldn't see the point of learning languages, geometry, etc. .... he mitched most of his last term, spent it in the billiards room of the Workmen's Hall .... County Councillor William Bowen helped to release him from the parental undertaking so that he could leave in March 1936. He started underground, at Llanbradach, the next day on the day shift, changed to the night shift at the earliest legal opportunity (aged 16) .... you were paid six shifts for working five. Llanbradach colliery was still worked entirely by hand (mandril and shovel), there were none of the mechanical cutters or conveyor belts found in the more modern Penallta Colliery. Ken worked in No. 3 pit (the house coal seam), never more than four feet high, had to work on your knees .... kept your food in a metal snapbox or hanging from the roof to prevent the mice getting at it. He attended evening classes at Coedybrain School run by Ellis Hughes, under–manager of No. 3 pit, eventually gaining many certificates and manager status.

Mrs Marion Williams, born 1923, and **Mrs Glenys Wallace**, born 1925, sisters (née Davies). Their father, Emlyn, was two months old when his family came to Llanbradach in 1896. His parents had worked in woollen mills near Lampeter and Newcastle Emlyn before moving to the South Wales coalfield. The family lived in nos. 1 and 2 Glen View Terrace and had a draper's shop next door to Seion, the Welsh Baptist Chapel. One of Emlyn's older brothers, Bill, worked underground in Llanbradach colliery from 14 until the age of 26 years. He then did a remarkable thing – he came out of the pit, studied at home for his matriculation and with the financial support of his father he became a medical student at the London Hospital, completing his training in 1918 at the age of 34 years. He held positions at Talgarth Sanatorium and Cefn Mably Hospital (re-paying his father's loan) before becoming the first medical superintendent of Sully Hospital when it opened in 1936, a position he held until his retirement in 1949. Both his son and daughter followed him into the medical profession.

Marion and Glenys had their early schooling at Llanbradach Mixed and Infants. Mr. George Evans was the headteacher, a short man who carried a short cane around with him .... he caned children who didn't come in after morning rain, he would come into a classroom and fire questions about arithmetic, etc. .... when the sisters' mother tried them out in the Coedybrain Schools for half a day Mr. Evans visited her at home to ask, "What have we done to you?" There was an open coal fire in each classroom, the pupils in front roasted, those at the back froze .... milk bottles were put around the fire to warm. When the Belisha beacon was installed on the main road in 1936 the children were taught a song which Gracie Fields sang at the time :

When you cross the road by day or night
Beware of the danger that looms in sight
Look to the left and look to the right
And you'll never never get run over

They remember family walks on Sunday after chapel, along "the old road" or onto Mynydd Dimlaith to the three-cornered field above Trehir quarry, some-times with a treat of Turkish Delight or whipped cream walnuts bought by their father from the shop at 41 Garden Street.

After finishing her schooling at Caerphilly Girls Secondary Marion worked from 1941 for Dr Willoughby Clarke (later, for Dr. Pendse) and John Bowen, the chemist (later, for Mr. Balkwill). Throughout WW2 she made notes of the daily wireless news at 8am (and sometimes 1pm) for her deaf father, handing two copies to him through the railings at the back of Rees Terrace, one for the coke-ovens men and one for the other surface workers. Emlyn Davies had worked underground until his deafness forced him in the 1920s to work on the surface. He was employed on the operation of the aerial ropeway which carried the slurry (resulting from the coal being cleaned) onto the hillside tip on Llanbradach Isaf farm .... three men operated the ropeway, filling the large "buckets" at one-minute intervals as the wire rope circulated endlessly, day and night, between the colliery and the tip .... Emlyn could sense from the tension in the rope if something was amiss .... when a fault occurred he or a workmate had to go up the hillside to investigate .... if the bucket requiring attention was any distance from the supporting pylons he had to reach it by clinging, hand and foot, to the parallel ropes high above the ground.

Glenys also "passed the scholarship" and on leaving the Secondary School she worked in the Pit Offices (Now the home of Bruce Print Services) between 1940 and 1946, starting as telephonist before moving into the wages section on the first floor to replace, along with other young girls, the men who had been conscripted into the Forces .... on the top floor there were rooms for Mr G D Budge, the managing director, who was also based in the company's head office in Cardiff, Charlie Chrismas, secretary or office manager, the stores manager, the surveyors, and their secretaries .... on the ground floor there were the compensation clerk, a meeting place for the timekeepers (who worked underground), and the telephone switchboards – an internal system for the Pit Offices and the Colliery surface, an external system which included a direct line to head office. During WW2 the switchboards were manned 24 hours a day to receive warning from Cardiff of any threatened air-raids .... red and green alerts were passed on to the colliery powerhouse for the warning and all-clear signals to be sounded on the pit hooter .... two men were employed to cover the out-of-office hours .... Glenys and another young woman were sometimes paid a shilling each to cover the calls up to midnight so that the men could have an evening off .... on these occasions they were expected to do some of their normal daytime work without overtime pay!

Gary Linder, born 1928, remembers the Cinema on the corner of Thomas Street. He began to help in the projection box before leaving school in 1942. While working in the colliery, and later for British Rail, Gary continued his involvement with the Cinema during many of his leisure hours, becoming almost a fulltime un-paid projectionist as well as helping the owner, John Lewis, to repair vandalised seats and put all the loose electrical wiring into conduits when new regulations came in about 1950. Travelling "reps" from the film distribution companies (RKO, MGM, Pathé News) called regularly for films to be booked several weeks in advance; the "Big Picture" always had a shorter feature film attached to it as part of the deal. The distributors took a fixed percentage of the box-office takings. The Cinema, in common with all other exhibitors, was obliged by law to show a 33 per cent quota of English films (including the old music hall "greats" – Old Mother Riley, Will Hay, Arthur Askey), whereas the children (and, perhaps, the grown-ups!) preferred Popeye, Gene Autrey, William "Hopalong" Cassidy, and the more slick Hollywood pictures. By the time the well-travelled films reached Llanbradach they had often been damaged through repeated or careless use, resulting in sudden jumps in the action, or a complete breakdown which produced a thunderous protest from the audience, especially the younger element! As a privately owned cinema it was run on a shoe-string – the projectionist had two 78rpm records with which to entertain the audience before the evening show ("Ramona" and "Dance, ballerina, dance"), and the lighting was subdued to conceal the faded décor. As television became popular the attendance dwindled. The Cinema closed down and was demolished in the early 1960s to make way for the Woodlands flats.

Dennis Sellwood, born 1932, remembers Coedybrain Infants .... the slate board around the classroom walls on which the children chalked their exercises .... the whole class sitting, hands on head, when told to be silent .... standing on the seats in the music lesson playing drums, tambourines, "clackers", and triangles .... gathered around the piano while Miss Olwen Thomas played the Gracie Fields' popular song of the time, "Wish me luck as you wave me goodbye". The day war broke out .... playing with a toy wooden fort and lead soldiers "out the front" in Tynygraig Road on Sunday morning as the paper boy came down the street shouting the news, the grown-ups indoors solemnly listening to the wireless announcement by the prime minister .... being issued with gas masks in the All Saints Rooms .... walking in the blacked-out streets by moon and star light. Coedybrain Boys .... Mr. Williams reading Brer Rabbit stories, a sharp stroke on the palm of the hand for indiscipline or inattention .... the strong, distinctive (and now so nostalgic) smell of the asphalt playground when it rained after a spell of hot weather .... the sycamore keys helicoptering down .... peeing contests in the outside lav while singing, "Hitler, you're barmy, go'n'join the army" .... playground games – strong horses weak donkeys, leap-frog, dicky-five-stones, conkers, swapping cigarette cards, fighting .... whenever there was an air raid warning, running across the street to the safety of Kenny Carter's house .... sitting the scholarship exam in the school hall, with a piece of coal on the desk "for luck" .... 'Puggy' Thomas, the class teacher, positively beaming when he later announced the successful results, being sent running home at once to pass on the exciting, hardly comprehensible, news. Street games – playing marbles along the street gutters, relieve-o, ball games against the pine end of 2 James Street, cricket in James Street (the wicket chalked on the wall of the Co-op bakery), giving way to the rare motor-car and watching it until it disappeared around the corner .... making pea-shooters from the stem of the wild rhubarb plant down by the river, with the fruit of the hawthorn as ammunition .... going to the Workmen's Hall on New Year's Day to be given a bright new penny, in through the front entrance, out through the back with hand indelibly stamped to prevent any attempt to re-join the queue! .... whenever there was a wedding in All Saints waiting in Pencerrig Street until the bridegroom came out and threw a big handful of pennies into the road for the children to scramble after .... helping Gran to make newspaper spills for pipe-smoking Gramp to light in the coal fire, bathing in front of the kitchen fire, reading in bed by candlelight .... Mam scrubbing the long tiled passage through the house, the front steps, and part of the pavement .... blackleading the grate and hob, polishing the silver fender .... up to her elbows in the tub every Monday in the bailey washing and wringing clothes and bed linen all day (always bubble and squeak for dinner on washday) .... the embarrassment of being sent by Dad into neighbouring streets, with bucket and shovel, to collect horse-dung for the allotment .... helping him to shift the monthly ton of concessionery coal from the back lane into the coal shed. Listening to the wireless – Children's Hour, Dick Barton, Workers Playtime, ITMA, Variety Bandbox, In Town Tonight .... taking the accumulator every week to be re-charged by Mr Briffert in Church Street .... going to the pictures two or three evenings a week, fourpence to get in, tuppence for an ice-cream .... Cowboys and Indians, The Dead End Kids, George Formby, gorgeous Betty Grable, outrageous Carmen Miranda, "The Man They Couldn't Hang" and "The Mummy's Hand"! .... trying to make the two ounces' sweets ration last all week. The mass of miners coming off shift down the Pit Road in their dusty pit clothes, the whites of their eyes startling in the blackened faces, "tootying down" on their haunches on the pavement in the typical collier's pose as they waited for the homeward bus .... carrying Sunday dinner (roast and a rice pudding) in a wicker basket to Dad when he worked his all-day shift on the mechanical boilers.

MY VILLAGE, by Molly Tudor

I have a secret corner
That is all my very own,
And I often hurry to it
When I want to be alone;
For it's here that I can sit and dream
And watch the world go by,
As visions of the past arise
Before my eager eye.
On the wings of memory
I travel back once more,
And see my little village
As it was so long ago.

The farms in isolation
Enjoying their mountain seat,
Looked down and watched the village grow
House by house and street by street,
Each street of terraced houses
Wound along the valley floor,
With homely smoking chimneys
And polished knockered door.
The friendly village shops
That stayed open late at night,
Displaying all their goods for sale
To all who came in sight,
The lazy River Rhymney
Flowing through the fields so green,
And the lovely fern-clad mountains.
Oh such beauty to be seen!!!

No roaring screeching traffic
Sped along this busy street,
Occasionally the clip-clop
Of noble horses' feet
As the baker and the milkman
Came delivering to your door,
And errand-boys on bicycles
Brought your groceries once more.

To the west, the colliery
Like a mighty giant stood,
The reason for the village
Being just where it should.

163

I hear again the "hooters"
That called men to the mine,
The sound of the great steam-engines
A - puffing down the line
Pulling the trucks stacked full of coal,
Rattling along with their heavy load.
I hear again the miners' boots
As they walked on the old pit road.
And when the shifts at the colliery changed
Two streams of men on the track,
Those going on had faces white
Those coming off - all black

Some men worked at the "ovens"
Converting the coal to coke,
And I often watched them hard at work
From the shade of a giant oak.
I still can see the fiery glow,
Flames that turned the sky to red,
As the coke was ousted and cooled
From out of its oven bed.
And as a child I often thought
That the heat and flames could foretell
That here was an earthly picture
Of a fiery, flaming Hell !!!

How well I remember the people
That lived in the village then,
Kind-hearted motherly women,
And upright hard-working men.
Times were hard, families large,
And the income earned very small,
Opportunities came very seldom -
Sometimes never at all.
For ours was a mining village,
Most men worked at the Pit,
Facing hardships and danger each day
With humour and sheer grit.
And when their shift was finished
They'd thankfully retire
Back home for a good cooked dinner
And a bath in front of the fire.
Sometimes they'd sing or whistle
As they washed off the dirt and grime
Grateful to see the end of the shift
To return safely one more time.

Life was hard for the women
Who worked from morn till night,
Keeping their sparsely-furnished homes
Spotlessly clean and bright,
Tending their many children
With infinite love and care,
Struggling to clothe and feed them well
On the very small wages earned there.
Washing day was a busy day,
Rub on the rubbing-board,
No washing machine or spin-driers
To lighten the heavy load.
Ironing then with the heavy "flats"
Heated before the fire,
Cooking and sewing hour after hour,
Never seeming to tire.

The chapels and church were full then,
And Sunday a day of prayer,
They were the centre of village life
For parents and children to share.
Practising for concerts and the Anniversary,
Parade through the streets and the Whitsun treat,
And the yearly trip to the sea.
The village "bobby" who walked the street,
Was looked-up to with healthy awe,
Keeping children and adults
Always within the law.
Our friendly family doctors
Lived in the village too,
Caring for the sick with devotion,
All their patients well they knew.
Teachers and heads were respected
Their discipline just but stern,
Classes were large but teaching made easy
By pupils eager to learn.

The streets and lanes were our playground,
And after school each day
We'd all meet in our happy crowds
To pass the time in play:-
Hat-ball, tennis and cricket,
Jumping, skipping and playing "top",
Collecting stones and slate for a scale
If you were playing "shop",
No television to claim our time,
No pocket-money to spare,

So all of our leisure was spent
In God's free country air –
Picnics on the mountain,
Walks through the fields so green,
Gathering wild flowers that grew in the woods.
Life was then so serene !!!
Sometimes on a Monday
The best of joyous treats,
Off to the penny matinee
And a half-penny to spend on sweets.

Sometimes we'd plan a concert,
And we'd practise very hard,
Our dresses we made of crepe paper
Our stage was our own back-yard.
We'd draw up a simple programme
And we'd try to get it right –
Someone to sing, someone to dance,
Then someone to recite.
At last came the day of opening
Time for the show to begin,
When the back-lane door was opened
To let the audience in.
They crowded in and sat on stools
When the space we could allow,
And heartily clapped and shouted
As each artist took her bow.
Looking back, I often think
What a wealth of talent lay
In the little home-made concerts
Of the children at their play.

Like all children we looked forward to Christmas,
And knowing that money was short
We'd decide to save up our pennies
For a present that could be bought.
About the end of October
Mr Nicholas' shop, top of the street,
Would display Christmas gifts in the window,
And there all the children would meet.
I can see again how eagerly,
With noses pressed to the pane,
We scanned the shelves of lovely gifts
Again, and yet again !!!
Each had a ticket showing the price
Of the items on display

Stating how many pennies a week,
And how many weeks to pay.
How proudly we took our cards each week
To pay till the gift was bought
And feeling rich as a millionaire
When home our purchase we brought.
Then at last came Christmas morning –
Christmas Eve had quickly sped –
Unpacking the bulging stocking
Tied on to the end of the bed.
An orange, and apple and lots of nuts,
A toy whistle and cardboard house.
Bundles of chocolates tied with colourful string,
And a white and chocolate sweet mouse.
Then hurry downstairs to discover
What other presents we had,
However small and simple they were
They made us children so glad.

Then the excitement of New Year's Day –
At Mr Nicholas' shop we'd all meet,
And each were given an orange
And a penny as a New Year's treat,
Then a free picture-show at the Workmen's Hall,
And when the show was through
We each had a shiny new penny
Given to all of us too.

Then came the strike of nineteen-twenty-six,
Miners' wages had always been small,
But now that the men were all out of work
There was no incoming money at all.
Poverty was rampant,
Despair and anger were bred,
People were forced to go into debt
To see their families fed.
The old pit-road was silent !!!
No tramping of miners' feet,
And men walked around aimlessly
And chatted when pals they would meet.
Soup kitchens were opened for children,
And charity concerts held,
To help ease the burden and hardship
That families encountered then.

But as week followed week and the strike still held,
And neither would give any ground,
They decided to start the jazz-bands
In the villages all around.
It gave the men an interest,
It kept them fit and strong,
And gave a boost to their morale
Which had been dormant for so long.
The crowds would gaily gather
To hear the bands' gay sound,
And to watch the judging of them
In the miners welfare ground.
What a glorious Summer we had that year,
The sun shone both strong and true,
As if to make up for the hopeless despair
Of the gloomy time we were passing through.
The river had never been cleaner,
And we children on a very hot day
Would paddle and bathe in its water
And splash each other in play.

But when the colder weather came
And the coal-houses were bare,
Men were forced to dig in the tip
For any coal they could find there.
To have a fire was essential, so
Raids were made on the ponds of "slurry",
And coal-wagons on the "siding"
Were emptied in a tremendous hurry.
But at last the strike was over,
The men went back to the mine,
Once more the sound of the engines
Transporting coal down the line.

How changed is my 'little' village now !!!
It has grown to double its' size.
Two estates of lovely new houses
And the old ones modernised.
The coke-ovens have long been demolished
And our Pit years ago was closed too.
But for years we were left with the coal tips,
To remind us of days we once knew.

Life moves now at a much quicker pace –
No time to "stand and stare",
Everyone always hurrying,

Rushing here and there.
The mode of life has altered –
Altered in lots of ways –
We've gained and we've lost as we've travelled
From what is known as the "bad old days".

They called the days of my childhood
"The bad old days" – and it's true,
They were "bad" because of the poverty
And hardship that everyone knew.
But they were "good" days for the fellowship
And the neighbourliness that existed,
They were fearless days of freedom
When crime was always resisted,
They were days when children and adults
Were safe to wander at will
Exploring nature's beauty
Of river, field and hill.

If I could choose to be born again
And could choose the place and the time
I would still choose to be born right here.
And the time? – When I was a child.

Mrs Molly Tudor (née Iris Wright) was born in 15 Rees Terrace, where she lives still, in 1918, the youngest of eight children. She was a pupil in the Coedybrain Schools before "passing the Scholarship" in 1930 to go to the Caerphilly Girls Secondary School. After completing one year in the Sixth Form she entered Barry Training College to qualify as a teacher. Unable to fulfil the Glamorgan County Council requirement to be proficient in the Welsh language (her parents came from Gloucestershire and Oxfordshire in about 1900) she was forced to seek employment in England for a number of years, and then Newport and Trelewis before eventually obtaining a post in Coedybrain Infants in the 1960s, from whence she retired in 1978 as deputy headteacher.

Note
The poem refers to Mr. Nicholas' shop on the corner of Rees Terrace and Morgan Street. The slurry ponds behind Rees Terrace held the coal dust washed from the coal – in 1926 villagers "stole" the sediment, dried it out, rolled it into balls by hand to burn on the kitchen fire; the laden wagons on the colliery sidings were also prime targets. The game of hat–ball was a variant of tag – boys and girls put their caps and hats on the ground, the ball was thrown, and the owner of the headgear in which it landed was "on it".

169

Appendix 1   List of Scholars, 1901 – 1950

The list is as full and as accurate as I have been able to make it, using a variety of sources. My thanks go to those former scholars who helped to fill some of the many gaps in the official records. I apologise for the inevitable errors and would welcome any corrections the reader can supply. Details of address and parent's occupation, when taken from the Admission Registers, are sometimes five years out of date by the time of the scholarship year.

The list includes children who "passed the scholarship" but did not, usually for financial reasons, take up their place in the secondary schools; others started but did not stay the course due to the pressure on family income or because they found the academic atmosphere of the schools uncongenial.

Some parents (usually shopkeepers, ministers of religion, or colliery officials) ensured their children against the hazards of the competitive County Entrance Examination by sending them, especially in the early years, as fee–payers.

The children of the Caerphilly district (from Taffs Well to Nelson) were competing for a limited number of places – a rough average of 55 for boys and girls in the 1920s and of 160 (secondary and technical) in the 1930s and 1940s – which inevitably resulted in many of them failing by the narrowest of margins (one mark out of a possible maximum of 300) to gain a place.

Name	Address	Parent's Occupation	School
1901	LLANBRADACH NATIONAL		
Gertrude FUELL	10 Glen View	?	Hengoed Intermediate
	COEDYBRAIN MIXED		
	None Known		
1902	LLANBRADACH NATIONAL		
	None Known		
	COEDYBRAIN MIXED		
Mary Ann JAMES	?	?	Pontypridd Intermediate
Gwladys WILLIAMS	?	?	Pontypridd Intermediate
1903	LLANBRADACH NATIONAL		
	None Known		
	COEDYBRAIN MIXED		
Edmund JARMAN	48 (now 1) High Street	Baker	Pontypridd Intermediate
1904	LLANBRADACH MIXED		
	None Known		
	COEDYBRAIN MIXED		
	None Known		
1905	LLANBRADACH MIXED		
Annie ALLSOPP	43 (now 11) High Street	?	Hengoed Intermediate
Catherine Lydia PROUT	9 (now 20) High Street	Shopkeeper	Hengoed Intermediate
Ellen WESTHEAD	15 Glen View	?	Hengoed Intermediate

	COEDYBRAIN MIXED		
Edith JONES	8 (now 18) High Street	?	Pontypridd Intermediate
David J WILLIAMS	11 De Winton Terrace	?	Pontypridd Intermediate

1906 LLANBRADACH MIXED
None Known
COEDYBRAIN MIXED
None Known

1907	LLANBRADACH MIXED		
Roy Meyrick EVANS	8 (now 18) High Street	Baker	Pengam Intermediate
	COEDYBRAIN MIXED		
	None Known		

1908	LLANBRADACH MIXED		
Cyril Joshua EVANS	8 (now 18) High Street	Baker	Pengam Intermediate
	COEDYBRAIN MIXED		
James BECK	14 Wilkins Terrace	?	Refused place at
or BAKER	Pwllypant		Pontypridd Intermediate
Florence EDWARDS	37 Coedybrain Road	Miner	Hengoed Intermediate
Edith HUGHES	?	?	Hengoed Intermediate
Susan WARREN	3 Lewis Terrace	Miner	Hengoed Intermediate

1909 LLANBRADACH MIXED
None Known
COEDYBRAIN MIXED
None Known

1910	LLANBRADACH MIXED		
Mabel Emily GRIFFIN	14 Ffrwd Terrace	Miner	Hengoed Intermediate
Gladys MOORE	10 Monmouth View	Miner	Refused place at
			Hengoed Intermediate
Mary THOMPSON	18 Tynygraig Road	Overman	Hengoed Intermediate
	COEDYBRAIN MIXED		
Elizabeth Lily JAMES	18 Rees Terrace	?	Refused place at
			Pontypridd Intermediate
Maggie Evelyn WHITE	Constitutional Club	Stewardess	Pontypridd Intermediate

1911	LLANBRADACH MIXED		
	None Known		
	COEDYBRAIN MIXED		
Hilda May TURNER	De Winton Hotel	Hotel Keeper	Hengoed Intermediate

1912	LLANBRADACH MIXED		
Lydia GRIFFITHS	?	?	Hengoed Intermediate

	COEDYBRAIN MIXED		(H.E.=Higher Elementary)
Edith BASSETT	16 Rees Terrace	Miner	Caerphilly H.E.
Annie BRAMBLE	60 School Street	Miner	Caerphilly H.E.
Beatrice COLMAN	18 School Street	Signalman	Caerphilly H.E.
Annie POWELL	Pwllypant Post Office	Miner	Caerphilly H.E.
Ethel WILLIAMS	102 School Street	Miner	Caerphilly H.E.
Lydia WILLIAMS	2 Central Terrace	Winder	Hengoed Intermediate
Thomas D WILLIAMS	Glasgow House, High St.	Draper	Caerphilly H.E.

1913 — LLANBRADACH MIXED

Hilda DAVIES	9 Central Terrace	Headteacher	Howell's, Llandaff
Lilian M WELCH	19 Victoria Street	?	Hengoed Intermediate

COEDYBRAIN MIXED

Arthur EVANS	18 High Street	Milk dealer	Caerphilly H.E.
Mary JENKINS	10 Energlyn Row, Pwllypant	Platelayer	Caerphilly H.E.
Mabel MITCHELL	8 Energlyn Row, Pwllypant	Signalman	Caerphilly H.E.
Bertie WHITE	Constitutional Club	Stewardess	Caerphilly H.E.

1914 — LLANBRADACH MIXED

None Known

COEDYBRAIN BOYS

John BOWEN	9 Garden Avenue	Miner	Caerphilly H.E.
Rufus CHURCHES	71 Coedybrain Road	Miner	Caerphilly H.E.
Cyril HOARE	94 School Street	Miner	Caerphilly H.E.
Clifford LEWIS	17 Lewis Terrace	Grocer	Pengam Intermediate
Jack LUCAS	41 Coedybrain Road	Sister	Caerphilly H.E.
William SKYM	24 Rees Terrace	Miner	Caerphilly H.E.
Lawrence WATTS	1 Coedybrain Road	Widow	Caerphilly H.E.
Henry WILLIAMS	9 Garden Street	Haulier	Caerphilly H.E.
John Hy WILLIAMS	14 High Street	Chemist	Pengam Intermediate

COEDYBRAIN GIRLS

Flossie M JAMES	13 Garden Avenue	Haulier	Caerphilly H.E.
Gladys H MARE	21 Thomas Street	Miner	Hengoed Intermediate
Dora ROSS	32 High Street	Collier	Caerphilly H.E.

1915 — LLANBRADACH MIXED

Arthur DAVIES	1 Glen View	Miner	Pengam Intermediate
Claude K DAVIES	9 Central Terrace	Headteacher	Pengam Intermediate
Edward Th WILLIAMS	Graddfa Farm	Farmer	Pengam Intermediate

COEDYBRAIN BOYS

John DAVIES	22 Thomas Street	Miner	Caerphilly H.E.
Horace DOWLING	42 De Winton Terrace	Grocer	Pengam Intermediate
John H JONES	6 James Street	Miner	Caerphilly H.E.
David E RIDGE	58 School Street	Miner	Caerphilly H.E.

172

	COEDYBRAIN GIRLS		
Sarah PEARSON	18 Church Street	Widow	Caerphilly H.E.
Annie D RICHARDS	38 High Street	Draper	Caerphilly H.E.
Louisa STEPHENS	5 Church Street	Miner	Caerphilly H.E.

1916

	LLANBRADACH MIXED		
	None Known		
	COEDYBRAIN BOYS		
Archibald DAVIES	44 School Street	Miner	Caerphilly H.E.
Charles ROSS	32 High Street	Miner	Caerphilly H.E.
Owen WILLIAMS	3 School Street	Miner	Caerphilly H.E.
	COEDYBRAIN GIRLS		
Cissie BRISTER	24 High Street	Butcher	Caerphilly H.E.
Josephine HOPKINS	Gwasted Cottage, Pwllypant	Widow	Caerphilly H.E.
Edith JONES	6 Tynygraig Road	Winder	Caerphilly H.E.
Enid WILLIAMS	61 School Street	Miner	Caerphilly H.E.

1917

	LLANBRADACH MIXED		
	None Known		
	COEDYBRAIN BOYS		
Harold GRENFELL	19 Rees Terrace	Coke Ovens	Caerphilly H.E.
Joseph H HEWER	7 Wilkins Tce, Pwllypant	Stoker	Caerphilly H.E.
	COEDYBRAIN GIRLS		
Ethel Mary BARTLETT	4 Morgan Street	Miner	Caerphilly H.E.
Blodwen CHARLES	10 James Street	Winder	Caerphilly H.E.
Lily Louisa CHURCHWARD	68 School Street	Stoker	Caerphilly H.E.
Margaret A CROMBY	25 Thomas Street	Pit Labourer	Caerphilly H.E.

1918

	LLANBRADACH MIXED		
Neteliah Jane REES	15 Oakfield Street	?	Hengoed Intermediate
Annie Maud WILSON	12 Ffrwd Terrace	?	Hengoed Intermediate
	COEDYBRAIN BOYS		
Harold DOWLING	42 De Winton Terrace	Grocer	Caerphilly H.E.
Reginald HANDCOCK	2 Pencerrig Street	Ostler	Pengam Intermediate
Lionel T MOORE	114 School Street	Miner	Caerphilly H.E.
	COEDYBRAIN GIRLS		
Blodwen DAVIES	Police Station	Police Sergeant	Caerphilly H.E.
Elsie THRESHER	Pwllypant	Coachman	Hengoed Intermediate
Muriel WATKINS	14 James Street	Miner	Caerphilly H.E.
Dora WILLIAMS	14 High Street	Chemist	Caerphilly H.E.

1919

	LLANBRADACH MIXED		
	None Known		
	COEDYBRAIN BOYS		
Joseph BISHOP	Oaklands	Cokeworks Manager	Pengam Intermediate
Herbert JAMES	31 High Street	Ripper	Caerphilly H.E.

173

Daniel T PHILLIPS	3 Tynygraig Road	Railway Clerk	Pengam Intermediate
Geo. Lionel WATKINS	14 James Street	Miner	Pengam Intermediate
	COEDYBRAIN GIRLS		
Emma Elvira EVANS	4 James Street	Miner	Hengoed Intermediate
Amelia POWELL	Pwllypant Post Office	Miner	Caerphilly H.E.
Margaret Ellen POWELL	16 Glen View	Ostler	Hengoed Intermediate
Eliz. Mary RIDDIFORD	18 James Street	Miner	Hengoed Intermediate

1920   **LLANBRADACH MIXED**

Rosemary DAVIES	25 Wingfield Crescent	Ostler	Caerphilly H.E.
Wm G PAYNE	12 Oakfield Street	Miner	Caerphilly H.E.
	COEDYBRAIN BOYS		
Wm. H. BISHOP	60 High Street	Cokeworks Manager	Pengam Intermediate
Donald HOARE	25 Coedybrain Road	Miner	Pengam Intermediate
John Ivor WILLIAMS	Graddfa Farm	Farmer	Caerphilly H.E.
Oswald J WILLIAMS	9 James Street	Miner	Pengam Intermediate
	COEDYBRAIN GIRLS		
Ethel Grace BOWYER	11 Rees Terrace	Fitter	Caerphilly H.E.
Gwladys M POWELL	16 Glen View	Collier	Hengoed Intermediate

1921   **LLANBRADACH MIXED**
None Known

	COEDYBRAIN BOYS		
Edgar DAVIES	34 High Street	Fruiterer	Pengam Intermediate
Albert E PHILLIPS	3 Tynygraig Road	Railway Clerk	Pengam Intermediate
Geo S WILLIAMS	3 School Street	Miner	Caerphilly Secondary
	COEDYBRAIN GIRLS		
Emily (Millie) BARTLETT	4 Morgan Street	Miner	Caerphilly Secondary
Phyllis B WILLIAMS	9 School Street	Miner	Caerphilly Secondary

1922   **LLANBRADACH MIXED**

Irene MASON	1 Garden Avenue	Lamp-room	Hengoed Intermediate
? POWELL	16 Glen View	Ostler	Hengoed Intermediate
? POWELL	16 Glen View	Ostler	Hengoed Intermediate
	COEDYBRAIN BOYS		
Richard C CONNICK	4 Tynygraig Terrace	Clerk	Caerphilly Secondary
	COEDYBRAIN GIRLS		
Millie BISHOP	13 Rees Terrace	Miner	Caerphilly Secondary
May E ECKLAND	10 Garden Street	Foreman	Hengoed Intermediate
Hilda FOWLER	36 High Street	Haulier	Hengoed Intermediate
Pauline M JONES	47 De Winton Terrace	?	Caerphilly Secondary
Mary (Molly) LEWIS	17 Lewis Terrace	Shopkeeper	Hengoed Intermediate
Betty V LLEWELLYN	Llanbradach Hotel	Hotel Proprietor	Hengoed Intermediate

1923   **LLANBRADACH MIXED**
None Known

	COEDYBRAIN BOYS		
Reginald C S BEVAN	2 Garden Street	Miner	Caerphilly Secondary
Richard Neville EVANS	Pwllypant Cottage	Schoolmaster	Caerphilly Secondary
	COEDYBRAIN GIRLS		
Doreena BAKER	3 Oak Terrace	Barber	Caerphilly Secondary
Kathleen M COLLINS	10 Garden Street	Housekeeper	Hengoed Intermediate
Enid TARGETT	4 High Street	Shopkeeper	Hengoed Intermediate

1924 LLANBRADACH MIXED

Nellie MATTHEWS	27 Rees Terrace	?	Caerphilly Secondary
Ronald L PIPER	39 Wingfield Crescent	Overman	Caerphilly Secondary
	COEDYBRAIN BOYS		
	None Known		
	COEDYBRAIN GIRLS		
	None Known		

1925 LLANBRADACH MIXED

Cecil N NEALE	2 Victoria Street	?	Caerphilly Secondary
Hilda M SMITH	10 Victoria Street	?	Caerphilly Secondary
Thomas F WATKINS	1 Graddfa Road	Colliery Manager	Caerphilly Secondary
	COEDYBRAIN BOYS		
Henry S COLES	11 Ffrwd Terrace	Miner	Caerphilly Secondary
Eric R ECKLAND	10 Garden Street	Stoker/Foreman	Caerphilly Secondary
Hurbert GRIMES	84 School Street	Pitman	Caerphilly Secondary
Ronald TUDOR	112 School Street	Miner	Caerphilly Secondary
John WILLIAMS	9 School Street	Miner	Caerphilly Secondary
C Thos. Leslie HEAD	4 Oak Terrace	Confectioner	Caerphilly Secondary
Joseph Lionel JOHNSON	58 High Street	Industrial Chemist	Caerphilly Secondary
	COEDYBRAIN GIRLS		
Winifred BASSETT	14 Rees Terrace	Miner	Caerphilly Secondary
Bronwen M J STUART	31 High Street	Miner	Caerphilly Secondary
Elsie M DAVIES	51 School Street	Collier	Refused place at Caerphilly Secondary
Annie LANNON	19 Thomas Street	Housekeeper	Hengoed Intermediate

1926 LLANBRADACH MIXED

Catherine (Kitty) HUGHES	2 Graddfa Road	Colliery Manager	Caerphilly Secondary
	COEDYBRAIN BOYS		
Robert GUMBLETON	26 Tynygraig Road	Miner	Caerphilly Secondary
Wilfred L PREECE	4 Tynygraig Terrace	Coke Ovens	Caerphilly Secondary
Horace WEBB	12 Coedybrain Road	?	Caerphilly Secondary
Frank WHITE	17 School Street	Miner	Caerphilly Secondary
	COEDYBRAIN GIRLS		
Phoebe E DAVIES	44 School Street	Miner	Caerphilly Secondary
Catherine (Kitty) GRIMES	84 School Street	Pitman	Caerphilly Secondary
Dorothy M SMITH	57 Coedybrain Road	Miner	Caerphilly Secondary
Mildred Cissie THISSEN	4 Morgan Street	Overman	Caerphilly Secondary

1927	LLANBRADACH MIXED		
Margaret E L SMITH	?	?	Caerphilly Secondary
	COEDYBRAIN BOYS		
Kenneth G BISHOP	60 High Street	Cokeworks Manager	Caerphilly Secondary
Fredk. Wm. COLES	11 Ffrwd Terrace	Miner	Caerphilly Secondary
Myrddin DOEL	21 Rees Terrace	Miner	Caerphilly Secondary
	COEDYBRAIN GIRLS		
Edith F PRITCHARD	14 Glen View	?	Treforest Commercial
1928	LLANBRADACH MIXED		
	None Known		
	COEDYBRAIN BOYS		
Gwilym Chas. DOEL	21 Rees Terrace	Miner	Caerphilly Secondary
Gilbert J SPAREY	27 School Street	Miner	Caerphilly Secondary
John Alfred SUMMERS	12 Garden Avenue	Fitter	Caerphilly Secondary
Eric Evan WILLIAMS	22 Grove Street	Carter	Caerphilly Secondary
	COEDYBRAIN GIRLS		
Lily G BUTT	23 Thomas Street	Collier	Caerphilly Secondary
Diana H JONES	40 High Street	Milkman	Treforest Commercial
Mgt. May JONES	Chapel House	Fireman	Caerphilly Secondary
Eunice E MALE	47 School Street	Miner	Caerphilly Secondary
Sarah J MOORE	12 Grove Street	Miner	Caerphilly Secondary
Winifred PEARSON	3 Coedybrain Road	Miner	Caerphilly Secondary
Winifred PREECE	4 Tynygraig Terrace	Coke Ovens	Caerphilly Secondary
Nancy THOMAS	1 Monmouth View	Miner	Caerphilly Secondary
Nancy THOMAS	8 Wilkins Tce. Pwllypant	Fireman	Caerphilly Secondary
1929	LLANBRADACH MIXED		
Leonard CARTER	42 Garden Street	Colliery Medical Attendant	Caerphilly Secondary
	COEDYBRAIN BOYS		
Trevor MORGAN	9 Pencerrig Street	Signalman	Caerphilly Secondary
Emrys John RALPH	42 De Winton Terrace	Collier	Caerphilly Secondary
Ronald WAYTE	26 Church Street	Clerk	Caerphilly Secondary
	COEDYBRAIN GIRLS		
Constance RICHARDS	26 Thomas Street	Miner	Caerphilly Secondary
1930	LLANBRADACH MIXED		
Emily BARBER	Maesycwmmer Road	?	Maesycwmmer Secondary
Ken JAMES	4 Wingfield Crescent	Miner	Caerphilly Secondary
Trevor MILLS	6 Wingfield Crescent	Miner	Caerphilly Secondary
Thomas PAYNE	12 Oakfield Street	Miner	Caerphilly Secondary
	COEDYBRAIN BOYS		
Sidney M BAILEY	11 Tynygraig Road	Miner	Caerphilly Secondary
Robert W REECE	9 Lewis Terrace	Miner	Caerphilly Secondary
Fredk. J SMITH	57 Coedybrain Road	Miner	Caerphilly Secondary
Leslie THORNTON	1 Morgan Street	Fitter	Caerphilly Secondary
Glanville WEBB	12 Coedybrain Road	Miner	Caerphilly Secondary

	COEDYBRAIN GIRLS		
Mavis BAILEY	11 Tynygraig Road	Miner	Caerphilly Secondary
Amy BASSETT	14 Rees Terrace	Miner	Caerphilly Secondary
Thurza EVANS	6 Grove Street	Railwayman	Caerphilly Secondary
Anewta FENNELL	9 Morgan Street	Traveller	Caerphilly Secondary
Betty POOK	18 Rees Terrace	Coke Ovens	Caerphilly Secondary
Gwyneth RICHARDS	26 Thomas Street	Miner	Caerphilly Secondary
Iris WRIGHT	15 Rees Terrace	Miner	Caerphilly Secondary

1931   LLANBRADACH MIXED
None Known

	COEDYBRAIN BOYS		
James BROWN	20 School Street	Miner	Caerphilly Technical
Francis H JACOB	8 School Street	Miner	Caerphilly Technical
Herbert Neil PENNINGTON	Graddfa Road	Engineer	Caerphilly Secondary
Glyndwr THOMAS	18 Garden Street	Miner	Caerphilly Technical

	COEDYBRAIN GIRLS		
Ivy D BUTT	23 Thomas Street	Miner	Caerphilly Secondary
Barbara A JONES	27 High Street	Milkman	Caerphilly Secondary
Nancy Keirle JONES	9 Grove Street	Dairyman	Caerphilly Secondary

1932   LLANBRADACH MIXED
None Known

	COEDYBRAIN BOYS		
Glanville DAVIES	10 Church Street	Coke Ovens	Caerphilly Secondary
Herbert J DAVIES	5 Stanley Terrace	Miner	Caerphilly Secondary
Albert EVANS	29 Coedybrain Road	Miner	Caerphilly Technical
Ivor G JENKINS	Cwmer Cottage (Mon)	Miner	Caerphilly Technical
David R JONES	40 High Street	Dairyman	Caerphilly Secondary
Victor G NOLAN	7 Ffrwd Terrace	Miner	Caerphilly Secondary
Trevor SPICER	10 Church Street	Driver	Caerphilly Secondary

	COEDYBRAIN GIRLS		
Rhoda BUNT	8 Lewis Terrace	Miner	Caerphilly Secondary
Ivy BRAMALL	80 School Street	Mason	Caerphilly Secondary
Edna HENDY	26 Tynygraig Road	Miner	Caerphilly Secondary
Olive H HUGHES	6 School Street	Miner	Caerphilly Secondary
Phyllis JACOB	8 School Street	Miner	Caerphilly Secondary
Dorothy LOGAN	26 School Street	Miner	Caerphilly Secondary
Ada P SHANNON	1 Garden Avenue	Miner	Caerphilly Secondary
Dilys M WEEKS	46 De Winton Terrace	Miner	Caerphilly Secondary

1933	LLANBRADACH MIXED		
Fred GOODE	16 Plasturtwyn Terrace	Miner	Caerphilly Secondary
Ron HAYTER	? High Street	Miner	Caerphilly Secondary
Evelyn LUCAS	29 Oakfield Street	Miner	Caerphilly Secondary
Cathleen MEYRICK	Castell Llwyd Farm	Farmer	Bedwellty Secondary
Sid PAYNE	12 Oakfield Street	Driller	Caerphilly Secondary

Ben PIPER	19 Glen View	Overman	Caerphilly Secondary
Arthur SMITH	25 Tynygraig Road	Shopkeeper	Caerphilly Technical
	COEDYBRAIN BOYS		
Idris BASSETT	Ranger Bungalow	Miner	Caerphilly Secondary
Tom BEEBE	20 RichmOnd Terrace	Miner	Caerphilly Secondary
Kenneth BOWEN	9 Garden Avenue	Checkweigher	Caerphilly Secondary
Cyril J BUSH	35 Thomas Street	Miner	Caerphilly Secondary
Wm G CHARLES	15 Glen View	Overman	Caerphilly Secondary
Jas. Symes HARDACRE	28 High Street	Coke Ovens	Caerphilly Secondary
Ken H G PLINT	3 Station Road	Miner	Caerphilly Secondary
Geoffrey THOMAS	50 High Street	Miner	Caerphilly Secondary
Derrick WHELAN	4 Coedybrain Road	Mother	Caerphilly Secondary
	COEDYBRAIN GIRLS		
Edna BUTT	23 Thomas Street	Miner	Caerphilly Secondary
Gwenllian DEARSON	8 Wilkins Tce, Pwllypant	Miner	Caerphilly Secondary
Pauline J EVANS	13 Garden Avenue	Miner	Caerphilly Secondary
Eleanor GARAWAY	20 Garden Street	Clerk	Caerphilly Secondary
Annie Jose GARBERTT	2 School Sreet	Miner	Caerphilly Secondary
Gwyneth HORTON	Caravan Maesycwmmer Rd	?	Caerphilly Secondary
Doreen LEWIS	24 Grove Street	Electrician	Caerphilly Secondary
Margaret O'BRIEN	5 Castle View, Pwllypant	Miner	Caerphilly Secondary
Nancy SPRAGG	11 Central St. Pwllypant	Miner	Caerphilly Secondary
Jean M STEWART	31 High Street	Mother	Caerphilly Secondary
1934	**LLANBRADACH MIXED**		
Wm MILLS	6 Wingfield Crescent	Miner	Caerphilly Secondary
Edwin SPENCER	40 Wingfield Crescent	Miner	Caerphilly Secondary
	COEDYBRAIN BOYS		
Henry W AMOS	26 High Street	Miner	Caerphilly Secondary
John R BISHOP	60 High Street	Cokeworks Manager	Caerphilly Secondary
Francis EDWARDS	7 Stanley Row	Miner	Caerphilly Secondary
Havril G EVANS	6 Grove Street	Fitter	Caerphilly Secondary
Norman E JACOB	8 School Street	Miner	Caerphilly Secondary
Harold LEWIS	14 Tynygraig Road	Miner	Caerphilly Technical
John E NOLAN	17 Ffrwd Terrace	Widow	Caerphilly Secondary
Arfon OWEN	"Caeglas", Pwllypant	Miner	Caerphilly Technical
Arthur J PROBERT	74 Garden Street	Checkweigher	Caerphilly Secondary
Maldwyn THOMAS	8 Grove Street	Miner	Caerphilly Secondary
Trevor THOMAS	16 Ffrwd Terrace	Widow	Caerphilly Secondary
	COEDYBRAIN GIRLS		
Violet BRAMALL	80 School Street	Miner	Refused place at Caerphilly Secondary
Dorothy Joan COPPAGE	5 De Winton Terrace	Butcher	Caerphilly Secondary
Cath (Kitty) DAVIES	6 Tynygraig Terrace	Widow	Refused place at Caerphilly Secondary
Sarah (Sallie) DAVIES	5 Rees Terrace	Miner	Caerphilly Secondary
Phyllis Joyce HAZELL	5 Ffrwd Terrace	Miner	Caerphilly Secondary

Emily JONES	58 De Winton Terrace	Miner	Caerphilly Secondary

1935 — LLANBRADACH MIXED

Marion DAVIES	2 Ffrwd Terrace	Ropeway Worker	Caerphilly Secondary
Joyce DYER	42 High Street	Miner	Caerphilly Secondary
Thomas PHILLIPS	11 Garden Street	Miner	Caerphilly Secondary
Mary PRICE	Ty Gwyn Farm	Farmer	Maesycwmmer Secondary

COEDYBRAIN BOYS

George ASHDOWN	10 Grove Street	Miner	Caerphilly Technical
Bernard Geo. LEIGH	27 Central St, Pwllypant	Miner	Caerphilly Secondary
Ivor Geo. PROBERT	74 Garden Street	Checkweigher	Caerphilly Secondary
John PUGH	35 Coedybrain Road	Miner	Caerphilly Technical
Wm. H ROWLANDS	23 De Winton Terrace	Miner	Caerphilly Secondary
Ronald J RUDGE	94 School Street	Miner	Caerphilly Technical
Sidney F SARGENT	46 School Street	Lampman	Caerphilly Secondary
Ronald B SMITH	57 Coedybrain Road	Miner	Caerphilly Secondary

COEDYBRAIN GIRLS

Edith Marg. AMOS	68 School Street	Miner	Caerphilly Secondary
Betty HAMMOND	21 Stanley Row	Coke Ovens	Pontypridd Intermediate
Velma J RICKS	8 Mountain View, Pwllypant	Miner	Pontypridd Intermediate
Mair T WATKINS	1 Graddfa Road	Colliery Manager	Caerphilly Secondary
Minna WHITE	17 School Street	Miner	Pontypridd Intermediate

1936 — LLANBRADACH MIXED
None Known

COEDYBRAIN BOYS

Kenneth CHARLES	15 Glen View	Fireman	Caerphilly Secondary
Ivor DAVIES	45 School Street	Miner	Caerphilly Secondary
Leonard Ivor DAVIES	110 School Street	Miner	Caerphilly Secondary
Noel FOWLER	20 Grove Street	Fitter	Caerphilly Secondary
Trevor R GARAWAY	20 Garden Street	Clerk	Caerphilly Technical
James HOARE	19 Coedybrain Road	Miner	Caerphilly Secondary
John MASLEN	5 Garden Street	Miner	Caerphilly Secondary
Edward MURPHY	24 Tynygraig Road	Widow	Caerphilly Secondary
Thomas T OWEN	"Caeglas", Pwllypant	Miner	Caerphilly Secondary
Victor G PROTHERO	24 High Street	Miner	Caerphilly Secondary
Wm. T STEPHENS	78 School Street	Miner	Caerphilly Secondary
Wm. TOVEY	57 School Street	Miner	Caerphilly Secondary
Bryan G WILLIAMS	5 Mountain View Pwllypant	Miner	Caerphilly Secondary
John E WRIGHT	14 Grove Street	Miner	Caerphilly Secondary

COEDYBRAIN GIRLS

Olive BALL	21 Central St. Pwllypant	Miner	Caerphilly Secondary
Gwyneth DAVIES	18 Glen View	Insurance Agent	Caerphilly Secondary
Margaret (Peggy) DAVIES	5 Rees Terrace	Mason	Caerphilly Secondary
Jose GARAWAY	? Morgan Street	?	Caerphilly Secondary

Betty LEWIS	24 Grove Street	Electrician	Caerphilly Secondary
Kathleen PERRY	2 Pencerrig Street	Miner	Caerphilly Secondary
Joan SHANNON	30 Tynygraig Road	Miner	Caerphilly Secondary

1937   LLANBRADACH MIXED

Glenys M DAVIES	2 Ffrwd Terrace	Ropeway Worker	Caerphilly Secondary
Daniel SHAUGHNESSY	3 Oakfield Street	Miner	Caerphilly Technical

COEDYBRAIN BOYS

Dewi G ASHDOWN	19 Garden Avenue	Miner	Caerphilly Secondary
Ronald DOLE	12 Mountain View, Pwllypant	Miner	Caerphilly Secondary
David J EDWARDS	22 Thomas Street	Miner	Caerphilly Secondary
Ronald EDWARDS	9 Rees Terrace	Miner	Caerphilly Secondary
Joseph H HUGHES	22 School Street	Miner	Caerphilly Secondary
Glyn JOHN	16 Garden Avenue	Miner	Caerphilly Secondary
Daniel LEWER	15 School Street	Guardian	Caerphilly Secondary
Norman E G LEWIS	19 Richmond Terrace	Miner	Caerphilly Secondary
Idris MINTON	15 Coedybrain Road	Miner	Caerphilly Secondary
Stanley PIPER	19 Glen View	Overman	Caerphilly Secondary
Wm. T SHANNON	13 Garden Avenue	Miner	Caerphilly Secondary
Ronald B THOMAS	33 Coedybrain Road	Shopkeeper	Caerphilly Secondary
Clifford WHITE	70 Garden Street	Miner	Caerphilly Technical

COEDYBRAIN GIRLS

Brenda CORNISH	2 Central St., Pwllypant	Miner	Caerphilly Secondary
Thelma EVANS	8 Pencerrig Street	Miner	Caerphilly Secondary
Dorothy J JENKINS	59 School Street	Miner	Caerphilly Secondary
Joyce Irene JOHNSON	88 School Street	Miner	Caerphilly Secondary
Mildred Betty LANGDON	31 Coedybrain Road	Miner	Caerphilly Secondary
Gwen LEWIS	9 Castle View, Pwllypant	Miner	Caerphilly Secondary
Marion RICHARDS	6 Rees Terrace	Miner	Caerphilly Secondary
Lilian E ROBERTS	6 Monmouth View	Miner	Caerphilly Secondary
Brenda WILLIAMS	7 Grove Street	Timberman	Caerphilly Secondary
Joan WITCHELL	11 De Winton Terrace	Miner	Caerphilly Secondary

1938   LLANBRADACH MIXED

William MARTIN	56 High Street	Powderman	Caerphilly Technical
Joyce L TUDOR	25 Rees Terrace	Pitman	Caerphilly Secondary

COEDYBRAIN BOYS

Chas. Leonard AMOS	68 School Street	Collier	Caerphilly Secondary
Walford BAILEY	11 Tynygraig Road	Engine Driver	Caerphilly Secondary
Wm G CHURCHES	2 Wilkins Tce, Pwllypant	Collier	Caerphilly Secondary
Derek S DAVIES	9 Garden Street	Coke Worker	Caerphilly Secondary
James DOLE	12 Mountain View, Pwllypant	Collier	Caerphilly Secondary
Dennis FORBER	3 Morgan Street	Traveller	Caerphilly Secondary
Harry FOWLER	20 Grove Street	Fitter	Caerphilly Secondary
Basil ISAAC	80 Garden Street	Miner	Caerphilly Secondary

Douglas LEEDS	6 Mountain View, Pwllypant	Miner	Caerphilly Secondary
Gordon J PERRY	2 Pencerrig Street	Ostler	Caerphilly Secondary
James RIDEOUT	23 Tynygraig Road	Coke Worker	Caerphilly Secondary
Graham H SHANNON	30 Tynygraig Road	Miner	Caerphilly Technical
Norman L WEBB	51 School Street	Widow	Caerphilly Secondary
	COEDYBRAIN GIRLS		
Gwyneira DAVIES	5 Rees Terrace	Mason	Caerphilly Secondary
Lavinia DAVIES	8 Coedybrain Road	Miner	Caerphilly Secondary
Patricia R HOARE	19 Coedybrain Road	Miner	Caerphilly Secondary
Betty M HUGHES	2 Tynygraig Road	Overman	Caerphilly Secondary
Mair JAMES	1 Lewis Terrace	Miner	Caerphilly Secondary
Anita C LEWIS	18 Garden Avenue	Miner	Caerphilly Secondary
Glenys M SHANNON	12 Garden Avenue	Miner	Caerphilly Secondary
Sylvia M SPENCER	27 Richmond Terrace	Miner	Caerphilly Secondary
1939	**LLANBRADACH MIXED**		
	None Known		
	COEDYBRAIN BOYS		
David Edmund JOHN	16 Garden Avenue	Time Keeper	Caerphilly Secondary
Clifford LEWIS	11 Monmouth View	Grocer	Caerphilly Secondary
Thos. Glyn MORRIS	54 School Street	Lampman	Caerphilly Secondary
Harry PIPER	19 Glen View	Overman	Caerphilly Secondary
Malcolm SHANNON	30 Tynygraig Road	Miner	Caerphilly Secondary
Joseph H SKINNER	5 Grove Street	Coke Man	Caerphilly Secondary
Cyril WATTS	27 Tynygraig Road	Miner	Caerphilly Secondary
Ronald W WESTHEAD	37 Coedybrain Road	Miner	Caerphilly Secondary
	COEDYBRAIN GIRLS		
Beryl DAVIES	6 Tynygraig Terrace	Shopkeeper	Caerphilly Secondary
Beryl METTERS	104 School Street	Miner	Caerphilly Secondary
Kathleen WOLFE	5 Graddfa Road	Engineer	Caerphilly Secondary
Marian GARRETT	28 Thomas Street	Miner	Bridgend Secondary
	Moved to Pencoed		
Glenys M GOODSHIP	8 Morgan Street	Miner	Refused place at Caerphilly Secondary
1940	**LLANBRADACH MIXED**		
Len DAVIES	3 Ffrwd Terrace	Miner	Caerphilly Technical
Glenys M LEWIS	?	?	Bedwellty Secondary
Desmond MORGAN	5 High Street	Munitions	Caerphilly Technical
Kenneth SMITH	23 Rees Terrace	Coke Ovens	Caerphilly Secondary
	COEDYBRAIN BOYS		
Leslie D COLE	11 Ffrwd Terrace	Miner	Caerphilly Secondary
Garnett COPPAGE	22 De Winton Terrace	Electrician	Caerphilly Technical
R John COPPAGE	22 De Winton Terrace	Electrician	Caerphilly Secondary
Leslie FLOWER	15 Thomas Street	Fruiterer	Caerphilly Secondary
Colin A MALE	30 De Winton Terrace	Miner	Caerphilly Secondary

181

Trevor ROBINS	3 New St., Pwllypant	Bus Conductor	Refused place at Caerphilly Secondary
	COEDYBRAIN GIRLS		
Patricia AUSTIN	22 De Winton Terrace	(Evacuee)	Caerphilly Secondary
Margaret LEWIS	3 Pencerrig Street	Miner	Caerphilly Secondary
Eira PERRY	16 De Winton Terrace	Miner	Caerphilly Secondary
Peris REES	40 Garden Street	Baptist Minister	Caerphilly Secondary
Ethel SARGENT	46 School Street	Miner	Caerphilly Secondary
June R STRONG	2 New St, Pwllypant	Miner	Caerphilly Secondary
Vera THOMAS	38 Central St, Pwllypant	Guardian	Caerphilly Secondary

1941 LLANBRADACH MIXED

Margaret BLACKMORE	38 Wingfield Crescent	Miner	Caerphilly Secondary
Glyn DAVIES	2 Ffrwd Terrace	Ropeway Worker	Caerphilly Secondary
Emlyn SAMUEL	9 Tynygraig Road	Miner	Caerphilly Secondary
Wm G SNOOK	32 Plasturtwyn Terrace	Shopkeeper	Caerphilly Secondary
	COEDYBRAIN BOYS		
Ian DAVIES	45 School Street	Miner	Caerphilly Secondary
Adrian HARDACRE	54 High Street	Civil Servant	Caerphilly Secondary
Harry F HARVEY	2 Thomas Street	Miner	Caerphilly Secondary
John HODGE	10 Garden Street	Miner	Caerphilly Secondary
John Wm JONES	4 Barry Cottages, Pwllypant	Miner	Caerphilly Secondary
Granville LEWIS	2 Rees Terrce	Miner	Caerphilly Secondary
Gordon NEWCOMBE	10 Rees Terrace	Coke Worker	Caerphilly Secondary
Colin PHIPPEN	11 Tynygraig Rd	Shop Manager	Caerphilly Secondary
Trevor ROBINS	3 New St, Pwllypant	Bus Conductor	Caerphilly Technical
Wm H THOMAS	24 Richmond Terrace	Miner	Caerphilly Technical
Alfred L WEEKS	46 De Winton Terrace	Colliery Rider	Caerphilly Technical
Leonard WILLIAMS	9 James Street	Coke Worker	Caerphilly Technical
	COEDYBRAIN GIRLS		
Catherine DAVIES	48 High Street	(Evacuee)	Caerphilly Secondary
Edna May JOHNS	1 Morgan Street	Miner	Caerphilly Secondary
Jean N REYNOLDS	56 School Street	Miner	Caerphilly Secondary

1942 LLANBRADACH MIXED

Kenneth A GARDINER	20 Plasturtwyn Terrace	Foreman	Caerphilly Secondary
Jean M GLASS	14 Oakfield Street	Miner	Caerphilly Secondary
Ben GOODE	16 Plasturtwyn Terrace	Miner	Caerphilly Secondary
Cyril PAYNE	29 Oakfield Street	Fireman	Caerphilly Secondary
Tony PREECE	20 Church Street	Miner	Caerphilly Technical
	COEDYBRAIN BOYS		
Terence J BURGAN	44 De Winton Terrace	Miner	Caerphilly Secondary
Clive DAVIES (Evacuee)	10 or 50 High Street	Dock Labourer	Caerphilly Secondary
Islwyn J DAVIES	58 Garden Street	Mason	Caerphilly Secondary
Malcolm DAVIES	17 Rees Terrace	Miner	Caerphilly Secondary
Arthur HAZELL	12 High Street	Miner	Caerphilly Technical
Norman JAMES	6 Tynygraig Terrace	Miner	Caerphilly Secondary

T Brynley JAMES	5 Tynygraig Road	Miner	Caerphilly Technical
Malcolm T E JONES	5 Wilkins Tce, Pwllypant	Miner	Caerphilly Secondary
Edwin C LEWIS	29 Coedybrain Road	Miner	Caerphilly Technical
Barrie MALE	30 De Winton Terrace	Miner	Caerphilly Secondary
Malcolm PUGH	69 School Street	Miner	Caerphilly Secondary
	COEDYBRAIN GIRLS		
Sarah Jane COLES	7 Lewis Terrace	Postman	Caerphilly Secondary
Peggy R DAVIES	21 Tynygraig Road	Miner	Caerphilly Secondary
Llinos M SHANNON	30 Tynygraig Road	Miner	Caerphilly Secondary
June WHITE	70 Garden Street	Miner	Caerphilly Secondary
1943	LLANBRADACH MIXED		
	None Known		
	COEDYBRAIN BOYS		
Vivian ADNEY	10 High Street	Builder	Caerphilly Secondary
Terence BOOSE	13 Richmond Terrace	Miner	Caerphilly Technical
Neville BRANGWYNNE	Colliery Police Station	Policeman	Caerphilly Secondary
Anthony DAVIES	67 School Street	Miner	Caerphilly Secondary
Ivor FOLLAND	39 Richmond Terrace	Warehouseman	Refused place at
			Caerphilly Technical
David A FOWLER	20 Grove Street	Fitter	Caerphilly Secondary
David JACKSON	15 Church Street	Guardian	Caerphilly Secondary
Giraldus J JAMES	22 Tynygraig Road	Miner	Caerphilly Secondary
Graham R KEIRLE	4 James Street	Miner	Caerphilly Technical
Claud MITCHELL	90 School Street	Miner	Caerphilly Secondary
Terence PLINT	3 Station Road	Miner	Caerphilly Secondary
Ernest A SPENCER	7 Richmond Terrace	Miner	Refused place at
			Caerphilly Secondary
Wm A VAUGHAN	59 Coedybrain Road	Miner	Caerphilly Secondary
Howell A WILLIAMS	9 Pencerrig Street	Miner	Caerphilly Technical
	COEDYBRAIN GIRLS		
Norma KEIRLE	1 Lewis Terrace	Soldier	Caerphilly Secondary
Margaret MORRIS	54 School Street	Miner	Caerphilly Secondary
(Doreen) Joan SWEET	Myrtle Bungalow	Coke Ovens	Caerphilly Secondary
1944	LLANBRADACH MIXED		
Jeanette EVANS	30 Plasturtwyn Terrace	Miner	Caerphilly Secondary
	COEDYBRAIN BOYS		
Wm F G BROOKS	12 or 62 School Street	Miner	Caerphilly Secondary
Sidney HOWELLS	16 Grove Street	Fitter	Caerphilly Technical
Robert A ROACH	50 High Street	Policeman	Caerphilly Secondary
Dennis G SELLWOOD	19 Tynygraig Road	Boilerman	Caerphilly Secondary
Stanley E SPENCER	2 Stanley Row	Miner	Caerphilly Technical
Bernard STONE	12 Ffrwd Terrace	Miner	Caerphilly Technical
Maldwyn W THOMAS	3 Horace Terrace	Miner	Caerphilly Technical
Calvin WILLIAMS	9 Pencerrig Street	Mine Traffic Manager	Caerphilly Secondary

	COEDYBRAIN GIRLS		
Jean BISHOP	1 Oak Terrace	Miner	Pontypridd Commercial
Jean R HASKINS	7 Coedybrain Road	Miner	Pontypridd Commercial
Margaret J KIDLEY	65 Coedybrain Road	Miner	Pontypridd Commercial
Joan SEABOURNE	7 High Street	Soldier	Caerphilly Secondary
Mary S STRONG	2 New St, Pwllypant	Miner	Pontypridd Commercial

1945	LLANBRADACH MIXED		
Percy S ALLEN	23 Oakfield St	Factory	Caerphilly Technical
Ronald A BIRD	4 Victoria Street	Steelworker	Caerphilly Technical
Thomas J HOLE	24 Plasturtwyn Terrace	Miner	Caerphilly Technical
James T MILSOM	9 Victoria Street	Factory	Caerphilly Technical
	COEDYBRAIN BOYS		
Howard T COLE	11 Ffrwd Terrace	Miner	Caerphilly Secondary
Denzil CORNISH	2 Central St, Pwllypant	Miner	Caerphilly Secondary
Roye DOLBELL	21 School Street	Boilerman	Caerphilly Technical
Brian HARPER	35 Coedybrain Road	Coke Worker	Caerphilly Technical
Keith HODGE	10 Garden Street	Fitter	Caerphilly Secondary
Gethin HUGHES	14 James Street	Fireman	Caerphilly Technical
Ken HUGHES	9 Morgan Street	Miner	Caerphilly Secondary
Vernon HUGHES	8 Lewis Terrace	Coal Hewer	Caerphilly Secondary
Leonard HUMPHRIES (Evacuee)	28 School Street	Royal Marine	Caerphilly Secondary
Clive ISAAC	80 Garden Street	Colliery Engine Driver	Caerphilly Secondary
Maldwyn JAMES	6 Tynygraig Terrace	Miner	Caerphilly Secondary
Brian W JOHNS	25 Coedybrain Road	Factory	Caerphilly Secondary
Donald KEYNON	7 Rees Terrace	Miner	Caerphilly Technical
Sidney KITT	11 School Street	Miner	Caerphilly Technical
Peter J POOLE	2 Church Street	· HM Forces	Caerphilly Technical
Kenneth WALDING	2 School Street	Miner	Caerphilly Secondary
	COEDYBRAIN GIRLS		
Gaynor BRIFFERT	10 Church Street	Railwayman	Caerphilly Secondary
Dorothy DEENE	14 De Winton Terrace	Coal Hewer	Caerphilly Secondary
Mair C HOARE	61 Coedybrain Road	Miner	Pontypridd Commercial
Elsie JONES	De Winton Hotel	Hotel Keeper	Caerphilly Secondary
E Mary JONES	27 Coedybrain Road	Winder	Caerphilly Secondary
Edith E MATTHEWS	78 School Street	Coal Hewer	Caerphilly Secondary
Shirley Margaret THOMAS	57 Coedybrain Road	Lorry Driver	Caerphilly Secondary

1946	LLANBRADACH MIXED		
Llewellyn G EDWARDS	3 Plasturtwyn Terrace	Surface Worker	Caerphilly Technical
Ronald J EDWARDS	3 Plasturtwyn Terrace	Surface Worker	Caerphilly Secondary
Donald H PLUMMER	5 Monmouth View	Miner	Caerphilly Technical
	COEDYBRAIN BOYS		
Dennis W BAYNTON	3 School Street	Navy	Caerphilly Secondary
Brian W CAMPBELL	6 De Winton Terrace	Newsagent	Caerphilly Secondary
Ken C CARTER	74 School Street	Coal Hewer	Caerphilly Technical

Name	Address	Occupation	School
Cyril G EVANS	23 School Street	Miner	Caerphilly Technical
Ivor EVANS	19 Glen View	Miner	Caerphilly Technical
Dermont Peter FOURNIER	22 High Street	Guardian	Caerphilly Secondary
Derek HARPER	35 Coedybrain Road	Coke Worker	Caerphilly Technical
Graham E C HITCHCOCK	14 Grove Street	Sgt. Major	Caerphilly Secondary
Malcolm HODGE	27 Garden Street	Fitter	Caerphilly Technical
Alan LEWIS	24 Grove Street	Electrician	Caerphilly Secondary
Nicholas SRODZINSKI	1 Church Street	Able Seaman	Caerphilly Secondary
Robert WALTON	Myrtle Dale, Corbetts Lane	Fitter	Caerphilly Secondary
Colin J WILLIAMS	Garth Owen	Coal Merchant	Caerphilly Technical
Barrie YOUNG	7 Oak Terrace	Miner	Caerphilly Technical
	COEDYBRAIN GIRLS		
Lorna BRANGWYNNE	Colliery Police Station	Policeman	Caerphilly Secondary
Gaynor JONES	12 James Street	Ostler	Pontypridd Commercial
Vyvyan JONES	De Winton Hotel	Hotel Keeper	Caerphilly Secondary
Marion RUDGE	24 Church Street	Miner	Caerphilly Secondary

1947 — LLANBRADACH MIXED

Name	Address	Occupation	School
Fredk. H LANGDON	14 Plasturtwyn Terrace	Miner	Caerphilly Secondary
Helen Molly PRICE	47 Wingfield Crescent	Mother	Caerphilly Secondary
Brian VINEY	9 Wingfield Crescent	Engine Driver	Caerphilly Secondary
	COEDYBRAIN BOYS		
Edw. Glyndwr BEVAN	7 Mountain View, Pwllypant	Army	Caerphilly Secondary
Grant COLSON	44 Garden Street	By-Product Plant	Caerphilly Secondary
Robert J DAVIES	3 Tynygraig Terrace	Coal Hewer	Caerphilly Secondary
Wm J DAVIES	16 Lewis Terrace	Miner	Caerphilly Technical
Robert J JONES	23 Church Street	Coal Hewer	Caerphilly Secondary
Peter R Keirle	1 Lewis Terrace	Collier	Caerphilly Secondary
Donald J KITT	86 School Street	Colliery Labourer	Caerphilly Secondary
Donald MUNN	55 School Street	Factory	Caerphilly Technical
Jas Arthur SMITH	Garth Owen	HM Forces	Caerphilly Secondary
	COEDYBRAIN GIRLS		
Anita CALLAGHAN	29 Richmond Terrace	Miner	Caerphilly Secondary
Audrey DAVIES	2A High Street	Carpenter	Caerphilly Secondary
Norma JACKSON	15 Church Street	Miner	Caerphilly Secondary
Joyce SPENCER	18 Richmond Terrace	Miner	Refused place at Caerphilly Secondary

1948 — LLANBRADACH MIXED

Name	Address	Occupation	School
Ernest Clive POOLE	12 Wingfield Crescent	Miner	Caerphilly Technical
	COEDYBRAIN BOYS		
Reg CRUMB	Quarry Cottage	Coke Ovens	Caerphilly Sec/Grammar
Martin Lloyd JONES	4 Barry Cottages, Pwllypant	Collier	Caerphilly Technical
Reginald Glyn JONES	De Winton Hotel	Licensed Victualler	Caerphilly Sec/Grammar
Thomas P LANE	2 Garden Street	Coke Ovens	Caerphilly Sec/Grammar
Colin MAHONEY	13 School Street	Munitions Worker	Caerphilly Sec/Grammar
Arthur OSBORNE	3 James Street	Miner	Caerphilly Sec/Grammar

185

Name	Address	Occupation	School
John PAYNE	64 School Street	Bricklayer	Caerphilly Sec/Grammar
Vernon SPRAGG	24 High Street	Army	Caerphilly Sec/Grammar
John SRODZINSKI	1 Church Street	Navy	Caerphilly Sec/Grammar
	COEDYBRAIN GIRLS		
Pamela JOHN	16 Garden Avenue	Colliery Timekeeper	Caerphilly Sec/Grammar
Olwen LITTLEWOOD	56 Garden Street	Colliery Fireman	Caerphilly Sec/Grammar
Shirley RICHARDS	17 High Street	Miner	Caerphilly Sec/Grammar
Valerie SELLWOOD	19 Tynygraig Road	Boilerman	Caerphilly Sec/Grammar
Gwyneth SKYM	11 Monmouth View, Pwllypant	Munitions	Caerphilly Sec/Grammar
Dilys STONE	2 Monmouth View	RAF	Caerphilly Sec/Grammar
Shirley WESTHEAD	37 Coedybrain Road	Cinema Manager	Caerphilly Sec/Grammar

1949 LLANBRADACH MIXED

Name	Address	Occupation	School
Graham DAVIES	1 Victoria Street	Miner	Caerphilly Technical
Keith D GARDINER	20 Plasturtwyn Terrace	Foreman	Caerphilly Technical
Janice M WILLIAMS	12 Glen View	Miner	Caerphilly Sec/Grammar
	COEDYBRAIN BOYS		
Keith BENNETT	14 Ffrwd Terrce	Munitions	Caerphilly Technical
David H BEVAN	7 Mountain View Pwllypant	HM Forces	Caerphilly Sec/Grammar
Dennis BROWN	98 School Street	Miner	Caerphilly Sec/Grammar
Gerald DAVIES	3 Tynygraig Road	Colliery Labourer	Caerphilly Sec/Grammar
Peter E DAVIES	22 Grove Street	Colliery Shotsman	Caerphilly Sec/Grammar
Michael E EVANS	6 Barry Cottages Pwllypant	Railway Fitter	Caerphilly Sec/Grammar
Richard EVANS	23 School Street	Miner	Caerphilly Technical
Robert GREENWOOD	50 High Street	Stationmaster	Caerphilly Sec/Grammar
Cliff HARMAN	23 De Winton Terrace	Coal Hewer	Caerphilly Sec/Grammar
Leslie R HUDD	Brynteg Bungalow, Pwllypant	Army	Caerphilly Technical
David LEEDS	6 Mountain View, Pwllypant	Munitions	Caerphilly Technical
John MEADE	11 School Street	Coal Hewer	Caerphilly Sec/Grammar
Eric V PHILLIPS	1 Barry Cottages, Pwllypant	Munitions	Caerphilly Sec/Grammar
Ioan Glyndwr PRICE	Graddfa Farm	Farmer	Caerphilly Technical
Keith THOMAS	24 Richmond Terrace	Coal Hewer	Caerphilly Sec/Grammar
	COEDYBRAIN GIRLS		
Gwyneth M BARTLEY	Bryn Heulog, Pwllypant	War Reserve P.C.	Caerphilly Sec/Grammar
Joan BUCK	37 Garden Street	Wagon Carpenter	Caerphilly Sec/Grammar
Marlene BURGAN	44 De Winton Terrace	Miner	Caerphilly Sec/Grammar
Iris Maureen DOLE	2 Horace Terrace	Miner	Caerphilly Sec/Grammar
Ella Marina HUGHES	11 Thomas Street	Miner	Caerphilly Sec/Grammar
Maureen MEADE	15 School Street	Miner	Treforest Commercial

1950

	LLANBRADACH MIXED		
Jennifer M McDOWELL	23 Plasturtwyn Terrace	Miner	Caerphilly Sec/Grammar
	COEDYBRAIN BOYS		
Glyndwr BAYNTON	41 School Street	Plant Worker	Caerphilly Sec/Grammar
John Hewitt CARTER	74 School Street	Coal Hewer	Caerphilly Sec/Grammar
David EVANS	6 School Street	Clerk	Caerphilly Sec/Grammar
Keith FOX	6 Garden Avenue	HM Forces	Caerphilly Sec/Grammar
Ronald HURN	30 School Street	Widow	Caerphilly Technical
Jeffrey JONES	36 De Winton Terrace	Coal Merchant	Caerphilly Sec/Grammar
Gerald D KEARLE	41 De Winton Terrace	Air Force	Caerphilly Technical
Frank T J PASCOE	2 Mountain View, Pwllypant	Factory	Caerphilly Technical
Maldwyn J PAYNE	19 Coedybrain Road	Coal Hewer	Caerphilly Technical
Lindsay B ROWLANDS	9 Garden Avenue	Painter	Caerphilly Sec/Grammar
Douglas Brian SMEATH	20 School Street	Army	Caerphilly Sec/Grammar
Granville H WISE	33 Coedybrain Road	Baker's Roundsman	Caerphilly Sec/Grammar
Peter WHATLEY	18 Grove Street	Railway Sheds	Caerphilly Sec/Grammar
	COEDYBRAIN GIRLS		
Gwyneira EVANS	2 Station Road	Miner	Caerphilly Sec/Grammar
Valerie GARBERTT	12 High Street	Coal Hewer	Pontypridd Technical
Hilary C GOUGH	50 School Street	Miner	Caerphilly Sec/Grammar
Ann Eliz. HARDWICK	2 Rees Terrace	Constructional Engineer	Caerphilly Sec/Grammar
Denise ROBERTS	4 Oak Terrace	Miner	Caerphilly Sec/Grammar
Janet Lorraine WILLIAMS	25 De Winton Terrace	Miner	Caerphilly Sec/Grammar
Ann WILTSHIRE	8 Grove Terrace	Fitter GWR	Caerphilly Sec/Grammar

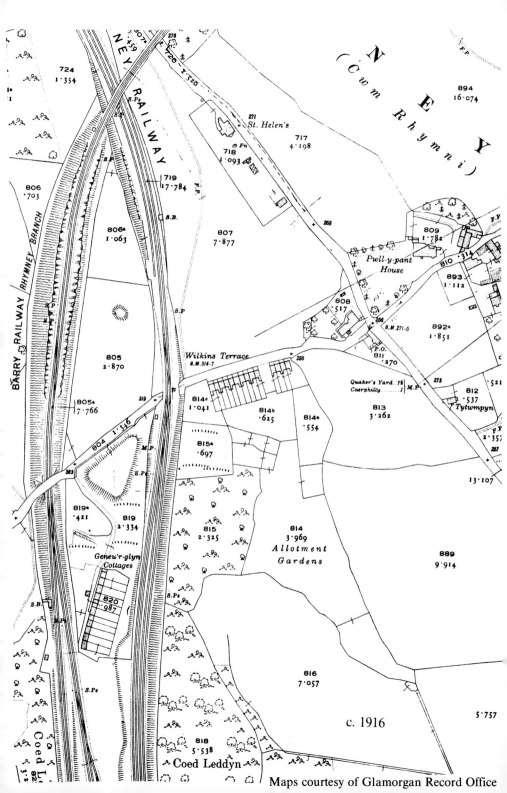

Maps courtesy of Glamorgan Record Office

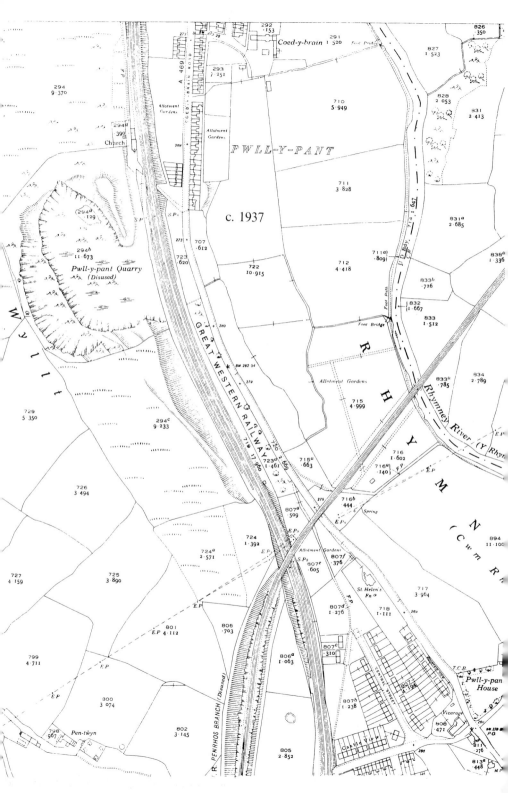

c. 1937

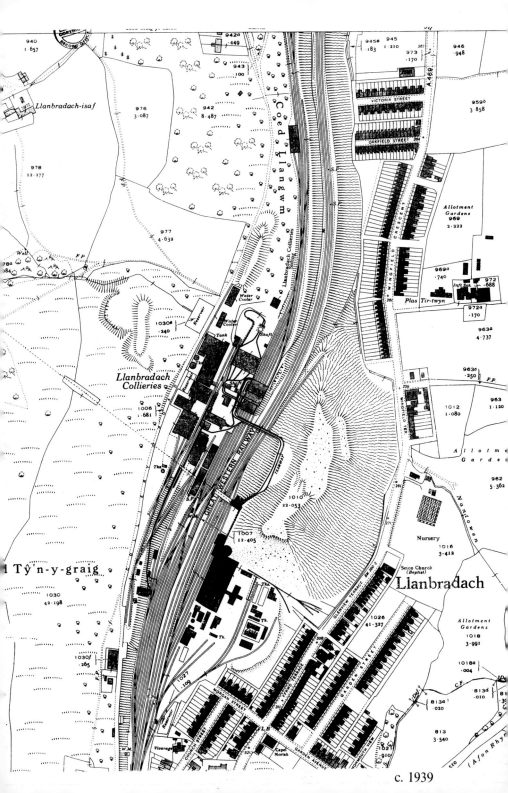

c. 1939

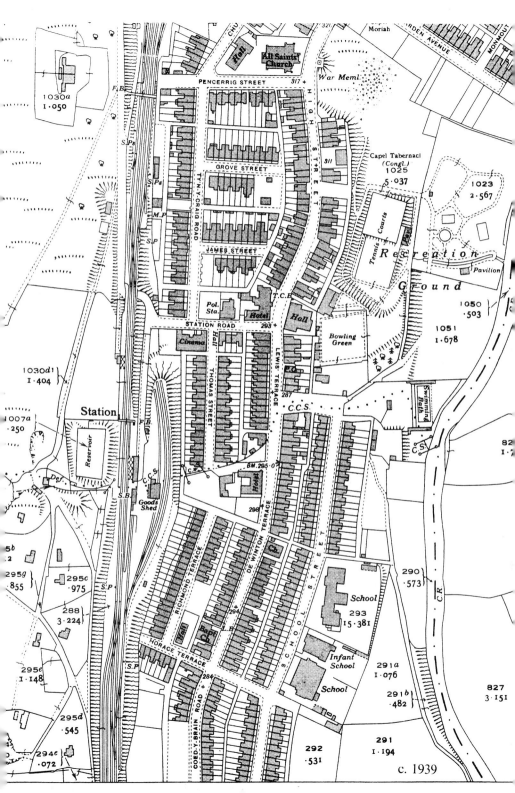

c. 1939

SOURCES

Logbooks, Llanbradach Mixed and Infants, 1892–1952   Glamorgan Record Office

Logbook, Coedybrain Infants, 1900–1952   Glamorgan Record Office

Logbook, Coedybrain Mixed, 1900–1913   Glamorgan Record Office

Logbook, Coedybrain Girls, 1913–1959   Glamorgan Record Office

Logbooks, Coedybrain Boys, 1913–1967   Glamorgan Record Office

Admission register,
Llanbradach Mixed and Infants, 1944–1950   Coedybrain Primary School

Admission register, Coedybrain Infants, 1900–1912   Coedybrain Primary School

Admission register, Coedybrain Mixed, 1903–1913   Coedybrain Primary School

Admission register, Coedybrain Boys, 1913–1944   Coedybrain Primary School

Admission register, Coedybrain Girls, 1913–1944   Coedybrain Primary School

Results of County Entrance Scholarship
Examinations, 1909–1927, 1936–1950   Glamorgan Record Office

Admission register,
Lewis Endowed School, Gelligaer, 1891–1923   Glamorgan Record Office

Admission register,
Pontypridd Intermediate School, 1907–1926   Glamorgan Record Office

Glamorgan Education Committee
Minutes, various 1903–1952   Glamorgan Record Office

Caerphilly Group Managers
Minutes, 1915–1922, 1925–1939   Glamorgan Record Office

Records of Cardiff Collieries Co. Ltd.   Glamorgan Record Office

Electoral registers various 1896–1948   Glamorgan Record Office

Correspondence,
Llanbradach Welfare Association, 1931   Coedybrain Primary School

Public Information Leaflets (Civil Defence), 1939

The Blitz in Riverside   Cardiff Central Library

40 Years On   Henry Simons, 1985

Cwm Aber Schools, 1909–1984   Basil Phillips

Education System in England and Wales   Sharp and Dunford, 1990

English History, 1870–1914   Sir Robert Ensor, 1936

English History, 1914–1945   A.J.P. Taylor, 1965

New Tredegar, Bargoed and Caerphilly Journal   Bargoed Library

Merthyr Express   Merthyr Tydfil Central Library